Questing Fictions

Questing Fictions

Latin America's

Family Romance

Djelal Kadir

Foreword by Terry Cochran

Theory and History of Literature, Volume 32

University of Minnesota Press, Minneapolis

863
K 11 q

The University of Minnesota Press gratefully acknowledges assistance provided by the Andrew W. Mellon Foundation for publication of this book.

Published by the University of Minnesota Press
2037 University Avenue Southeast, Minneapolis MN 55414.
Published simultaneously in Canada
by Fitzhenry & Whiteside Limited, Markham.
Printed in the United States of America.

Library of Congress Cataloging-in-Publication Data

Kadir, Djelal.
    Questing fictions.

    (Theory and history of literature ; v. 32)
    Includes index.
    1. Spanish American fiction — History and criticism.
2. Quests in literature. I. Title. II. Series.
PQ7082.N7K33   1986   863   86-16019
ISBN 0-8166-1516-0
ISBN 0-8166-1517-9 (pbk.)

An abbreviated version of Chapter 3 was published in *Studies in Twentieth
Century Literature* as "Same Voices, Other Tombs: Structures of Mexican
Gothic" (vol. 1, no. 1, 1976). Thanks are due the editor for permission
to republish parts of that essay.

The University of Minnesota
is an equal-opportunity
educator and employer.

Contents

Theory and History of Literature
Edited by Wlad Godzich and Jochen Schulte-Sasse

Foreword
History and Exile
Terry Cochran

Writing on Latin American literature is a task that often fails, for success is measured by the degree to which one's conception undermines its own foundation. The failure relates to the way the project has inevitably been conceived: to see one's task as that of establishing the specificity of Latin American literature means that in terms of historical development it is lagging behind other, already established literatures (namely those of the "developed," or less "exotic," world). The solution, however, is not to abandon the historical in favor of an explanatory model that takes for granted its specificity: as is often said, that too is a very specific conception of history. And it is along the fractures of this contradiction — involving "specificity" and "history" — that one must situate Djelal Kadir's text: while the specificity of Latin American literature does have to do with its belatedness, this does not mean it is derivative or secondary but rather that the very conditions of its production force the question of history into the open as one of its constitutive elements. The history that emerges can no longer take for granted the temporality it seemingly depends on: if the specificity of Latin American literature is that it foregrounds the historical, the primary area of concern must be the way in which one inscribes oneself within that history. Kadir's very careful reading of several key Spanish American texts takes as its point of departure that inscribing activity — inscription as the historical necessity propelling one's reading and writing.

Although former "colonies" evince obvious similarities, both conceptual and historical, that result from the shared patterns of the various modes of conquest during the so-called age of colonization, here we will restrict ourselves to a brief discussion of Latin America; the conquest of Latin America (and North America as well) is particularly revealing because the course it took — the almost total annihilation of indigenous peoples and their culture — turns out to be what makes its experience of colonization universalizable. The scarcely existing remnants of indigenous cultures — in comparison to what they must have been — make Latin America an extreme instance of the process by means of which one culture, more powerful and globally articulated, seeps into the empty spaces left by less hegemonic cultures. As might well be expected, the indigenous cultures (and the further — perhaps even more extensive — creolization brought on by the influx of African peoples) are later recuperated by nation-building historians who, contrary to their intent of proclaiming true independence, certify the victory of European concepts and social formations. In fact, what we must confront in describing Kadir's project is the tension between these concepts and the theories of history that inevitably accompany them.

Therefore, we must first address the broader contexts — theoretical and narrowly historical — that inform Kadir's analysis, thereby taking into account the historicity of our own — and Kadir's — formulations. The culture of the "Third World" — whether that culture is literary, linguistic, or political, and whether that "world" is India, Africa, Latin America, or elsewhere — poses frequently unacknowledged questions for anyone wielding the more privileged European discourse. The problem is compounded by the fact that acknowledging the questions in no way leads to their resolution: because the "European" discourse (itself a construct) is the discourse of knowledge, recognizing the challenge of non-European cultures to accepted modes of thought only reaffirms that knowledge. In a very real sense this recognition represents the Hegelian residue that marks all Western discourse (which in this context must also include that of Eastern Europe); to acknowledge what would question — to be more specific, negate — one's knowledge is to increase one's knowledge at the expense of its negation. While to the nonphilosopher this formulation may seem unduly complicated, it is a very straightforward and perhaps simplistic description when juxtaposed to the international debates that are currently taking place (including, for example, the controversy regarding which discourse will control the pronouncements of organizations such as UNESCO).

A well-known anecdote expresses very precisely the relationship of colonizers to the colonized space they would inhabit, if only by proxy; the anecdote emerges as a result of the single most important act in the annales of Latin American history — Napoleon's intra-European colonization. To give in succinct narrative form the background necessary for understanding the anecdote: when, after having conquered Spain, Napoleon's armies invaded Portugal, the Portuguese royal court set sail for Brazil; during the voyage many women of the court had to shave their heads to eliminate vermin, which gives rise to the story: upon the court's arrival several ladies of the colonial "aristocracy" had their heads shaved, thinking that in this way they would become participants in a new European vogue.[1] The modalities of this encounter, in themselves trivial, deserve closer attention, for the episode contains *in nuce* the recurrent issues of Latin American discourse. On a very superficial level, one must note that this anecdote manifests the structure of fundamental misrecognition inherent in all relationships between colonizer and colonized, but at the same time one cannot refer to it as a "misrecognition," for the structure does not permit of a recognition that is not misrecognition. In terms of the story itself, then: the Bahian ladies imitated the sea-worn ladies of the court, but the story would never have been told if its significance had resided in mimetic accuracy. Its "significance" (i.e., "humor") derives from the fact that the perfect mimetic image is the most distant example of that which it would imitate. The lateral circumstances of the recounted event are much more articulate, for the "original" depilation not only occurred *en route* from the fatherland to the colony but it also was a direct result of that voyage: within the narrative, the shaved heads mark the difference between colonizer and colonized, and their imitation merely reaffirms the unbridgeable gap separating them.

Yet critical discussions of the twentieth century inevitably fall within the framework established and held in place by the reign of very specific concepts that cannot render an account of the above anecdote. In what has been conveniently demarcated as the economic or socioeconomic sphere one immediately thinks of "development" and "progress," concepts that not by chance originate alongside the "modern" State — a social configuration irrevocably linked to the constitution of overseas domains and national hegemonies. These same concepts implicitly operate in literary discourse, not simply in reference to periodization (baroque, romanticism, modernism, etc.), but more insidiously by keeping in place a history that will only generate more and more periods. Several noteworthy attempts have been made to treat some of these historically defining concepts without making recourse to developmental history (specifically Lyotard's assertion that the "postmodern" is not a temporal concept in the sense of "after the modern," or Paul de Man's demonstration that "modernity" certainly cannot be explicated on historical grounds), but such unmaskings still do not render the concepts any more effective: although they show the faultiness of representational history, they also stop short of theorizing the historical. However, they and others point out two aspects of the debate that are frequently ignored and which we, along with Kadir, will have occasion to return to: 1) if representational history operates according to the precepts of narrative to the same extent as does a fictional text, this does not mean that the representations are arbitrary but are historically constituted, structured in relation to specific interests; 2) if one wishes to put forth a history to "unmask" the representational (or, if one prefers, the "official") history that by definition is oppressive to those whose point of view is not represented, then one unfortunately must duplicate the representational mode of the history that is rejected.[2] An extensive analysis of representation has yet to be carried out (and may in any event prove to be impossible), but it must be said that every serious study of the logic of representation — and particularly when it relates to a given historical milieu such as Latin America — cannot avoid addressing, however cursorily, these two questions.

As a text *Questing Fictions* makes strenuous demands on the reader, demands that are linked to its own attempt to grapple with the representational without falling prey to representation. Yet it does not renounce representation (if indeed it were ever possible to do so completely), for that would be to renounce the critical project; at the same time, however, it does not embrace representation with open arms, for that would be to operate with a concept of history that was only able to ground itself on the basis of hierarchical distinctions it itself instituted, most notably the "backwardness" of marginal societies (Latin America, the "Third World"). This difficult "in-between," which is "between" in the sense that it partakes of the representational even as it disavows it, is textualized in the difficulty faced by the reader who would take representation for granted: the representation cannot be separated from the act constituting it. Kadir's concern with representation is not, however, reflected explicitly in a theory of reading, even if it makes itself felt there; instead, his focus is primarily one of textual production, a producing that never becomes a product, that never coalesces into a representation:

> In other words, a sought-after destination becomes perpetually dislocated into endless deferment through the agency of a supreme fiction's ciphers, that is, through the acts of writing. (p. 5)

The question turns out to be the force that powers the writing, and the peculiar temporal structure that has haunted all Latin American writing, whether about Latin America from the vantage point of Europe or from Latin America in imitation of Europe, does not allow one the option of taking refuge in an easy concept of textuality that somehow powers itself; it is this 'mechanism' that refuses to be reduced to 'textuality' that Kadir calls ". . . constant *erring* or perpetual quest" (p. 12).

That "erring" or "quest" is both the condition of literary production and the agency whereby it is being produced; and it remains distinct from solely textual concepts of "errance" because of its *historical* necessity. To understand this "quest" — here distinct from the medieval quest-for-self — in Kadir's terms, one might consider it the state of homelessness in which one endlessly seeks a home to call one's own. Nevertheless, we can make it more precise by virtue of the above-mentioned anecdote: irrevocable marginality determines all attempts to arrive at the center as mere affirmations of the impossibility of ever arriving. What arrives at the margins — Siberia, if you will — can no longer recover its identity, whether one conceives of the separation from the 'origin' in a physical sense or as an introduction of instruments of acculturation, i.e., whether one conceives identity as the possibility of returning to an already constituted identity or constituting a future one. Kadir's project is not, therefore, wholly new in its formulation, although it has never been articulated as a general theory of textual production: the problem is one of *exile*, and while it obviously relates to an empirical, physical exile, it just as evidently can take the form of cultural or, to emphasize its pervasiveness, discursive exile (and one can think of many instances when the two coexist: in a Gombrowicz, for example). The overriding significance of Kadir's text derives from its treatment of "exile" — which he most frequently refers to as "homelessness" — as a concept instead of merely a result of physical expatriation. Therefore, Kadir's textual analysis of exile could never be called a thematic one, nor does it constitute an arbitrary choice on the part of a critic who wants to stake out his own territory; here exile should rather be viewed as the nexus where all the above-mentioned questions of representation intersect.

To articulate the very precise stakes that inform Kadir's readings we must first attempt a rigorous and careful description of the dynamics of exile. Perhaps the most complete discussion of exile occurs in a brief text by Julio Cortázar;[3] that a Latin American delivered and then published the text in French only underscores its appropriateness. For Cortázar there is a refracted relationship between the present-day "exile in Europe" and what for preceding generations was the "voyage en Europe":

> What we perceive today as a constraint was then a voluntary and happy decision — the mirage of Europe as the catalyst of forces and of talents not yet born. That voyage of a Chilean or Argentine to Paris, Rome, or London was a voyage of initiation, an impetus without substitute, access to the Holy Grail of Western knowledge. (p. 121)

The strategy of argument is no less important than the argument itself, and while it unmistakably derives from a Hegelian model of history, it introduces an important element that cannot be accounted for in that model. More explicitly: the text juxtaposes two ways of conceiving the difference between Latin America and Europe, but this juxtaposition is represented in temporal terms, i.e., the way it was "then" and the way it is "now." "Then" one went to Europe to gain access to knowledge, or, rather, to achieve consciousness; one had to go to Europe in order to recognize oneself. "Now," however, in looking back, it becomes obvious that such a concept of Europe derived from a colonized mentality; now we recognize *clearly and undistortedly* what our predecessors failed to see: the mirror of self-recognition was in fact a mirage. In other words, the relationship between the "then" and the "now" is no less Hegelian than the "then" being critiqued. The distinction between the colonized consciousness and the exiled consciousness resides in the localization of the possibility of activity. The generation of the "voyage en Europe" seemingly drew its impetus from Europe and willfully decided — leaving aside the question of ideology, which is obviously implied here but which cannot be dealt with in this introduction — to make the journey, whereas the exiled have no choice and cannot endorse the fiction that they are their own agents. In fact, the difference that Cortázar has narrativized can now be pinpointed as the difference between acting and reacting, i.e., between localizing the impetus to act in the subject or elsewhere.

The issue for Cortázar, then, is not one drawn solely from empirical history, although one can certainly cite historical examples; it rather relates to the more pressing aspect of exile, the form of activity the exiled individual must historically assume. And that activity must always result as a reaction to exile itself, to the fact that one is exiled, for exile is not a choice, a matter of subjectivity, but an imperative. As alluded to in the above quotation, Cortázar describes this imperative to exile as a violence inflicted upon one: "The notion of exile, for me at least, carries with it a constraint and very often a violence" (115). One has no choice but to react, and one's modalities of activity are circumscribed in the very conception of exile that confirms the loss it implies: exile is seen as

> a denial [di-valence], a derogation, a mutilation against which one reacts.
> . . . One almost always departs from the negative (. . .); making use of
> the poor trampoline of denial, one tries to leap forward and recuperate
> what has been lost. (117-18)

Here we must follow Cortázar's argument very closely, for the Hegelian concepts are just as misleading as they are necessary; the Platonic "recuperation" inserts a contradiction that not even the dialectic can surmount: whereas the Hegelian dialectic is *historical* and makes use of the negative only to propel itself into greater self-consciousness, "recuperation" represents an attempt to render the historical static, to idealize a present conception of the past. The Hegelian stance of beginning with the negative in order to negate it and move beyond is stalemated: one experiences an illusion of movement but that is the nature of the trampoline.

A more coherent and less contradictory alternative to this reaction to exile would be to allow the dialectic to annihilate the negative, which in this case would mean to purify it of the drive to recuperation. Superficially such a purification resembles Cortázar's own analysis that the text at first alludes to in recognizably Hegelian terms: exile as "the object of an internal critique that annuls it as denial so as to project it on a positive ground" (117). Nevertheless, the reaction that he describes here receives a more extensive treatment that belies the dialectical project and introduces the most important elements of any theory of exile as a concept that cannot be reduced to the effect of distance separating one from a cultural, linguistic, and geographic origin. As the text expands on its first allusion to a positive theory of exile, it begins to skew the termini:

> Those who exile the intellectuals believe this act to be a positive one

because it leads to the elimination of an adversary. But what if those who
are exiled also consider their exile as positive? (118)

The encounter is set up initially as an agonistic relationship in which one has
absolute power over another: the positive act becomes positive only to the extent
that it negates an Other or "eliminates an adversary"; the following question
poses a conceptual problem that disrupts the totalization proper to the dialectic.
If those who are eliminated, geographically removed, simulate the positive, i.e.,
fail to conceive of exile as a loss, this does not mean that exile is in any way
overcome or negated. The positive act that institutes exile does not parallel the
positivity of exile: the former is simultaneously cognitive (the elimination of an
adversary) and instrumental (in this instance the possibility of the cognitive act
depends on the ability to execute it), while the latter seems to be merely cognitive.
Yet it would also be a grave mistake to equate the two modes of cognition; the
continuation of passage makes this cognitive difference increasingly clear.

> I believe it is more than ever necessary to transform the negativity of
> exile — which as such assumes the triumph of the enemy — into a new way
> of conceiving reality [*en une nouvelle prise de réalité*]. This reality would
> be based on values and not denials and would be rendered positive and
> effective by the specific labor of the writer who completely reverses the
> adversary's program and faces it in a way the adversary could not imagine.
> (118)

The conflictual agnostics of the dialectical model characterize exile as occupying
one negative pole of opposition; to conceptualize the act of exile in this way
"assures the triumph of the enemy" because for the dialectic to function — historically and/or conceptually — one must possess the power to enforce it. In the
case of *exile* one cannot reduce such a discussion to metaphorics — exile is an
undeniably palpable experience. Yet one should note that what Cortázar refers
to here is rather a conceptual mode that opens up the possibility of an activity
that refuses to be complicit in the positivity of the master. In fact the dialectical
model of history — the dialectic is always a model of history — is inconceivable
without the correlative centrality of the subject. Thus only one in exile, exiled
from one's identity, from a home, can defuse the dialectic. The dissolution of
the negativity of exile takes place cognitively, as we began to describe above,
but the cognitive mode does not correspond to a mental act; the negative is
dissolved in a new *prise de réalité*. It is not a question of the *prise de conscience*
that might be expected — there is no "coming to oneself," the activity cannot
be located simply in the mind — and it would be premature to dismiss this passage
as the reintroduction of some form of "objective reality," the counterconcept
of all epistemologies where cognition is theorized as emanating from the subject.
In effect, it is a reality rendered positive(ly) and effective(ly) through discursive
labor, which inverts the dialectical program.[4] But how does one invert the

dialectic? In this very specific instance one in exile does not have the power necessary to negate the negation of exile and return *home*: the inversion, the text makes very explicit, does not operate by means of negation but by affirmation.

* * *

Kadir's text does not present an overarching theory that seeks to render an account of all these concerns. Instead, his study is a series of readings of specific Latin American texts and their responses to the conditions of their production. And as is frequently the case, these readings are more significant for theory than a text about theory. What the subtitle designates as the "family" of Latin American writing emerges from the common elements these diverse texts express vis-à-vis these socio-historical and literary conditions. In Kadir's words, the writings' "creative performance," their " 'negative,' or critical quest . . . constitutes an originary act that self-consciously knows itself not to be wholly original but a repetition of the founding act which it violates, which it transgresses" (p. 139). Although the problematic is explicitly Hegelian — particularly in the last chapter, where the various aspects of the analysis are most fully articulated — Kadir takes great pains to distinguish the open-ended dynamics of his description from Hegelian teleology. The text, in adopting the Hegelian dialectic, dispenses with the promised moment of totalization that guarantees the unfolding of history.

All of these lines of argumentation come together in Carlos Fuentes's *Terra Nostra* or, rather, in Kadir's reading of it. The novel is well-chosen, for it represents an attempt to come to terms textually with the predicament of New World — and specifically Latin American — discourse; the only North American novel that operates within a similar framework is William Gaddis's *The Recognitions*, which is comparable both thematically and from the perspective of the dynamics of its narrative.[5] *Terra Nostra's* importance for Kadir's analysis derives from its simultaneous articulation and disarticulation of the Hegelian dialectic: to read the progression of sections — from "The Old World" to "The New World" to some kind of final resolution in "The Next World" — as a simplistic thesis-antithesis-synthesis cannot be maintained on the basis of the text itself that displays no temporal progression: what it displays might be better called "temporal collusion." This relationship between the historical totalization of the dialectic and the text's thwarting of any such totality serves as the context for Kadir's remark about his procedure of "holding Fuentes up to Hegel's mirror" (p. 122). In fact, a great deal of the difficulty the reader will experience with Kadir's text has to do with what can only superficially be dismissed as "wordplay" (the "mirror" being a description of Hegelian self-reflection but also a reflection of the way Fuentes mirrors or does not mirror Hegel); in this instance, for example, the mirror is a major thematic element in Fuentes's novel (as it is in *The Recognitions*) and reference to it should be taken literally.

The complexities of any novel can never be exhausted or wholly explained, but *Terra Nostra's* lack of a center can in part be attributed to its multiplicity of mirrors: they are one of the most essential parts of the text and inevitably appear in the innumerable discussions of secular history and self-recognition. An important scene in the relationship between history, self-consciousness, and writing — a relationship that recurs throughout the entire novel — takes place, predictably, in the "Old World" section; El Señor is dictating an alternative and heretical history not to his scribe but to Guzmán, the administrator of his kingdom. In this text the mirror is a frightful instrument for it contradicts the historical and philosophical role it has represented as the reflection of the mind divorced from the practical sphere, also its role as the promise of a future when the reflection is no longer an *other*. In response to Guzmán's question about the origin:

> the life of the mirror, of all the mirrors that duplicate the world, that extend
> it beyond all realistic frontiers, and to all that exists, mutely says: you are
> two. But if this mirror had an origin, it was crafted, and used, and passed
> from hand to hand and from generation to generation; so it retained the
> images of all those who had viewed themselves in it, it had a past and not
> only the magic [*mágico dueño*: the magical master] of a future that El
> Señor had seen one morning as he ascended the stairs with the mirror in
> his hand. (192-93; 198)

As in the case of all descriptions of self-consciousness, the temporal allusions are very much at odds with the visual image that is to express them; here, however, self-reflection does not culminate in an identity that can stand alone from its past. But the past inscribed on the mirror — the images can retain their presence on the surface of the mirror only by overlapping and intersecting with one another — cannot be assigned to a given subject, for the self gazing into the mirror is not privileged and becomes only one reflection among a multiplicity. And no history can be written to render a complete account of its subject. The mirror of this description becomes an unavoidably secular one, crafted and passed from hand to hand, historically inscribed with the images intersected with it. As benign as it seems to any reader accustomed to "modern" writing, History without a reason, without an underlying purpose, becomes plurality of histories, which leads to a situation hostile to established social order.

Such a situation would be unstable and not by chance reminds one of the ideological controversies of sixteenth- and seventeenth-century Spain: to mention one very obvious characteristic of what has come to be designated the modern state (a characteristic that in the sixteenth and seventeenth centuries certainly gave concern to the rulers), the greater the number of people having access to reading and writing, the more and more difficult it is to control what is written and read. The implications become clear in the context of El Señor's dictation to Guzmán, in the ongoing discussion of heresy:

"Let us be reasonable, Guzmán, and let us ask ourselves why we have accepted as truth only one series of events when we know that those events were not unique, but common; that they are ordinary [*corrientes*], multiplicable into infinity in a series of plots that repeat into exhaustion: look at them, look at them filing by, interminably, century after century, in the glass of my mirror." (194; 199)

Perhaps one should be surprised that such a modern conception of history should come out of the mouth of an early king of Spain: the leveling of *absolute* hierarchical distinctions between histories and the right of freedom of expression are supposedly precepts of modern democratic societies. How, then, is the social order to be stabilized and authority to be reinstated? If one cannot look into the past, for the past is a series of irreconcilable events and stories of those events, then perhaps one could turn toward the future, project a reconciliation in whose name one could act. As has long been recognized, the historical conceptions of Christianity and of Hegel do not — structurally, at any rate — differ greatly in terms of the "moment of fulfillment": in both instances history ends, with the distinctions between past, present, and future becoming annihilated. Nevertheless, in *Terra Nostra* it is the impossibility of envisaging such a future that precipitated the crisis of history in the first place:

"Guzmán, look at it; I challenge you to climb to the end and origin of everything, but like me, you will not see the Creator in the mirror, and that absence, more than the announcement of our irremediable senescence, of our mortal death, will be what terrifies us." (190; 195)

The solution lies neither in the past nor the future: the past can only be told and retold inexhaustibly but never definitively, truthfully, and the mirror of the future, which should allow for the advent of absolute self-consciousness, only reveals an absolute nothingness that can never be recuperated by the self (the first Spanish text cited above underscores the significance of the nothingness by making an explicit — and somewhat ironic — reference to Hegel's *master*, that is, the mirror as the magical master versus the enslaved other, in this case, the future). We should at this point remind ourselves that despite its intimate concern with history *Terra Nostra* makes no pretense of being *history*; yet it is at the same time a rigorously historical work. The motivation for this very logical contradiction — only partly related to the preceding discussions of negativity — becomes apparent in the ultimate scheme of El Señor, the one most significant for colonization: "Let us struggle, not against heresy, but against the pagan and idolatrous abomination of the savage nations that do not believe in Christ" (195; 200). Establishing the otherness of the non-European and, principally, non-Christian "nations" permitted the reinstitution of history as true discourse of a relative difference: this is the frequently mentioned notion of belatedness that was necessary for a secular history to come into its own; here a "secular" history refers to the history of the state, a state that emerged in a society that could no longer be governed or stabilized on the basis of god's revelation.[6]

The complex irony of *Terra Nostra* is owed to the very limitations of Third-World writing: to write the history of *Terra Nostra* (the ambiguity should be maintained — *Terra Nostra*: "our land" when from the perspective of the Americas, "our earth" when from the vantage point of the Spanish empire) means to renounce even the structure of history, for history was invented in and for Europe to deprive non-Europeans of the possibility of a history that might take another course. To write a Latin American history today merely helps enforce the loss of its history, and while one cannot claim that "fiction" has come to constitute the writing of "authentic" history, it inscribes that loss as an affirmation. This activity of inscribing affirmation not coincidentally resembles the exile that Cortázar so carefully described:

> The first task of those who are exiled would be to strip in front of the terrible mirror that is the solitude of a foreign hotel; there, without the easy alibi of localism where the terms of comparison are lacking, they must try to see themselves as they are. (122)

Looking into the mirror of exile is hardly the affirmation of one's own identity, but the affirmation of its impossibility; for Cortázar gazing into such a mirror opens up the question of one's activity (122). And it is this activity, this "exile" as a structure of the marginalized understanding, that Kadir has first pointed out in Latin American discourse; while one might wonder whether it could still be called a "self-conscious critique," he has presented us with the necessity of thinking through that affirmation.

Preface

The filial line that extends the imaginative life of Latin America is an inventive, perpetually self-inventing, line. This thread, this clew that guides literary tradition, restlessly weaves, unweaves, and reweaves itself into a tapestry depicting a culture's tireless peregrination. In this process the journey and the object of the journey become one; the thread's path becomes a bias always bent on extending its line by depicting its own odyssey.

This metaphor is a way of saying that *quest* in Latin American literature figures as family history; that the errantry which resulted in the discovery of the New World has become internalized by that world's imagination; that the first voyagers' error which led to the necessity of *inventing* a reality for an unexpected world, the happenstance discovery, serves as precedent for the ever-errant inventiveness of Latin American fictions. Indeed these fictions trace the imaginative outlines of an errant family history in endless errancy. Lest the procession, the internalized impulse to wander, attain its goal, that measure of the founding error from the accidental discovery is built in so that the quest may perpetuate itself. This built-in mechanism and its errant itinerary are the object of our study.

The present book, then, is an attempt to chart the byways of erring, to map this self-deflecting peregrination in fiction's textual enterprise, in the bias of the fictions' own fabric. Our progress will take us from the generic to the specific manifestations of this quest: It begins by surveying the terrain and contingencies through which quest becomes internalized as operating principle; the way it manifests itself as family history as exemplified in Jorge Luis Borges; the ways it is diagnosed as congenital characteristic by such essayists as Octavio Paz and José Lezama Lima.

The second chapter is an attempt at plotting what Wallace Stevens calls ''ghostlier demarcations,'' here the pilgrim's progress of author as wanderer in Borges. These ''demarcations'' are the ploys by which the authorial figure self-effaces into phantomness so that he may haunt unimpeded, quest in perpetuity through thresholds of time and book-scapes of culture.

Quest in the most traditional sense occupies the third chapter. Examined here are two faces, two specters of timeless seeking-after: A Telemachiad — the search for the father — in Juan Rulfo's supremely Mexican version of that topos, and Narcissus as Mexican reflection dissolving into the mirror, the violent mirrors of history as skewed by Carlos Fuentes.

Baroque as the infinite yearning for the Infinite has found its resurgence as irrepressible energy in the profuse verbal flow of Latin America's Neo-Baroque. After tracing the proliferation of this resurgent errantry as desire, as yearning insufficiency with a guarantee of necessity, of necessary longing, the fourth chapter examines the way a particular Neo-Baroque project, Alejo Carpentier's, thwarts its own fulfillment so that the Baroque peregrination may carry on in its prodigious prodigality.

Finally, in the fifth chapter, we witness a clear demonstration of quest that only arrives at the impossibility of self-seeking. The focus here is on Carlos Fuentes and the author's attempts to arrogate to himself critical as well as authorial authority. After studying the self-reflective strategies of *Terra Nostra* as novel bent on critically mediating itself, this novel and Fuentes's reflections on Cervantes and the *Quixote* are examined as mirrored phenomena engaged in a Hegelian enterprise which mimes (and compounds) the problematics of self-mediation in *The Phenomenology of Mind*. The textual quest here turns most blatantly on itself, re-inventing itself as its own haunted spectacle into endlessness.

In keeping with Giambattista Vico's apothegm that a method should take its principles from the object of its treatment, the methods and language of the present study hark, self-consciously, to the voices of their objects. Accordingly, the problematics embedded in the writings treated here are mirrored intentionally in the critical exegeses and speculations which attempt to elucidate them. More recent philologists, such as E. R. Curtius, teach us to recognize the necessity of an unimpeachable continuity from the itinerary of poetic fictions to the enterprise of a critical pursuit. In the spirit of this necessity, I have endeavored to discuss the fictions treated here in a critical language that the shape of such fictions, in mutual interaction with our current contexts of critical understanding, makes inevitable — a critical discourse which this mutuality makes virtually necessary. Beyond this Vichian principle of procedure and this philological imperative, I adhere to no particular critical school or fashion. My only adherence is to the principle of non-adherence — the irreverent agnosticism and questioning spirit which by definition constitute the task of criticism and critical reading. This is not to say, however, that I deny a historical ''present'' and critical context (what Emerson might have called our ''hodiernal facts'') which, perforce, shape our modes of non-adherence. I merely wish to hold that the shape of the critical modes with which our working life may coincide should not remain immune to the questioning and antithetical differentiations of criticism's critical task. In the light and heat of that questing spirit, I can say, without anxiety, that I have learned most from those with whom I may ''disagree.'' I shall not enumerate names, a practice vitiated by the inevitably exclusionary results which accrue to it. My heresies and fidelities, such as they may be, should speak for themselves in the pages that follow.

Dj. K.

Questing Fictions

Chapter 1
Overture: Errant Landscape/ Untimely Pilgrimage

Romance, Harold Bloom has taught us, is a journey toward home. Or, notes this agonistic Qabalist, "romance is a journey toward a supreme trial, after which home is possible, or else homelessness will suffice."[1] In a highly suggestive way the fictions of Latin America, particularly in the last two or three decades, seem to vindicate this observation; for the "romance" of Latin America's fictions is above all a family romance. It is a quest for beginnings whose vicissitudes go beyond a supreme trial to emerge as the strategy of a supreme fiction, a paradoxical supreme fiction that locates its "home" in the homelessness of originary ciphers. Those beginnings are in themselves embattled scenes of imaginative romance, for they trace the illusionary history and chronicles of utopic pursuits and serve as primal map of filial fictions that trace the family history. Latin American fiction, then, is a supreme fiction because it is necessarily fictitious and the origins of that necessity are imaginatively engendered.

I am not unaware of the predictable expectations evoked by the phrase "family romance," particularly for students of Freud. I should make clear that my use of the phrase intends to twist those Freudian expectations in the direction of a particular metaphor. The family line of the romance we shall be tracing is a genealogy of literary texts. The itinerary of this romance refers to the way-stations of a literary tradition. As in all plots of the romance mode, the desired end of the pilgrimage is a homing. In this sense, Latin America's literary history does not differ from other literary traditions. As in other national literatures, literary tradition in Latin America moves toward an encounter with a self-definition which might constitute the homecoming. Although this trajectory may be taken for granted in other traditions, in Latin America it emerges as self-conscious, problematic itinerary, if for no other reason than that, far from being a homologous certainty, the phenomenon we refer to as "Latin America" is an artificial and debatable construct. As we shall see, the specific ways in which Latin American writing accommodates such differentia constitute the particular nature of its textual filiations. While many of its poetic strategies may be recognizable in other literatures, Latin America's literary enterprise acquires a specificity by virtue of being the product of an especially problematic history.

I do not wish to imply by this that I aspire to an *essential* definition of Latin American culture. Nor does this study pretend to reduce Latin America's literary history to the quest for marks of identity. However, the poetic devices deployed in these fictions inevitably internalize the formal strategies of the written histories to which they and their hemisphere pertain. To this extent, the literary family romance is inextricably enmeshed in the broader family history, the history of the histories of Latin America. And, while my aims are a good deal more modest than the documentation of Latin America's quest for a homing in self-definition, the peculiarities of textual filiation elucidated here may become more meaningful if we remain alert to certain historical precedents. Fictions may well be the poetic correlatives of those historical antecedents. As poetic images in which empirical events find their articulate realizations, these fictions have helped, from the very beginning, to shape the history which has engendered them. In this sense it is difficult, and less than wholly desirable, to try to establish an order of priority for the historical "determinants" of this family romance.

Imaginative writings have contributed to the physiognomy of Latin American history from its problematic inception. Because of this persistent reciprocity between history and fictions, our focus on poetic stratagems and their filial entanglements will not preclude a constant vigilance toward certain historical considerations of which poetics may be, simultaneously, a cause as well as a symptom. I shall be dealing with some of these historical elements very shortly. For now we might recall, in a highly synoptic way, that Latin America is itself the product of a textual strategy. Like the fictions it has elicited (from the journals of Columbus to the novels of today), Latin America is the reification of imaginary and imaginative poetic structures — whether these be the eschatological visions of Columbus and the early missionaries, or the chivalric chimeras of the Conquistadors.

Latin America, we should recall, begins its history as impediment, as incidental difficulty which persistently deflects the oriental odyssey of its discoverer. In continental obstinacy the impediment persisted, so much so that it took on antipodal weight, becoming New World to the Old, Terrestrial Paradise to the Orbis Terrarum, and, as Columbus baptized one of the capes in his path, Alpha and Omega of longitudinal cardinality for the planetary sphere. These were more than random linguistic epithets to Columbus and those of his contemporaries who applied them to the topography of this accidental discovery. It was not long after Columbus that this stubborn continental mass which he placed East of Eden became the West — the diabolical, obdurate West for a number of Court physicians and Scholastic humanists, and certainly so for later dramatic almegists such as Lope de Vega. This Edenic Arcadia was, also, Apocalyptic Utopia, as we shall see.

We can readily appreciate how this self-contradictory history of origins engendered a literary tradition whose itinerary becomes congenitally equivocal, ambivalent, self-conscious, manneristic. We can appreciate, too, that its textual family romance should thrive on impediments by internalizing deflective difficulty, by engendering in its poetic strategies tortuous and insurmountable byways so that its pilgrimage might extend itself through the thwarting of its own arrival at that ever-deferred destination. Certainly Latin America's political ethos evinces, through its chronic revolutions, the symptoms of having internalized that originary history; and its literary politics, that is, the romance of its textual family history, seems to have done likewise. Thus, the poetic quest in the texts we now read carries on as unremitting peripeteia. Products of an antipodal "other world," these texts obsessively move to engender and flaunt their own "otherness," their own non-identity to themselves. No straight path here, no linear, univocal, progressive pilgrimage, rather a sinuous movement through twists, turns, skewed lines, and deflecting figures. The mediate agents of this arduous family romance are the questing heroes, the romancers — identifiable as members of this family and its history by a self-recognition whose salient trait, to borrow from Chesterton, is being "homesick at home." By this constant attribute, we are to understand that the journey is desired more than the destination and that the impending arrival is chronically displaced by anxious postponement. (The reasons for that anxiety will emerge further on in our discussion.) As a result, the quest becomes forever extended and the destination rendered perpetually abeyant. The continually suspended goal, then, becomes the suspense of the romance; the imminent and always impending decipherment emerges as a "new" cipher; the radical home, forever absented, is read and reread as a fiction. The repeated readings weave a provisional presence whose fictions, the "supreme trial" of the quester, substitute for that perpetual absence. In other words, a sought-after destination becomes perpetually dislocated into endless deferment through the agency of a supreme fiction's ciphers, that is, through the acts of writing.

The fabric of this fictional substitution is woven by diverse threads. These we tend to identify by the traits that correspond to each quester's name: Jorge Luis Borges, José Lezama Lima, Alejo Carpentier, Juan Rulfo, Carlos Fuentes, to mention only the few who fall within the purview of the present study. The pattern each contributes to the texture of this fabric becomes distinctly identifiable. Jorge Luis Borges, subsuming, consciously or coincidentally, Wordsworth's "something evermore about to be," deploys the congenital suspense and trials of this family romance as strategy of an unending threshold. In questing after what he calls the "aesthetic phenomenon," Borges defers that destination of vision by re-enciphering the threatening disclosure as the "imminence of a revelation that does not take place."

Alejo Carpentier straddles the Atlantic, dialogically. His quest proceeds between the polar points of a European historical consciousness and the belated vision of an Afro-Antillean primordial scene in which he self-consciously seeks to recognize himself as pre-self-conscious sensibility: A questing after the enchantments of the marvelous that he enciphers as "lo real maravilloso." He forestalls the homecoming or arrival at either of the antipodes, as well as the possibility of permanence at any conciliatory midway point, through an exuberant inventiveness, a profuse Baroque of linguistic plenitude whose figurative-fictional presence interdicts the quester's destination. That blockage, that hindering, guarantees a continued yearning, a sustained awe of insufficiency before the *horror vacui* of an opulent *barroquismo* — an abundance whose self-sufficiency belies and accentuates the absence it engenders.

In Juan Rulfo the fabric or texture of the text as cipher ensuing from the pursuit of deciphering becomes overtly compounded. Here the family romance is at once figurative (a trial fiction) as well as "literal" at the plane of narrative *récit*. On both levels, however, we are left with the hard presence of love's body (paternal and erotic). The desire of that body marks an absence that leaves presence behind as corpse and wanders off to haunt as questing passion. Rulfo's only novel, *Pedro Páramo*, is a graphic trace of murmuring voices (a novel muttered, not "written") and, also, a ghost space of haunting memory where mnemonic specters wander in erotomania in pursuit of origins in spectral perpetuity.

A successor to the pursuits of these latter day Quixotes in a New World, Carlos Fuentes's quest becomes spectrally compounded by subsuming the romance of the precursors' specters. The "holy grail" of his endeavor is transformed into the reflection of his ghostly hosts by sublimating them, as in his *Terra Nostra*, through the medium of Thomas Aquinas's Scholastic formula: "Nihil potest homo intelligere sine phantasmata," which Fuentes dilates into "Man can understand nothing without images. And images are phantoms." These images for Fuentes become haunting *locum tenentes* that pullulate as mediations, trace the time of memory in the ever-extended heterotopias of textual space.

My own goal here is not a "history" of this quest romance. That would compound redundancy. My object is a glimpse of a metaphor, of a sanctioning discourse, for a process — a process as new as the New World, as old as the proleptic texts that conceived its invention and prophesied its discovery, and as constant as the perpetually unfolding fictions that endlessly re-make the New World anew. I seek to elucidate that constancy in "making it new" become an obsession on which Oscar Wilde was moved to quip: "The youth of America is their oldest tradition. It has been going on now for three hundred years." That it continues unabated is vindication enough for the perspicacity of Wilde's ironic witticism. The "youth" or "newness" of the New World, as I already suggested, figures as an ongoing problematics, starting from that October day in 1492 when Columbus, the "Knight Errant" of the high seas, *erred*, thereby perpetrating the suggestive first chapter of a necessary fiction. The process I refer to as quest can be characterized best by the duality of the portmanteau term *errant*: a pursuit or questing after and, at the same time, never an over-taking, always a mis-taking, an *errant* accommodation displacing the pursued cipher by endless re-encipherments. The process is obviously problematic, and necessarily so, since the operation whose metaphor we are after is itself a metaphor.

In *Beginnings: Intention and Method*,[2] Edward Said perceptively suggests that all beginnings may well be a necessary fiction since all points of departure are ultimately recursive. Said's insight, I believe, has one of its stark vindications in what many consider the most significant event of the Renaissance: Columbus's discovery of what would be known as the New World. Columbus's accomplishment, however, may be characterized best by Paul Valéry's renowned phrase for the most original of deeds — "a derived achievement." Granted, Said and Valéry are referring to poetic texts while we are speaking of a historical "event." But this, precisely, is the point, as I hope to make clear in short order. That is, the process of Columbus's achievement as we historically know it and the process of poetization referred to by Valéry and Said are not constitutively different. Within each process the paradox of derived originality and secondary and repeated inaugurations is of the same order.

I refer to Columbus as a "Knight Errant" of the high seas. I do so for a number of reasons, the most blatant being that he hired himself out to run an errand for whichever court would engage his services, and the fortuities of history chanced that it should be the Catholic Monarchs of Castille and Aragon. Like his land-locked Medieval precursors on horseback, however, his wanderings had mediating and controlling factors of a more transcendental character founded in the tradition of errantry. Columbus's sally was literally a *peregrinatio*, that is, not just a parabolic gesture for a circuitous journey back home, but an attempt at a world-circumnavigation which would indubitably ascertain that the *peregrinatio* was not only an allegorical trope but, as well, an actual circuitous journey back home. Like his chivalric antecedents, Columbus undertook a task that signified an act of continuity, the continuity of a tradition whose formal structures necessitated their contingent correlative in history, even if that historical event meant a break, a discontinuity within this very tradition. In this sense, the paradox of America as belated original or secondary beginning is already embedded in the pre-discovery tradition of European consciousness. Paradoxically enough, centuries before the discovery, the very possibility of "another" world was interdicted by medieval church fathers such as St. Augustine who condemned as heretical the notion of undiscovered antipodes or inhabited lands. After all, had the Word not reached to all corners of the world already? The "Newness" of the New World, then, is necessarily problematic even before the New World was discovered and so dubbed. Columbus's accomplishment, its *prima facia* happenstance nature aside, is a contingent event, a historical contingency that spells a historical discontinuity. But it is a contingent event that emanates from a necessary structure, or from a congeries of structural necessities that anticipate the event in philosophical, mythological, and eschatological structures. These are the source, the radical antecedents of the "derived achievement" performed by Columbus's "original deed," or "new beginning." The most commonly recalled of these structures comprise the antipodean speculations of Parmenides, reauthorized by Aristotle — the notion that the *oikoumene*, man's home in the cosmos, the world, must have a balancing counter-ballast; Plato's mythological Atlantis; the New World prophesied by the biblical Book of Revelation — a new earth, a millennial kingdom, the eschatological other world; the Hermetic Utopia of Hermes Trismegistus' Adocentyn, later become Tommasso Campanella's City of the Sun.

When Columbus's errantry beached on *terra firma*, that untimely event took on the character of a very problematic beginning. Rather than a constative act of founding, that event signified a performative act of finding, a *découpage*, or meaningful culmination, of a constructive tradition whose radical structures reached down to antiquity. What was to become known as the New World, in fact stood as the historical, corroborating prop for a pro-visional, or previously envisioned, structure; it stood as event which in itself attained the status of an enduring and ever-recurrent topos. The phenomenal event which was to be a New World, in short, figures as topo-graphic cipher, as tropological signature. To put it more radically, the New World becomes the "culmination" of an imaginative trope whose writing and repeated re-writings already dated back to classical Europe. As a structural "closure," or completion, this dénouement emerges as a problematic, literally pre-posterous beginning, an eventuation of a necessary structure into a contingent episode which partakes simultaneously of perennial continuity and chronic discontinuity. This disjunction too is radical, in the sense that it goes back to the roots, to the problematic beginning, for the discontinuity spelled by the discovery consists in a drastic reversal: Formal structures (scripture, philosophy; imaginary, poetic, visionary tropes of fiction) are no longer analogical correlatives of the world; now, a world geo-graphy with empirical entailments of its own emerges as the corroborative reality (or so it has been understood by our questing romancers, from Columbus to García Márquez) of these imaginary forms.

This radical inversion, this momentous discontinuity, I believe, is what con-figures the "New" in the New World. The "New," in other words, is *not* in the World; it does not obtain in geography necessarily, but in the discourse it makes necessary, in the imaginative form, the necessary fiction that obtains in the precipitated *topo-graphy*. Therein lies the structure of quest and its chronically inopportune object. Therein, too, lie the problematic origins of our family romance — culminating from and eventuating in a necessary fiction of poetic discourse. Exemplary instances of this problematics abound in Latin America. One thinks immediately of Sor Juana Inés de la Cruz and her "new" world cosmogony in "Primero sueño," of Andrés Bello, and his anxious georgics of primacy, of Gabriel García Márquez and his primal/apocalyptic America in *One Hundred Years of Solitude*, as well as a number of authors we shall be discussing in this study at length. The most succinct poetic metaphor articulating this process may well be the work of T. S. Eliot, an American writer who self-consciously problematizes his own Americanness with characteristic ambivalence toward the "New" and the New World. I refer to that standard chiasmus of return in Eliot's "East Coker" which, suggestively enough, opens with "In my beginning is my end" and whose closing line recursively reads, "In my end is my beginning." Eliot forces us to confront a compounded equivoque by troping — in spectral mirror inversion — the proemial line and coda of his poem. Beyond the circuitous figure of *peregrinatio*, however, Eliot's opening gambit articulates the preposterousness of America's proemial predicament and its equivocalities — a predicament of self-entrapment since, with the poem's "closure," we are remanded back to its beginning to begin anew. Our homecoming after the circuitous journey of the *peregrinatio* is in the poem itself, that is, in the repeated turns, the tropes of its necessary fictions, the discourse of its textual *topo-graphy* and its discursive practice.

In this same poem, the second from Eliot's *Four Quartets*, we read, "Home is where one starts from." Where we do start from, whether in 1492 or in the opening line of "East Coker," is that culmination and departure point of proemial paradox. Thus, born of a necessary fiction, the American romancers *qua* American (in the hemispheric sense), like the poetic persona and implied readers of Eliot's poem, inevitably will seek after a homecoming in a necessary fiction. Their quest will beach, inexorably, on the slippery shore of fiction's topo-graphy. As much may be said not only of the poetic persona, but of T. S. Eliot the poet, whose return to East Coker, the ancestral English home of the Eliots, could be seen as a reversion, the seeking after a corroborative geography for an imaginary and imaginative topo-graphy, a necessary fiction in the best American tradition.

In this sense, one cannot help but see in Eliot's backward glance, which is also a forward gaze, a spectral avatar of Inca Garcilaso de la Vega, yearning in sixteenth-century Andalucía for the imaginary topography, the sublimated fiction of an Incaic homeland in America which was more a poetic construct inherited and engendered by his fecund poetic powers; or of Andrés Bello, whose twenty-year stint in the nineteenth-century London of Blake engendered the romance of a neo-epic quest — the *Silva a la agricultura de la zona torrida* with its enchanted topo-graphy and timeless nostalgia for the future. That Eliot should turn East while Inca Garcilaso and Andrés Bello turn West when looking homeward does not alter the essential act of the quest or its family history, the romance. That incidental difference is explained by Octavio Paz as a function of the past's significance to Latin Americans and to Anglo-Americans. The latter, Paz notes, have eradicated the past in favor of an endless future. Eliot, then, can only seek after an inaugural space beyond America, in a past beyond the effaced American past, in Europe. The Latinate American line, on the other hand, has compounded the fabric of its "New World" past through cumulative accretions of heterogeneous cultural elements that have succeeded in integrating themselves into a whole only partially and problematically, yielding thereby not only one past but a plurality of pasts in simultaneous space(s) — with many places.[3]

Octavio Paz, a supremely American poet who has done a great deal to Americanize T. S. Eliot through sublimation and subversion of that reluctant native son of St. Louis, notes that the unique character of American literature "resides in the fact that the reality against which it contends is a utopia . . . we are a chapter in the history of European utopias." And of European history, he notes, "we are its premeditated creation."[4] The ways in which American literature "contends" with this predicament are exquisitely illustrated by the poetic discourse of Paz himself where, and one thinks immediately of such exempla from the Paz canon as "Vuelta" or "Piedra de sol," utopia time *and* again (always anew, recommencing again) is subjected to the chastisements of repetition, of "revolution," to the differentiation of originary acts in a ceaseless replay of "new" beginnings. The process is summed up by Harold Rosenberg's now commonplace conundrum "the tradition of the new" and is incisively delineated by Paz in his 1971-72 Charles Eliot Norton Lectures at Harvard.[5]

America, as "premeditated creation" of European history, as "a chapter in the history of European utopias," *contends* with the previously mentioned structures of its founding by constantly refinding those inventive frames, appropriating them; America subsumes them into a process of what Giambattista Vico called "secular history," synonym for "poetic history" or a history continually self-made, a historical self perpetually self-invented. Thus, lest a "premeditated" utopia wrought by the European imagination in order to escape the burden of its own history become consecrated into a central Imago, a mystified and portentous myth, the inventive impulse of that utopia, its necessary fiction, is internalized as quest. In that internalized phase it becomes manifested as perpetual operation, unending event, ceaseless contingency, self-de-centering re-play, ever-errant and deliberately erring. It emerges, one might say, as a quest strategy deployed for its own sake and against its own ends, a drive that oscillates between its pre-posterous beginning and its equally waylaid destination. Revolution chastises utopia through the constant repetition of "making it new" in a redoubled strategy; it deploys at once an analogical and an ironic tactic. The errantry of "beginning anew" emerges as spectral analogue, as recursive reflection of its founding fictions. Like all analogues, however, the process points as much to the relation between terms of correspondence as it serves to engender or heighten difference between those analogous terms. In this sense the quest for the new points to itself as difference. It pursues the attainment of novelty by constantly aiming at displacement so that *it* may move to the originary point of departure, to the beginning. The doubly meaningful term *recapitulation* is a perfect equivoque for describing this operation. For recapitulation signifies at once a gathering or summation and a re-move back to the head (of the line), back to a beginning which antedates all that becomes recapitulated.

The quest turns to stratagem of irony when, self-consciously, it reflects on its necessary errancy. The realization that the project must be necessarily delay-ridden, ineluctably erring, precipitates the irony of self-deflection. The quest must "speak" against itself so that its enterprise of beginning anew will not be interdicted, foreclosed, relinquished by peremptory completion or totalization. The problematically originary past, then, must always be made present, as com-memorative analogue, as mnemonic reflection. But its presence must never attain completion, *coup*, or sufficiency. That plenitude must be forever pro-scribed. The inventive past, rather, must serve as on-going activity; it must haunt as ghost of a beginning assumed to have been, but to have been only as necessary fiction, as poetic history not as totalized (completed) history. It must, too, be a "present" that supplements and is supplemented by the future. In that way, the projected quest, the errant project, may always dwell as unconsummated desire, as nostalgia or as future-directed recollection, displaced and ever-displaceable by the seeking *after*. In this sense, in this radical and revolutionary chastisement of utopia — that topo-graphy which is no-place other than in time — becomes ceaselessly deposed from a no-where to perpetually "new" now-here. Call this a *uchronia* in which all time attains to the timeless, to a "present absence" or an "absent presence." The oxymorons point to a temporal figura of irony in which time and presence become counter-self-directed so that the proemial fiction of "a new beginning" may begin anew, as for example, in the radical irony of Borges's title "A New Refutation of Time."

If, then, Renaissance Europe tried to overthrow the burden of history by stepping "outside of itself" into the Utopia of a New World, the New World contends with the burden of being what Paz calls "a premeditated creation" of European history. It steps out of utopia or, more accurately, it exacerbates utopia into *heterotopia* and, further, into *uchronia*. This radical intensity displaces utopia from no-place further into no-time, that is, into *uchronia*. *Uchronia*, in this sense, is not ontological timelessness. Rather, it is the ever-slipping project of the *timeless* which obtains in continuous repetition.

Uchronia is the breaking of form, the form which dwells in time, that is, the form of utopia. That break constitutes a rupture which shatters the dwelling, the mediate and hypostatized structure of utopia. Our Romance idioms, French and Spanish in particular, possess a linguistic figure that connotes this shattering disintegration, this undoing which exposes, unshelters, opens up to homelessness and adversity. The French *contretemps*, primarily grammatical, its denotation more tied to rhetorical operations of syncope, is clearly a violation of structural integrity, a "thorough breaking" or "severing" which the Greek etymons of "syncope" suggest. The Spanish *destiempo* and the more common *contratiempo* are more broadly connotative, more inclusively suggestive. Here the breaking of form, or shattering of temporal dwelling, skews the timeless, the *uchronic*, into adversity to be weathered, a connotation inherent in the French *contretemps* as well. We might say, then, that the American imagination contends with structures of historical determinacy by consigning those structures to a condition of indeterminacy (to an endless "ante-predeterminacy," if one could forge such a compounded figura) in the rarefied air of the timeless.

By self-dislocation into a recurring homelessness, the continuous project of beginning anew will not be impeded. Relentless *adversity* (literally turning toward, toward the un-timely and the counter-time, or *contratiempo*) propitiates the timeless, self-decentering errantry/errancy. Carlos Fuentes tersely distills the process I have been describing: "Escribir es combatir el tiempo a destiempo. . . . Escribir es un contratiempo" (To write is to combat time *untimely*. . . . To write is an *adversity*).[6] Flaubert's characterization of writing as enduring lie against time clearly reverberates in Fuentes's apothegm. A compelling difference, however, separates the Mexican's *escritura* from the *écriture* of Flaubert. Whereas for Flaubert writing constitutes a "lie," a Bovaristic utopia or "utopiography," Fuentes's writing, in its post-European, American, duplicitous irony, already knows itself to issue from and against utopia — a necessary fiction centered in the counter-time, the *uchronia* of American temporality. That centeredness is what the American's *escritura* aims to dislocate, *à contretemps*, *à outrance*, into a timeless breach of the "timely."

The negative valence of this dislocating "counter-time" directed against the time-centered myth of utopia, ironically enough, has its precedent in the figure of utopia itself. For utopia, Thomas More's master irony, has its genesis in a counter-statement, itself a negative or critical valence. Utopia, we must recall, stands as contrary trope of affirmation, as negative space, as critical deconstruction and ironic disfiguration of *Eutopia* — the *locus amoenus* of a Golden Age ironically displaced by *Nusmquama*, a nowhere land of temporal perfectability or perpetual futurity. A tropological stock market, so to speak, whose futures acquire their value in their endless promise and perpetual futurity. This compounded trope or multiple irony is another name for *utopiography* traced by our romance texts and their supreme fictions as constant *erring* or perpetual quest with a built-in mechanism that forever guarantees the post-ponement of its object or goal. The paradox of a nostalgia for a future or a mnemonic yearning forever pushed into futurity is another name for desire, itself more desired than its object or destination. A desire whose pursuit, lest it over-reach and overtake its object, removes the danger of its fulfillment not only by apotropaically extenuating the future but, also, by spectrally equating the object of nostalgia that lies in the future with the object of nostalgia whose recovery is sought after (and after the fact), that lies in the past. We could term this a constantly receding horizon in both directions at once, whose ends are spectral and mutually reflecting: "In my beginning is my end . . . In my end is my beginning," to recall Eliot once more. Or, what is before us lies behind us.

We read this paradox of desire in America's textual romance within the problematical quest of the nineteenth-century Anglo-American Edward Bellamy's *Looking Backward: 2000-1887* (1887) and in our contemporary Spanish-American (Mexican) Elena Garro's *Los recuerdos del porvenir* (1963) — "Memories of the Future." Both are visions of the un-timely, nostalgias *a destiempo*, yearnings *à contretemps*. They project a *locus* in time, in future-time, from which to reflect, recursively, the past and what by then (in that future perfect) will have been a past — a circuitous desire, a *peregrinatio*, that displaces a present and its presence so that the goal, the homecoming into the present is already made absent, emptied out, rendered and maintained object of desire before that destination is reached. In the best American tradition of intensifying the pursuit of utopias, an obsession with necessary fictions inherited as tradition from the Old World, both of these works are utopiographies: That of the New Englander a nostalgia for a promised time in a promised land, that of the novelist from New Spain a yearning for the meliorating future of a Revolution (in both senses of social and temporal revolution) and its promises. But both end up as reversed images of their object of desire. That is, they emerge as utopiographies of inverted utopia, as figures of dystopia — yet another ironic twist of a Eutopia skewed by the paradox of Thomas More's master irony. For Bellamy's idealistic projection bespeaks more the nightmare of historical reality between 1887 and the bimillennium, just as Elena Garro's acrimonious memories of the future become haunted recollections by specters of a betrayed and failing revolution (the specific allusion is the Mexican Revolution of 1910).

If we keep in mind the antipodean tenets that go back to Parmenides and consider not only their cosmological significance but also their rhetorical implications, we should not be surprised at the inversion of Old World structures within the *topography* of the antipodal New World. If the "New World" is an antipode, a counter ballast and inverse image of the "World," it is logical that those Old-World structures should follow suit in that New World reversal. But this logical expectation also takes on an added dimension, yet one more deflective turn. For the very notions of the *Utopia Moriana* are in some measure New World founded. More's reliance on the *materia* of New World chronicles — the accounts of Amerigo Vespucci, for example, or Columbus's first letter from the New World — is common knowledge. Thus, the New World is in fact a key coefficient in the transformation of Eutopia into the ironic and critical trope of Utopia. Equally intriguing in this regard is what Harry Levin points out with respect to that dramatic reversal which was to displace the ideal of a *locus amoenus* from Arcadia and its Golden Age in a commemorative past to a utopia in a visionary future. "If old Europe was no Utopia," Levin concludes, "there was still the New World, which had helped inspire the dream and would witness many attempts toward its realization." [7] Levin reminds us on that score of Vasco de Quiroga, the kindly Bishop of Michoacan (he was also the translator of More's *Utopia*, obviously in more than one sense) who sought to put into practice the tenets of More's New World-inspired ideals. What More had borrowed from New World accounts, then, to forge the mordantly critical ironies he aimed at European, and specifically English, (mis)governance *re*verts back to the New World as "practical principles." This may well represent one of America's extenuating counter-statements or spectral reversals, as we shall see shortly.

In the same year that More was tried, condemned, and beheaded (1535) by the Court of Henry VIII, Vasco de Quiroga would write back to Europe, justifying his experiment, "Not in vain but with much cause and reason is this called the New World, not because it is newly founded, but because it is in its people and in almost everything as were the first and golden ages." [8] Vasco de Quiroga's comment may well be a problematic beginning as revolutionary inversion, or as double reversal, that exacerbates Europe's utopic vision in America, for what he sees in the *New* World of Europe's future is *Old* Europe's Arcadian past, the mythological Golden Age. The Eliotic turn of "In my beginning is my end . . . In my end is my beginning" takes on a concrete figuration in Bishop Vasco's retrospective vision, brought forth to justify his utopian experiment. What is most compelling in this dramatic spectacle shows up in the interweaving of biography and utopiography.

We should recall that the administration of the Colonial First Audiencia in Mexico was a dismal failure. Cortés was moved to write to Emperor Charles V in response to that ill-fated misgovernance, recommending, in a widely disseminated letter, that Charles prohibit henceforth the assignment of lawyers to administrative posts in the New World. The consequences of these unfortunate events and Cortés's recommendations are twofold, and the elements of that duality become strangely intertwined as American quest romance, as elements of a historiographic and biographic family history. First, the recommendation of Cortés's letter regarding lawyers finds a precedent in Thomas More's *Utopia*. All lawyers are banished from More's ideal Nowhereland. Second, the Spanish court's answer to the tragic administration of the First Audiencia turns out to be the translator of More's *Utopia*, Bishop Vasco de Quiroga, who is dispatched by the court of Charles to ameliorate the effects of the administrative disaster. Bishop Vasco's remedy is the application of More's utopian principles.

I read in this intermediation of utopian structure and historical event, of *theoria* and *praxis*, an instructive parable of quest or self-perpetuating desire; the trope of an ironic quest whose terms (structure and event) entail a principle of mutual reversibility. Structures, that is, are brought to the fore when the events they precipitated turn back on them, shedding light on them as the events' generative principles, or beginnings. Mutual reversibility, however, implies, as well, a relationship of supplementarity; that is, an adversative play of substitutions whereby structure and event breach, displace, and subsume each other, antithetically. It is precisely on this contentious ground, this arena of "contending," to use Paz's verb from our earlier discussion, that structure (utopia), becomes chastised by the "revolutionary" or recurrent performance of the structure's repetition as event. A proemial or founding structure, in other words, finds at once its inaugural vigor and its superannuation in the recurrent event of commencement or "making it new." This, in short, may be another way of characterizing the perpetual process of decipherment through endless re-encipherment, a project which constitutes the supreme trials of our necessary fictions. We could call it an adversative quest in which the questing romancer, the errant pilgrim, must always find himself between homes, introjecting the past's beginning as prophecy and projecting the future as commemorative yearning. This adversative, revolutionary quest entails and becomes entailed in the imaginative life of self-begetting artifacts — America's necessary "supreme fictions" — which betray and extend homelessness or ceaseless transience between homes. We can appreciate in this regard Jorge Luis Borges's predilection when he confesses in one of his innumerable interviews that his favorite American story is Hawthorne's *Wakefield*, a work he characterizes as being "about the man who stays away from home all those years."[9]

"Making it new" or beginning anew — our critical, modern consciousness as self-begetting sensibilities — then, is a fictional locus, a fictitious point always between homes. The necessary fiction is the American uchronia, the hyperbolic extenuation of utopia, a uchronia which is never present or in the present. If this reads as a pleonasm, it does so by dint of being the irony of an obsession. The object and arena of this paradoxical obsession is a scene of recognition where all discernment is a self-recognition, and the consummation of that perspicacity runs the sure risk of proving fatal. Call it an apocalyptic crisis, an eschatology to be errantly mis-taken in order to be overcome, lest the future cease to be future by becoming present, and lest the cumulative weight of the past prove an overwhelming burden — an impending threat recurrently to be overcome by scurrying back to its incipient generation when it was new and weightless, even if that "newness" be the specter of self-delusion or a fiction of necessity. Although, it must be said, that specter in America is neither purely weightless, nor exclusively the product of self-delusion. The fact is, American history affords us a precedent in the plight of Moctezuma II and the Aztec Empire at the time of the Spanish conquest, as Archibald MacLeish, Octavio Paz, and Carlos Fuentes remind us. We see in the fatal immobility of Moctezuma the insurmountable burden of a recognition scene as apocalyptic crisis when the future becomes present by giving substance to the prophecy of the past. I am referring to Moctezuma's predicament on the occasion of the prophesied Second Coming of the beneficient, but fallen, Quetzalcoátl from the shores of the East and Cortés's landing on the Mexican mainland on the very day marked for that return by Moctezuma's ancestors and their prophetic calendars. Tomorrow, then, must always remain tomorrow and today must always begin anew lest it be taken for an overtaken tomorrow. "The time of old Mexico, in the conquest, fulfilled its promise only to find its death," Carlos Fuentes reminds us.[10] The Latin American imagination takes Moctezuma's fall as primal scene of instruction, a lapsarian scene whose lessons of recognition exact the dark and costly price of gnosis and eschatology.

Necessity is insufficiency, especially so in the quest romance, and its sufficient fulfillment is a totalization that spells the fatal blow. Thus, America's quest romance is a necessary fiction whose necessity stands for the desired insufficiency that must forestall fulfillment. Should it prove otherwise, the fatal consequences must repeat themselves. Such a dire eventuality, it would appear, haunts the American writer, from Borges to Carpentier to Fuentes. Borges dramatizes this predicament as gnostic parable, as for example, in his story "The Life of Tadeo Isidoro Cruz (1829-1874)," where Borges charts a biography of self-entrapment issuing from a recognition scene and its attendant retribution.[11] The Argentine romancer problematizes the beginning of this biography, as beginning, with a proemial augury, itself already problematical as contradictory prolepsis, as seeking *after* what already went before. I am referring to the story's epigraph from William Butler Yeats's "A Woman Young and Old," which becomes here an ominous predicament of apocalyptic self-recognition for the hero as questing protagonist and, ultimately, as we shall see, for Borges as romancing quester: "I am looking for the face I had / Before the world was made." Borges does not divulge that primal countenance, neither as revealed physiognomy nor as mnemonic presence. He merely alludes to its qualitative nature as dreamscape of phantasmagoria, as mantic nightmare whose augury becomes, in ultimate decipherment, a self-recognition in a fatal hour of final reckoning — when the remembered future falls into a present as deadly revelation.

And here, too, the structure of temporality is subjected to the subterfuge of uchronia by an attenuation of time wrought through the conscious exaggeration of temporal specificity. We encounter that duplicitous precision not only in the title of the story but also in the scrupulous and reductive pinpointing of events in their most incipient instant of origin or conception. The punctiliousness of Borges's tale is an inaugural exactitude centered on both the biography and the life-subject of that biography. This mirrored beginning in the beginning, where narrative structure and biographical (i.e., historical) event or incident overlap turns out to be an ingenious ploy, a deflective ruse. For the conception of the hero's biological life and the genesis of the tale become undermined *qua* inaugural moments by the supernumerary repetitions "beginnings" ultimately must endure.

Borges's narrative and Tadeo Isidoro Cruz's biography begin: "On the sixth of February, 1829 . . . along about dawn." At that moment, one of the men of a gaucho militia had a "haunting nightmare and, in the dim shadows of a shed where he lay sleeping, his confused outcry woke the woman who shared his bed. Nobody ever knew what he dreamed, for around four o'clock that afternoon the gauchos were routed by a detachment of (Suárez's) cavalry . . . in the thickening twilight, in tall swamp grasses, where the man died in a ditch, his skull split by a saber that had seen service in the Peruvian and Brazilian wars. The woman's name was Isidora Cruz. The son born to her was given the name Tadeo Isidoro" (p. 81).

The enigma of the gaucho militiaman's nightmare is sealed by his brutal death. But the mystery may well have its adumbration in that sudden demise, if we read his nightmare, that is, as precognizance whose contents hauntingly assail the man's sleep with the imminence of his untimely fate. Be that as it may, we are given only a glimpse of this gaucho, a glimpse into only one of his life's nights, a night of ominous terror by virtue of what is revealed to him in haunting nightmare. That single night of terrifying disclosure stands, nonetheless, as both primal scene of recognition and a final scene for the gaucho. His traumatic revelation ends up being an apocalyptic discernment dreamed in what proves to be his last dream. From that encirclement, a new spiral, a new concentric movement is inaugurated. That inauguration in this same primal scene consists in the rudimentary origins, the conception of the tale's hero, the life-subject of this bio-graphy.

Beyond this at once final and inaugural night, Borges as biographer tells us that his concern is a "single night" in the life of Tadeo Isidoro Cruz, a night which I am reluctant to qualify as *another* single night, *other*, that is, than the cyclical night we have just discussed. I believe the augmentative adjective is superfluous, for in this concentrically spiraling scheme a "single night" is a figure of speech that connotes neither uniqueness nor enumeration. Rather, it denotes a timeless instance, a uchronic figura that traces a *poetic history*, as we shall see shortly, whose itinerary is its own "truth," whose project is the performance of the acts that constitute the history, whose countenance is the face of that very history which, once revealed, once become present to itself in self-recognition, achieves the exhaustion of its trajectory; that is, it reaches the end which spells mortality. In this sense, the "single night" of the gaucho father and the "single night" of the "biographised" son are of one piece and writ within each other *as a single night* in which converge at once in timeless perpetuity beginning and end, "In my beginning is my end . . . "

The biographer Borges certainly manifests an insight into this economy. His penchant is clearly for such a concision or paucity which diminishes temporality into its own ghost, into the timeless ghosts of uchronic figurae. "Of the many days and nights that make up his life, only a single night concerns me; as to the rest, I shall tell only what is necessary to that night's full understanding" (p. 81). The possessive here is double and denotes a duality of understandings — ours, the readers' understanding of this poetic history which disseminates itself from a uchronic scene, and the hero's understanding as self-discernment. I shall return to the first of these in short order. For now I merely wish to comment on that understanding as self-re-connaissance. This is how Borges maps that recognition scene where self-encounter is tantamount to self-exhaustion of the quest's itinerary: "(What lay in wait for him, hidden in the future, was a night of stark illumination — the night in which at last he glimpsed his own face, the night in which at last he heard his name. *Fully understood, that night exhausts his story*; or rather, one moment in that night, one deed, since deeds are our symbols [read: our poetic history].) Any life, no matter how long or complex it may be, is made up essentially of a single moment — the moment in which a man finds out, once and for all, who he is" (p. 83, added emphases).

One readily recalls that the Borges *oeuvre* comprises a congeries of such exhaustive moments, visionary moments of autoscopy and self-recognition whose perspicacity exacts, in return, the final diacritical mark in the life-sentence of the seer, a gnostic self-gain at the sufficient cost of self-loss, a fulfillment of the quest that nullifies its necessity. Instances of this peroration from the Borges canon which immediately occur to one include "The Circular Ruins," "Death and the Compass," "The Garden of the Forking Paths," "The Secret Miracle," "Matthew XXV:30," "Snorri Sturluson (1179-1241)," "The Cyclical Night," and, most problematically, "Borges and I." Ultimately, however, as American romancer Borges is not reducible to that romantic irony of self-loss in self-gain. And at this juncture the isomorphic relationship between Yeats (the story's epigraph) and Borges's map of a quest romance breaks apart. This disjunction is founded in the fact that Borges's quest romance is fundamentally a family romance, a biography become autobiography, a poetic history which is a "tribal" or genealogical poetic history, in the most profoundly Vichian sense of "gentile" or "secular" history to be elaborated on later in our discussion.

Borges's is a poetic family history, or a family romance, in more than one sense. First, because the self-recognition discerned by Tadeo Isidoro Cruz on that night of "stark illumination" emerges as commemorative repetition with a built-in mechanism ensuring that it perpetually repeat. The face that Cruz encounters, "the face . . . / Before the world was made," is the face he will always have in what is the Argentine's national epic, the *Martín Fierro*. Second, because Tadeo Isidoro Cruz finds himself retracing in space the steps of his father, closing in on the geography of his conception for repeated convergence of beginning and end, conception and finality, in a primal and innumerable scene of transgression and recognition. For after many vicissitudes, Cruz finds himself in the very spot where he was hunted down as an outlaw after having killed a man, the very spot out of which "had come the unknown man who fathered Cruz and died in a ditch, his skull split by a saber that had seen action on the battlefields of Peru and Brazil. Cruz had forgotten the name of the place. Now, after a vague and puzzling uneasiness, it came to him" (p. 84). No longer a fugitive, rather as lawman, Cruz now leads a troop in pursuit of an outlaw-deserter, Martín Fierro, whose entrapment in the same spot elicits from Cruz "the feeling of having lived this moment before." The recognition of himself in the encircled outlaw, whom "he understood [to be] himself," leads him to throw down his officer's kepi and begin fighting, shoulder to shoulder, with Martín Fierro against his own men.

Beside Tadeo Isidoro Cruz's discernment in the tale, there is that other understanding in the possessive of "that night's full understanding," alluded to a moment ago. This is our, the readers', understanding that Borges's tale is in itself a repetition, a specular reflection of the repetitions in the story. What is mirrored within and between these frames are the events of a national poem written in the nineteenth century by José Hernández. While the biographical subject of our tale, then, repeats the deeds of the outlaw Cruz in the *Martín Fierro*, the biographer Borges repeats the graphic traces of José Hernández. In retracing those inventive lines of a national poetic history, Borges suggests the supernumerary repetitions and variations which endlessly extend those lines into timeless perpetuity. Borges tells us that that moment of "stark illumination" in that single night which reveals and exhausts all moments is an "episode [which] belongs to a famous poem — that is to say to a poem which has come to mean 'all things to all men' (I Corinthians 9:22), since almost endless variations, versions, and perversions have been read into its pages" (p. 82).

Inasmuch as Borges augments this repetition with *his own version*, he partakes of the process which he describes. Repetition is a fiction, a necessary fiction, for what is repeated is not the constancy of "same" but of self-differentiation or, as Borges notes, "endless variations, versions, and perversions." This errant course comprises the necessary errancy, the continuous mistaking whose one *mis-take* constitutes Borges's own story on that unending continuum of self-making and remaking. Supplanting *and* subverting at once all privileged points of inauguration, "The Life of Tadeo Isidoro Cruz (1829-1874)" configures a paradoxical primal scene, a self-recognition scene whose "ultimate" insight belies the myth of origin and of originality. For Borges's hero recognizes himself as the hero of another poem ("Tadeo Isidoro Cruz had the feeling of having lived this moment before''), and we recognize in Borges, the romancer, the voice and authorial quest of a poetic ancestor, José Hernández.[12]

But the family romance here goes beyond a poetic history whose questing fictions extend perpetually into the future of "repeatable" textuality. For in his re-encipherment of the *Martín Fierro* episode, Borges's graphic or poetic family history becomes, as well, a family romance that bears the marks of consanguine filiation. In Borges's *mistaking*, his "version" or willing errancy, of this epic's episode, the author goes beyond poetic affiliation into genealogical filiation. We read, for example, that the demise of the unnamed gaucho who fathered Cruz the night of his haunting nightmare, "his skull split by a saber that had seen service in the Peruvian and Brazilian wars," is at the hands of "a detachment of Suárez, cavalry." One recognizes in this Suárez, and Borges corroborates this in his own commentaries,[13] Borges's great-grandfather who led brilliant military expeditions in Peru and Brazil. The ranch from which Cruz sets out on a cattle drive to Buenos Aires in 1849, the ill-fated occasion on which he would kill a man, belonged to Francisco Xavier Acevedo, one of Borges's maternal ancestors. Poetic structures, historical details, and empirical contingencies thus become interwoven into the textual emplotment of this "poetic history," a strategy which places historical event and poetic structure on an equal footing — both equally subsumed by the event of Borges's re-encipherment of an episode from the national epic into recursive parable of recurring substitution and convertibility.

Borges's activity, then, substitutes its own version, its own poetization of a poetic episode. It does so, however, by a problematic repetition (itself "repeatable") of a poetic structure identified as a mark of national selfhood, a family romance further interlaced with the marks of consanguine filiation. In the obliquely American sense of T. S. Eliot's "Tradition and the Individual Talent,"[14] Borges's performance evinces the problematics of a supplement, a supplement which becomes an aggregate extending and simultaneously modifying tradition. The radical irony of that supplement, however, becomes clearer if we read *supplement* in the sense given to it by Jacques Derrida (as substitute, as surplus, as compensatory "other" that displaces, replaces, and extends the hegemony of that which it has replaced by calling attention to itself as its replacement), a sense which is very much to the point since the frenzy of American obsession with deauthorizing inaugural acts, with disprivileging any and all beginnings through their appropriation and exacerbation, would seem to offer a tenable exemplum of Derrida's idea of decenteredness.[15] In this respect Borges's supplement to the "original" poetic structure becomes a substitution that displaces, suspends, internalizes, and re-places. This is a replacement, however, in whose own figuration are embedded the seeds of its own displacements and substitutions, as well as its sundering or dissemination. As I have already noted, what is repeated in Borges's rendering of the *Martín Fierro* episode is at once the "same" and different — the same insofar as there is a movement back to the beginning; different since that inauguration is a *new* beginning. Like Cruz's discernment, it is a self-re-cognizing in which the discerning self defers to the re-cognized self, both rendered different by dint of this momentary perspicacity.

The measure of insight, therefore, is the measure of difference. And self-differentiation becomes a problematic movement toward and from that locus in time perceived as "originary" beginning but *known* to be a fiction, an imaginary and imagistic landscape. I emphasize *known* here by way of pointing to the problematic scene of that gnoseology, of that epistemology. For what is "known," in the words of one of America's most discerning sensibilities, is the image of *incunabula*. I am referring to José Lezama Lima, who suggestively equates *incunabula* with the *image* of *terra incognita*, that is, the "image of Latin America."[16] I find Lezama's equation of America with the "infancy" or cradle-stage earliness of text and textual space ("incunabula") illuminating. In this provocative association or "baroque metonymy," as Lezama himself would have it, we can truly appreciate the resonances of what Vico termed a "poetic history," as I hope to make clear in short order.

The opening lines of José Lezama Lima's essay "Image of Latin America" read: "After the image served as impetus for the most frenetic or meticulous expeditions through the *terra incognita*, through *incunabula*, it had to slacken. Columbus, like Marco Polo, suffered imprisonment after his discoveries and adventures, as if an imposed respite were necessary after the fever of the *imago*. Perhaps thanks to their imprisonments they achieved an ambivalence between what they had really seen and what they were going to relate, so as not to remain prisoners of the image from which they had departed even before touching and recognizing it." The critical semantic register in Lezama's insight here is what he alternately calls image and *imago*. "Image" stands as conjunctive term which the author uses to equate, by apposition, *terra incognita* and *incunabula*. The enunciatory linkage performed by Lezama has its grammatical precedents in the Classical rhetorical tradition, a tradition supremely (and idiosyncratically) familiar to Lezama's philological obsessions. The same tradition of rhetorical schemas modulate the dynamics of the *image* that are operative, even controlling, in the pursuit of these expeditions. In both undertakings — Lezama's and the two adventurers', Columbus and Marco Polo — we see a Classical mediation, what the rhetors called a *modus transumptivus*. This technical operation makes possible the figurative connectives, such as metaphor, metonymy, synecdoche, of which Lezama avails himself in making the connections between *terra incognita* and *incunabula*. The *imago* has its genesis in this same *terminus technicus*. "Image," then, that radical and radial focus, that field of energy whose force serves as impetus to the errantry of these questers, is not a transcendental, metaphysical, or mythological Imago numinously consecrated.[17] Rather, that potency is the energy generated from language under stress, rhetorical figures in tension, the text as difficulty, the dynamic force of culture, what Lezama enciphers as "gnostic space." That is, a "cultured" knowing which yields the *image*. The *imago*, we might say, is "gnostic space" through which *nature* becomes *landscape* and landscape dwells in *incunabula* — the cradle of text, the early scene of textuality, the primal scene of writing. In this sense, I find a supportive and felicitous consonance between what I have been referring to as a "necessary fiction" and Lezama's shorthand notation "image." An earlier and more extensive version of this Cuban writer's essay adumbrates and, to some extent, helps us to decipher the studied difficulty (so characteristic in Lezama) of this necessary fiction that he refers to as the "image."

In the opening lines of Lezama's *La expresión americana* we read: "Only the difficult is stimulating; only the resistance which challenges us is capable of confronting, provoking, and sustaining our powers of knowledge, but in reality, what is the difficult? . . . It is the form of becoming in which a landscape moves towards a direction, an interpretation, or a simple hermeneutics, in order to then move toward its reconstruction, which is what indicates definitively its efficacy or obsoleteness; its rigorous force or its extinguished echo; that is its historical vision. . . . Historical vision which is that counterpoint or texture [*tejido*, fabric] transmitted by the *imago*, by the image participating in history" (pp. 9-10).

I believe I read Lezama accurately when I take "image" as correlative of what he characterizes by the provocative and contending term "difficulty." At the heart of that difficulty lies a "hermeneutic principle," or as Lezama would have it, "the form of becoming in which landscape moves towards . . . an interpretation." That interpretation, the "reconstruction" of landscape, in turn, precipitates a historical vision through the dialectical mediation (counterpoint) of *imago*. Lezama equates "historical vision" with what he terms *tejido* — fabric, or the weaving of a text, of "incunabula." Image, then, points to a process of hermeneutical invention, of interpretation; to a landscape *fabricated* or invented rather than found. In other words, "historical vision," the "fabric" woven by the mediation of the *imago*, is the product of a deliberate operation, a technical process which we traditionally associate with the inventive production of texts and textuality, of incunabula. We can now see how incunabula become a corollary of *terra incognita*. In Lezama's insight *terra incognita* emerges as *landscape* in the process of "becoming," as what the Classical rhetoricians called a *topografia*, a commonplace of epic landscape, a rhetorical figuration or schema of a *terminus technicus*. The fabric which is contrapuntally woven "by the image participating in history," then, is a vision of a "poetic history," of history of/as self-invention. Our attainment of that vision, Lezama tells us, must inevitably be sought through the same inventive processes, the performative acts of *fabrication* — the technical procedures of weaving and textualizing — that accrue to the figurations of the "poetic history" whose operations we seek to comprehend. Our own vision of a cultural landscape inevitably must become a landscape of culture. Accordingly,

Lezama tells us, "that the valuation of historical links and of critical appraisal had to move necessarily to a new order was happily awaited. An Ernst Robert Curtius or a T. S. Eliot anticipate it with signs and intuitions. 'With time,' Ernst Robert Curtius says, 'it will become manifestly impossible to employ any technique which is not that of fiction.' . . . Now then, that technique of 'fiction' has nothing to do with the criticism of evocation, made fashionable by Walter Pater in his studies on Joachim Du Bellay or Watteau. *A technique of fiction will have to become indispensable when the historical technique can no longer establish the mastery of its data.* An obligation almost of reliving once again what can no longer be ascertained" (pp. 17-18. Emphases added).

Lezama exemplifies well in praxis what he propounds in theory. In that internal consistency we see him not only speculating theoretically but reflecting, too, in his practice the tenets of a technique of fiction which seeks to "establish the mastery of its data." In his supremely American task of errantry, Lezama ventures into what Harold Bloom has taught us to read as *misprision*,[18] a facet of what I have been characterizing thus far as a characteristically American *errant* or *mis-taking*. It is difficult to ascertain how consciously antithetical Lezama is being here. It is not difficult, however, to detect his errancy. He imputes an originality, a novelty, an inaugural voice and method to what in fact is a belated, secondary, and already established tradition when he tells us that the "new order" of "valuation of historical links and critical appraisal" is anticipated by Curtius and Eliot "with signs and intuitions"; when he purportedly cites Curtius, mis-attributing to this thorough twentieth-century philologist the words of Ernst Troeltsch and his unfinished *Historismus und seine Probleme* (1922), a work conditioned by the nineteenth century's acute consciousness of "historism" and infused with the spirit of Nietzsche's unseasonal essay *The Use and Abuse of History*.[19] By making Curtius and Eliot mantic or proleptic sensibilities, Lezama, one suspects, would have us take him as the full-blown development of their annunciations. However, that suspicion is strategically undermined (and thereby reconfirmed, some neo-Freudians might quip) by Lezama in his emphatic denunciation of what Nietzsche, in the essay alluded to here, called the *epigone*, the latecomer, who sees himself born to an autumnal scene of history, where he is pre-empted from the process of invention by those who preceded him.

Lezama feels in his own *modus vivendi*, in his "technique of fiction," an obligation, as he terms it, to "re-live once again, what can no longer be ascertained" or established by "mastery." In other words, he espouses an obligation to re-structure in repeating the process of invention, a process which derives its authorization from Vico's *ritrovare*, a theoretical, sanctioning precedent for the American impulse of "beginning anew" that we have already discussed. That is, a "repeating" with a difference, a recommencement which is not epigonic or secondary emulation, a beginning anew without "repetition." To that end, Lezama becomes eristically emphatic by pointedly distancing himself from Pater and Eliot. As if his pointed allusion to Walter Pater, an exquisite epigone *par excellence*, and to his "criticism of evocation" were not enough, Lezama draws an unmistakable distinction between Eliot and Curtius, identifying his own method with that of the latter in order to underscore his dissociation from the two Anglo-Saxon *epigonoi* of belatedness. To that end, Lezama cites from and discusses the second of Eliot's *Four Quartets*, "East Coker," to which we referred earlier. In "East Coker" Lezama reads Eliot's centripetal involution. He considers the poem an emblem for the Eliot parable of self-entrapment, an inexorable fall into a predicament of constative repetition, of fey emulation, of mythical re-enactments or, as Lezama puts it, "In reality Eliot does not try to draw close to the new myths . . . or to the vitality of ancestral myths, but to the safeguard that those myths offer to contemporary works, those which confer a classical nobility. Because of this, his criticsm is essentially pessimistic or crepuscular, for he believes that the old masters can not be surpassed, that only the satisfaction of repetition remains, perhaps with a new accent. An appraisal similar to Spenglerian pessimism" (p. 20).

By contrast, speaking of himself, Lezama declares: "Our method would rather come nearer to that technique of fiction proclaimed by Curtius, than the mythical, critical method of Eliot. *Everything will have to be reconstructed, invented anew, and the old myths, upon reappearing anew, will offer us their conjurations and their enigmas with an unknown face. The fiction of myths are new myths*, with new fatigues and new terrors" (p. 20. Emphases added).

Lezama's antithetical posture toward Pater and Eliot points to a significant problematics in America's family romance and its errant quest. Despite his protestations, or because of them, Lezama evinces a commonality with Pater, and with Eliot to some extent. At the very heart of his own *aporia*, his own self-consciously proclaimed *difficulty*, Lezama shares with Pater the exquisite sensibility, the sybaritic aestheticism of an inventive reader. His philological obsessions and his Classical preoccupation with the rhetorics of fiction make him a kindred spirit of what Lezama dubs Eliot's "neoclassicism *à outrance*." In Lezama's insistence on a "technique of fiction" for an appreciation of fictions, we can sense the resonances of Pater's own articulate eradication of that artificial distinction between creative and critical performance (I am thinking of Pater's grievance against Matthew Arnold, in his "Conclusion" to *The Renaissance* and in his "Postscript" to *Appreciations*). In his unyielding obsession with the "image" of culture, the "cultured landscape," Lezama shares Eliot's tenacious "each venture a new beginning, a raid on the inarticulate." In this sense Lezama partakes of the supremely American voice that resounds in the Emersonian declaration as proclaimed in "The American Scholar": "One must be an inventor to read well. As the proverb says, 'He that would bring home the wealth of the Indies, must carry out the wealth of the Indies.' There is then creative reading as well as creative writing. When the mind is braced by labor and invention, the page of whatever book we read becomes luminous with manifold allusion.''[20] Neither Walter Pater nor T. S. Eliot can be denied the brawn of pertinacity implicit in the Emersonian dictum. ''Braced by labor and invention'' as Pater and Eliot may be, however, the weight of ''the wealth of the Indies'' proves overwhelming and here Lezama's antithetical insight into these two sensibilities finds its mark. For in Pater and Eliot the extended shadow of the past and of tradition render the ''luminosity,'' what Lezama calls ''historical vision,'' crepuscular, autumnal, ''epigonic.'' As Lezama observes, in the case of Pater the ''technique of fiction'' becomes ''criticism of evocation'' and in the case of Eliot a Spenglerian pessimism, a seeking after a ''safeguard'' in ancestral myths, in the ''wealth of the Indies,'' which might ''confer a classical nobility.'' The price exacted by such anxious seeking after ''respectability,'' however, proves very dear. Anterior authority casts a long shadow over Eliot, as Lezama perceptively reads in ''East Coker,'' and Pater's pursuit of atonement for what he later saw as ''excesses'' of *The Renaissance* render the ''wealth of the Indies'' all too burdensome. The ''myths'' of established canon become a weighty encumbrance in Lezama's Anglo-Saxon counterparts, while Lezama himself eristically, antithetically, in the best American tradition and its Emersonian brazenness, adheres to the feverish task of debunking canon in favor of unending invention of canon (re)formation. He clings irreverently to the attainment of ceaselessly kinetic ''historical vision,'' what he terms ''that counterpoint of fabric'' transmitted by the ''image participating in history.''

I should like to turn to a closer scrutiny of Lezama's chosen procedure — ''technique of fiction.'' It may help elucidate not only Lezama's own preferred ''difficulty,'' but may help us, as well, in better understanding Latin America's quest romance in general. Such close scrutiny may help, too, in our elucidation of those perpetual displacements of the desired object, the necessary fictions in the quest's supreme trials. In this respect Lezama's reliance on the poetics and hermeneutical principles descried by Ernst Curtius becomes very revealing.

More than three decades before Roland Barthes problematizes the equivocal act of reading in his essay on Balzac's *Sarrasine*,[21] Curtius was teaching the art of *rereading* and the critical vicissitudes of its fictions.[22] Like the long line of works born of wrenching cultural crises and discontinuities enumerated by Curtius (Thucydides' history as consequence of the Peloponnesian War; Augustine's *City of God* as result of Alaric's conquest of Rome; Machiavelli's treatise in reaction to the French incursions in Italy; Hegel's *Philosophy of History* as a consequence of the revolution of 1789 and the Napoleonic wars; Taine's revision of French history provoked by the defeat of 1871; Nietzsche's *The Use and Abuse of History* spurred by the establishment of the Hohenzollern empire; Spengler's *Decline of the West* in response to the end of the First World War, which also provoked Ernst Troeltsch's *Der Historismus und seine Probleme*) — like these pivotal works of cultural disjunction and self-appraisal, Curtius's own

European Literature and the Latin Middle Ages is born of equally disjunctive imperatives or, as Curtius himself confesses, "vital urges . . . under the pressure of a concrete historical situation." Curtius is referring to the apocalyptic millenarianism of the Third Reich that brought civilization to the threshold of a new lapse into primordial chaos. Curtius's then is a work born of necessity, a necessity to maintain the civilizing acts of imagination alive lest the world lapse into mindless repetition.

The intellectual impetus behind Curtius's work is "historism," that great debate of the nineteenth century which made culture synonymous with self-consciousness (good or bad; happy or unhappy) and self-consciousness tantamount to historical consciousness. In this regard the nineteenth century has its immediate precursor in Giambattista Vico and his *New Science*,[23] for whom knowledge, *scienza*, was a cognate of *conscienza*, self-knowledge. The "knowing" implicit for Vico was an insight into the history of self-knowing, that is, what we have already spoken of as a "poetic history" founded on the processes of philology, which Curtius now defined as "the foundation of all historical investigation." Curtius then is in a direct line of nineteenth-century "historism" which has its immediate antecedent in Vico. But Curtius's genealogical line through the nineteenth century extends particularly to those historians who — notwithstanding the attacks of relativism, nihilism, or ironic skepticism — were able to steer clear of formidable currents that were programmatic, millenarian, and scleroid orthodoxies; historians such as Jacob Burckhardt and Friedrich Nietzsche who took as their preferred tack the open-ended, regenerate, and irreverential powers of the imagination, to be exemplified in this century by Ernst Troeltsch whom Curtius cites and whose words, which I cited earlier, Lezama Lima mis-appropriates. "The principle of construction," Troeltsch notes in another Curtius citation, "is to go beyond history through history and clear the ground for new creations" (p. 4). We can appreciate how such statements awaken the curiosity of America's questers for the generative impulse that resonates in these statements.

This apparent digression furnishes the background for that "technique of fiction" which Lezama appropriates. But I offer this historical reminder for another reason as well, which makes this backdrop very germane. The nineteenth century, as we shall see, exacerbates new beginnings or the process of self-conscious founding in Latin America. Thus, the historical consciousness of the nineteenth century and its inseparable association with the *imago* of culture, what Lezama calls "historical vision," encompasses, as well, Latin America's self-conscious and deliberate attempts at arriving simultaneously at a poetic and political history. I shall take up the itinerary of that enterprise later. For now, I should like to focus more intensely on the actual processes of this "technique of fiction" whose historical map we have just glimpsed in passing.

"The only thing that creates culture," Lezama asserts, "is landscape" (p.

27). Lezama's peculiar usage of *paisaje* — "landscape" — invokes the grammatical *figura* of *topografía* as well as the rhetorical *techne* of *topothesia* on which I shall elaborate shortly. In the tenth chapter, "The Ideal Landscape," of his seminal *paideia*, Curtius traces for us the varied career of these technical operations from Greek poetry through Romance epics. His procedure, which he calls "the science of philology," is a systematic, self-conscious analysis of a process of sedimentation. Like an archaeologist, he uncovers layer by layer the sedimental accretions of poetic operations, that is, of technical processes which have superimposed landscape upon landscape of culture. His own operation is de-scriptively hermeneutical, a delivery through un-writing and *de*scribing, a participatory performance in the fabric of a landscape. His characterization of this critical involvement comes in the opening paragraph of his first chapter. He calls it voluntary participation. Conscious of his own place and his own involvement in the scene of this history of poetics, Curtius comes to the realization that his own activity extends that history and becomes part of it. To put it another way, his history of poetics becomes subsumed by the poetic history of a scene of culture, of a "landscape," of a *topography*. Having traced his own intellectual genealogy to a particular strain of historism spun by the previous century, Curtius comprehends that, as he put it, "poetic form appears as the extreme concept of historism" (p. 7), because, he continues, "our survey of the modern historical method has led us to the concept of poetry in the sense of a narrative produced by the imagination ('fiction')" (p. 8). It is at this point that Curtius cites Troeltsch: "It will eventually become patently impossible to employ any technique except that of 'fiction'," a citation taken over by Lezama and misattributed to Curtius himself, harmlessly so since its import characterizes Curtius's own method as well.

I opened this segment of my discussion by alluding to Curtius as someone who, in a philological tradition liberated from theology, has been teaching us how to *reread* long before Roland Barthes's attempts at foregrounding the problematics of such activity. In light of what has followed, perhaps I can justify that allusion more intelligibly. Curtius's "voluntary participation" in "poetic history" (I hope it is clear by now why this phrase preempts "history of poetics") anticipates the acts of critical reading as we have come to understand that enterprise in the last two decades, since structuralism, deconstruction, and their aftermath. I make such claims for Curtius because it is clear to me that in his systematic self-consciousness, in his analytic, textual archaeology, and in his appreciation of historical narrative as production generated and emplotted by poetic imagination, Curtius is a critical reader in the sense that he reads with a difference — not only the difference he as a reader makes and of which he is clearly aware, but also the successive differences engendered by the occasions of reading and rereading *within* the works themselves. By this I mean what Borges has been teaching us in Latin America for a long time now, and that is that the operations he renders or describes themselves become operative in the rendering, thereby making each operation different in itself on each occasion of de/scription. The result is not a uniqueness which perdures in repetition, as we have already seen in our family romance and its poetic history, but the discovery of a different *uniqueness* which is different with each reading, with each description, with each repetition that makes "repetition" impossible. So much so in the case of Curtius, from whom Lezama and other American writers have learned so much, that the occasion of discussing *topothesia* itself configures a *topothesia*. That is, the rendering of a poetic operation, of a technique of fiction, is not only performed by a technique of fiction but, as well, it is the re-invention of a technique of fiction. The temerity, the adventure, of such "making it anew each time" is precisely what Lazama sees himself and Latin American writing since Columbus imbued with, the verve he saw lacking in the epigonic "judiciousness" of Pater and Eliot. The "technique of fiction" for Lezama, in short, is the code term for this daring adventure. It is what transforms nature into landscape, into *incunabula* which, for Lezama, is equivalent to *terra incognita* or "gnostic space."

The terrain is *incognita* in the differential sense of reading just outlined above. That is, "unknown" here imparts a sense by which we are to understand that the terrain is *not* constantly or immutably knowable. As "gnostic space" its gnoseology always re-verts to a clear, "empty" area, a *space*. Lezama calls the apprehension of this experience "strength germinating in empty space." This problematically knowable area is tantamount to the poetic performance, to the *terminus technicus* carried out and which must be carried out each time and again, after which it becomes emptied out *space* once more. As Lezama puts it, "it is the form of becoming in which landscape moves toward a direction, an interpretation, or a simple hermeneutics." In other words, a temporary arrangement unlike the enduring myth of Eliot which lingers long enough to cast a weighty shadow, or, as for Pater, to become evocation. (I am reminded here of Eliot's plaintive reminiscence, in the essay already referred to above — "Tradition and the Individual Talent" — on Emerson's notion that history is biography translated into institution. And an institution, in Emerson's phrase, is "the lengthened shadow of a man." Eliot sees that shadow extending into and eclipsing poetic history as well). "Landscape" in this Lezamian sense reaches back to the *topografia* of the Greeks. *Topografia* was a rhetorical figure, a tropology — literally the writing of a place. This landscape points as well to *topothesia*, which was the arrangement of a setting, the particular placement of a scene. In poetics the process would become what we now call emplotment, *epeon thesis*, a particular setting of words in verse, that is "a technique of fiction." Lezama's landscape, his *paisaje*, and his "gnostic space" are of one piece with this topography, this cultured terrain, always invented not found, always refined, produced, performed. And the momentum, the driving impetus for that performance, that errant venture, is rooted in the radical *image*. As I hope to show, *imagen* for Lezama the philologist consciously resonates in the sense of its Classical etymons — the Latin *imagines* which the Greeks had referred to as *phantasmata*. Lezama's uncanny sensibility in this regard surfaces, for he knows full well that phantoms do not cast shadows, *pace* Eliot, nor do they constitute or reify an immutable presence, except spectrally. But that, of course, is the ghost of presence, that is to say, a *fiction*, more precisely, a "necessary fiction" where necessity stands for the unfettered haunting of insufficiency, of a desired absence.

Latin American history for Lezama, as for many of his fellow errant questers for whom he speaks so articulately, is an imagistic history radiating from the generative powers of the image and its prisms. American space is a gnostic space, in the Lezamian sense, and the historical visions it engenders are the function of a method, a *modus transumptivus*, whose inventions are generated through a technique of fiction. "The chronicler of the Indies," Lezama tells us, "carries the romance of chivalry to the landscape. Bernal Díaz del Castillo's way of writing reveals that he read and heard stories from books of chivalry. The forest teems with enchantments and the flora and the fauna are recognized insofar as they correspond to those described in old bestiaries, collections of fables and magic plants. . . . Gonzalo Hernandez de Oviedo calls the lizards dragons. Every little animal as it is discovered leads the conquerors to recall Pliny the Elder. *First he carefully establishes the similarity and then the difference . . . in a form of violent emphasis. . . .* In America, during the first year of the Conquest, *imagination was not 'the family lunatic' but a principle of organization, of recognition, and of legitimate differentiation*" ("Image of Latin America," p. 323. Emphases added). The legitimacy of that differentiation is the measure of a "historical vision" that attains to a peculiarly American landscape, that is, America's scene of culture — the incunabula wrought as and by the image under the differential signature of what Lezama, in his Hispanisized Greek, calls "el plasma de su autoctonía" (p. 27). *Plasma* and *placenta* are two recurring terms in Lezama and they are invariably associated with *imagen*. That affiliation foregrounds and exposes, lays bare the surface texture and texturing devices of the image. It unmasks the image's fictions and technique of fiction, an exposure which ultimately serves to rescue historical vision and cultural landscape from the daemon of mystification, from metaphysical grounding, from the tenebrous myth of a logos and its theologos. In doing so, the landscape is humanized, kept circumstantial, contingent, and re-cognizable, or as Lezama puts it, within the possibilities "of legitimate differentiation." For *plasma* and *placenta* are surface terms, stylistic facets, circumjacent superficies — all attributes which bespeak the *aesthetic*, literally what can be sensibly perceived (*aestheta*), sensually apprehended, bodily knowable. (*Plasma* is from the Greek root and its Latin derivative meaning "mold" or "image" and its verbal form in the Greek *peplasmai* means to fashion, to model, to figure, or to image. Metaphorically it means "to make up," "forge," "fabricate." The Latin *placenta* is from the Greek *pláx*, plain, table-land, or surface). In this foregrounded, differential, unmasked sense of *imagen* Lezama and the necessary fictions of an ever-errant quest romance become more comprehensible, more figuratively intelligible. Here is Lezama articulating that necessary demystification or safeguard against metaphysical transcendentalism: "The gravitation of the image takes root among us right from the beginning, the image aimed toward the center of the earth and . . . totally liberated from magical reason. The image produced by this space which knows, which creates a *gnosis*, covers us like a *placenta* which knows, which protects us from the chthonic world, from the mortal darkness which could destroy us before our time" ("Image of Latin America," p. 324). And like his chronicler-precursors from that problematic beginning who "carried the romance of chivalry to the landscape," Lezama proceeds to differentiate, to "note the differences" as he observes: "Thus as Europe as Vico was able to note, moved from fables to myths, in America we have had to go from myths to the image. How the image has created culture, how that image has been most stimulating, how and when the image can no longer be fabulation or myth, are questions which only poetry and the novel can gradually answer. And above all, in what form the image will take part in history, will have effective powers, metaphorical strength so that the stones may again become images" ("Image of Latin America," p. 324).

Like the language of the best Latin American fictions, Lezama's idiom is skewed. It is an idiolect with a deliberate obliqueness, a self-conscious errancy. His studied difficulty, his declared and exercised *aporia* make his language eccentric, or ex-centric, and deliberately so. As statement which is accompanied by its simultaneous demonstration, as fiction displaying a technique of fiction, as deflective performance which flaunts its own difficulty, Lezama's is a self-decentering discourse. His language constantly moves to displace the concretions or accretions which its fictive performance might have left behind as sediment. His optimum value is in the fictions' making, and the charted landscapes move toward regenerate emptiness — the "gnostic space" in which discourse, like the image and historical vision it errantly pursues, seeks what Lezama calls "strength germinating in empty space." It follows that what becomes apprehended by such vision should be equally eccentric or self-decentering. In the first passage just cited, for example, Lezama speaks of the image "aimed toward the center of the earth and . . . totally liberated from magical reason." What is this chthonic "center" which is at once in the earth, totally liberated of magical reason, and "protects us from the chthonic world"? For Lezama there is no enigma involved here, just displacement, disconcerting and disconcertedness that liberate through "exile and captivity" — exclusion, circumscription, envelopment — exile of the Old World image in the New, the captivity of the New World image by the Old, and the mutual convertibility of exile and captivity, of "outside" and "inside," into each other. The result is a heterogeneous, imagistic locus; never a fixed and privileged center, never "There," but always in transit, always between. It is a spectral *imago*, a mirror of "nature" (in the sense of nascence, birth), at once reflecting and permeable, a radial omphalos of intermediacy and heterotopia in which dwell equally the indigenous American's "total divinization of the entire external world" and the European's "old image, nourished with infinite analogies." The interpenetration, Lezama tells us, "encounters a new space which disconcerts it and makes it tremble." That seismic reverberation is felt as displacing *imago*; it resonates as self-decentering, eccentric landscape, identifiable by its ceaseless qualitative movement more than by its quantitative, reified concretions. I follow Lezama's triadic plotting of that itinerary:

> What we have called "the American era of the image" has its evident expressions in the new meanings of the chronicler of the Indies, the baroque dominion, the rebellion of romanticism. There the image acts as a *quantos* which is converted into a *quale* by the discovery of a center and the proportionate distribution of the energy. Exile and captivity are at the very root of these images. The chronicler of the Indies brings his already-formed images, and the new landscape bursts them open. The baroque seigneur begins his contortions and repolishings anchored in fable tradition and Greco-Roman myths, but very soon the incorporation of the phytomorphic and zoomorphic elements which waylay him . . . create new collections of fables which grant a new center of gravity to his work ("Image of Latin America," p. 326).

From this point, Lezama moves on in his unfettered Vichian sweep to extend the periods of Conquest and Colonial Baroque flowering by the third term of his ternary scheme — an all-important third term, as suggested earlier — of poetic and historical self-consciousness in the nineteenth century. "The romantic rebellion among us," Lezama continues, "is something more than a rupture or the simple demoniac search for something else; on the contrary, it forms part of and expresses the historic circumstance. The verbal rebellion of the great romantics, from Sarmiento to Martí, equates their inventions in language with their creations as builders of nations. Our romanticism fused Callimachus and Lycophron with Lycurgus and Solon."

If the first two stages of discovery/conquest and seventeenth-century baroque of the Latin American landscape were fraught with the periphrastic energies of disconcertedness, dislocation, and self-decentering dynamism, the nineteenth century, the century of Latin America's literary romanticism and political self-determination, *redoubles* the intensity of those energies. That redoubling, however, is a compounded, exponential arithmetic of intensity. For as I have suggested earlier, the initial moment, the inaugural phase of Latin America's history, is already a problematic, pre/posterous, and errant beginning. As with the birth of nations and of secular or "poetic history" in the *New Science* of Giambattista Vico, the historical scheme of the New World figures a recommencement, that is, a secondary and belated "original," a beginning anew. That second inauguration in Vico begins with the castoffs after the Flood. In America it commences with "exile and captivity" — for the European, an irrevocable estrangement from the self-centered *oikoumene*; for the Aztec and Inca, the baneful consummation of a second coming augured in theogony; for the African black, an outrageous deracination. The violence of that mutual dislocation sunders the centeredness in each, giving way to differential *imago* that de-secrates each sacral *logos* and primal myth. "Burst open" by landscape, subsumed and transmogrified as and by topo-graphy, geography — natural and human — suffers the fierce mediations of the baroque, characterized by Lezama as "tension and plutonism." This baroque, second stage of an already secondary moment, is no less disconcerting in its differential displacement, in the dislocations of its language. For the baroque is the language of the image *par excellence*. It is surface in tension, eristic plasma, embattled fiction. Second stage of a secondary displacement, the baroque in America is truly "dialectical," truly a "counterpoint." But this is not a syllogistic dialectic of thesis, antithesis, synthesis, as we shall see at greater length in a later chapter. Rather, and Vico becomes more pertinent than ever at this point, it is a dialectic of exchange between language and the New World reality which language seeks to contain; an antithetical confrontation between the inventive/invented sign and the irreducible Continent as recalcitrant signified — the first fashioning and imaging the latter, the latter skewing, deflecting, evading the former as a protean rebus for a poetic image. The incunabula, the textual fabric, becomes the everchanging record, landscape, *terra incognita,* spectral "presence" emanating from that contentious "gnostic space."

The nineteenth century, the century of rebellion and historical consciousness, of disjunction and self-continuity, seeks to *read*, to decipher the fabric of incunabula and finds itself reflected in the prismatic facets of an already self-reflexive and self-conscious history. As Lezama puts it, "the romantic rebellion among us is something more than a rupture or a simple demoniac search for something else; on the contrary, it forms part of and expresses the historic circumstance." The romance (which has traditionally defined or traced a quest for self-identification, a pilgrimage toward one's home) of romanticism in Latin America, then, becomes a redoubled replay, a compounded secondariness. That is, it emerges as a re-discovery of a problematic discovery, a re-invention of invention, in a double sense, at that of political self-affirmation and poetic performance. Thus historical consciousness necessarily becomes meta-historical self-consciousness and its deployment in quest of a *landscape* configures a metalepsis, a trope on a trope, a technique of fiction of what already is a fiction. Hegel would have us understand this plurality of mediations as an "unhappy consciousness." Marx would have us apprehend secondariness, and certainly this compounded secondariness, as "farce." And we very well might. But only if we succumb to their programmatic, progressive, totalizing ideologies. We might even see, then, this hyper-self-consciousness as epigonic, autumnal predicament of decadence in the fatedly cyclical Spenglerian vein. But (and the contestation of these ideologies will surface throughout our discussion, particularly in our last chapter dealing with a problematically Hegelian enterprise) that, however, would mean turning our blind side to the other visage of historical consciousness which extends from Vico to Troeltsch, and through Curtius to contemporary Latin American writers, such as Lezama Lima as well as others whom I shall be discussing in short order. That epigonic view would imply our deliberate ignorance of and erudite blindness to such principles as Vico's *verum ipsum factum*; Troeltsch's *sententia* that "the principle of construction is to go beyond history, through history and clear the ground ['the gnostic space'] for new creations"; and Curtius's "voluntary participation" through a hermeneutical principle predicated on the insight that "poetic form appears as the extreme concept of historism." Finally, it would mean turning a blind eye on Lezama Lima's regenerative predilections for a "technique of fiction." Only then could we indict Latin American consciousness as a "bourgeois" sensibility whose cultural quest inexorably founders on culture. Only if we succumb to such thorough mystification can we convince ourselves that culture can have an object other than culture itself.

My comments here are intended, in part, as corrective swerve from one of the most intelligent readers of Latin-American literature who has addressed these problems head on and who has done so with acute sensitivity. In his ground-breaking study on the Cuban Alejo Carpentier, Roberto González Echevarría notes that the "question of Latin American identity has to be traced back to that second birth, propitiated by figures such as Andrés Bello. Being bourgeois and post-Romantic, Latin American literature centers around a lack, an absence of organic connectedness, and its mainspring is a desire for communion, or, in a Hegelian sense, for totality through reintegration with a lost unity. That lack leads Latin American writers to invoke 'culture' as the ontological and historical entity from which their works have sprung and to which they must return. But the lack is never overcome, for culture becomes in their works an entelechy (in its etymological sense of a finished teleology), a static, reified end product lacking a temporal dimension. Like the mothers in Carpentier's "Journey Back to the Source" and "Manhunt," culture appears as a dead, though always desired source."[24]

As a thoroughly cultured Latin-American intellectual González Echevarría embodies his statement's self-contradiction. Hegel is certainly most apt here since González Echevarría is the exemplary embodiment of a dialectical tension in a culture's creative negation, or self-mediating criticism — a process of culture that extends and extenuates itself without attenuation. My complaint against this incisive sensibility, the crux of our difference, that is, resides in my viewing this process, after Vico, Curtius, and Lezama, as perpetual and self-perpetuating, as endless and regenerative quest, as opposed to González Echevarría's hypostatizing of the process into "entelechy," what he amplifies as "static, reified end product lacking a temporal dimension." Even more fundamentally, whereas González Echevarría speaks of a "product," much less of an "end product," I insist on "process." Theoretically speaking, and our differences are primarily theoretical since his critical praxis evinces much greater rapproachement to my own, González Echevarría attributes to Latin American literature an *en soi*, im-mediate, transcendental onto-teleology ("outside" or "above" culture's enterprise) which founders, as it well must, on necrophilic and necro-mantic presence. I suspect that the overdetermination that mystifies González Echevarría into this search for "a lost unity" (an illusionary non sequitur in Latin America's *heterotopia*) is, more than Hegel, Spengler's dirge on Western culture and his droll of historical cyclicalism. While Spengler's significance for Latin American writers cannot be denied, and González Echevarría's expatiation of that connection is highly informed, we must account for and differentiate the deflections and skewed transfigurations a philosophy such as Hegel's or Spengler's must endure when translated to America. In view of those corrective calibrations, I maintain that the project of Latin American literature consists in a vital and self-generating pursuit, self-generated rather than motivated by a dead or lost object; a quest whose "mainspring" is not a Hegelian reintegration, especially since the very possibility or existence of a "lost unity" or originary center is itself problematical, as González Echevarría concurs. We agree too that the "mainspring" is a lack or an absence, but I hasten to amplify with the qualification that this "lack" is a desired and self-guaranteed absenting mechanism, a necessary insufficiency, as I have noted, pleonastically, already, rather than a reified dead weight. It is a desired necessity so that the questing after its fulfillment (which is deferred, postponed, *not* mortified) may be endlessly perpetuated — as in Lezama's "gnostic space" ("strength germinating in empty space"), as in Borges's unending postponements of onto-aesthetic phenomena ("the imminence of a revelation that does not take place"), as in Alejo Carpentier's equivocal ironies deployed against reason's discourse in *Reasons of State*, as in Carlos Fuentes's tactical inadequations of literary discourse and "poetic history" in *Terra Nostra*.

As he eloquently articulates his own program for charting Carpentier's itinerary, González Echevarría demonstrates that he is far from being insensitive to the paradox or ironic predicament of this project. "To read Carpentier," he avers, "without taking into account the contradictions of this dialectic would be naively to accept a fictional philosophy that allows for the coexistence of intolerable paradoxes" (p. 21). Far from being intolerable, however, I believe these "paradoxes" are *desirable*. And "taking into account the contradictions of this dialectic" does not mean their eradication, resolution, or undoing of the paradoxes. Far from being a desideratum, that dénouement would lead the quest of literature and the project of this culture unto the "dead source," the corpse of that culture's own past. It is precisely the tensions, the "difficulty," or what Lezama calls this "plutonism" of conflictive and contending contradictions that propel and energize the indefatigable process of the cultural enterprise. To extirpate the contradictions or paradoxes from a literature's landscape as "intolerable" would, indeed, translate into the remanding of that literary corpus to the necromancy of a corpse desirous of its "dead source." In that dire eventuality, America's poetic history would be deprived of its lifegiving "necessary difficulty," that desideratum to which Emerson refers in his own American context as "our poverty."

Fortunately, González Echevarría's displays no such "intolerance" in his own critical praxis. His characterization of what he aptly terms our "fictional philosophy" betrays his sensitivity to the ironic signature, to the difficulty or aporia of our contemporary post-Vichian readings: "In a post-Romantic literature that must base itself in fiction (even while claiming the opposite), philosophical systems are not present in a radically coherent form but merely stand for what could be considered belief. For this reason, philosophical systems are dealt with here as metaphor or conceits — and I use 'conceit' both in its present meaning and in its old poetic sense of binding image and concept" (pp. 21-22). Clearly, these shifting postures illustrate González Echevarría's own self-mediated, dialectical consciousness, yet another instance of an unfolding process in Latin America's cultural enterprise. Both in spite and because of himself, at once, González Echevarría's own intellectual difficulty and its plutonism betray him as initiate of the "technique of fiction" and its attendant blindness *and* insight. I shall return to this maieutic confrontation, this Socratic dialogue, in a later chapter dealing with Carpentier and the Baroque. For now, suffice it to say that I believe, *pace* González Echevarría, that the romance of Romanticism — inevitable antecedent of our contemporary fictions, philosophical or otherwise — is a historical corroboration of Vico's *verum ipsum factum*; that is, that human beings are capable of knowing, or misknowing, only what they have made themselves or are capable of making in principle; that what is "true" *is culture*, in other words, what has been *cultivated, made, fabricated. Factum*: truth and fabrication, "historical fact" and "historical fiction" evince a synonymy, a mirror convertibility in a process Vico encoded as "poetic history."

The nineteenth century's conscious self-rediscovery figures as moment of coalescense, as confluence, of these factitious facticities. Latin America re-discovers simultaneously its "true" fictions and the rebellious impulse to forge, to fabricate a new historical-political "truth" of liberation and democracy, which time proves, and continues to prove, as yet another fiction of linguistic extravagance and rhetorical errancy. These vicissitudes of nation-building in Latin America thus coincide with the resurfacing and first-time publication of a good number of literary works of the Colonial period that divulge the "true" poetic history, the hidden face of incunabula, a hitherto apocryphal landscape of the American *imago*. The list is long and I shall mention only the most obvious: Pero Vaz de Caminha's letter on the discovery of Brazil which was written in 1500 sees publication for the first time in 1817; Father Bartolomé de las Casas's *The History of the Indies*, begun in 1527 but still unfinished in 1566 when las Casas died, is published in 1875; Francisco Núñez de Pineda y Buscañán's *The Happy Captivity and the Reasons of the Numerous Wars of Chile* which dates from 1629 comes to publication in 1831; Juan Rodríguez Freile's *The History of New Granada*, finished in 1636, finds its way into print in 1859; Gregorio de Matos's biting poems which circulated in manuscript form during his lifetime in the second two-thirds of the seventeenth century appear in print in 1831; Bartolomé Arzáns de Orzua y Vela's *History of the Imperial Town of Potosí*, written around 1705, sees partial publication for the first time in 1872; Inca Garcilaso de la Vega's *Royal Commentaries* (I, 1609; II, 1617), which were circulated in published form in Spain, were prohibited from circulation in the New World for another two centuries. Emir Rodríguez Monegal, whom I follow in this printing history of Colonial works, aptly observes that "books written in Colonial times really became nineteenth-century books. Only after independence did a true picture of the state of letters during the Colonial period begin to emerge, and this picture is even today constantly being revised by the discovery of long-forgotten or unknown works. In reading these texts now we see them as they were never seen before: as the fabulous source of a literature to be. They are closer to us than they were to their nominal contemporaries."[25]

With his characteristic knack for simplifying "difficulty," Emir Rodríguez Monegal manages to telegraph into his propaedeutic prefaces the intricate itinerary of Latin America's family romance. In the process he discloses the perduring efficacy of the nineteenth century's problematic self-rediscovery. The most blatant manifestation of this symptomatic *rereading*, in Barthes's differential sense discussed earlier, is found in Rodríguez Monegal's revisionary *El otro Andrés Bello*.[26]

In consciously seeking a historical self to mold, to image into/as poetic history, Latin American romantics, from Andrés Bello to José Martí, discover themselves as poetic history already writ in the palimpsests, the heterogeneous superscriptions in the fabric of incunabula, in landscape's textuality wrought by the imago for more than three centuries. Just as significantly, romanticism discovers its self-consciousness, its self-knowing, in the *eccentricity* of that textuality, an eccentrism which kept those Colonial works from being *centric* to Colonial America and now makes them eccentric "nineteenth-century books." The nineteenth century finds itself in the self-difference which obtains within those Colonial works, a differentiation which makes them other to themselves, other than Colonial works, allowing their coming to life in the nineteenth century. By extension, the Colonial period is re-discovered by these romantics to have been other than what it was legitimately sanctioned to have been. In short, legitimacy itself is discovered to lie outside the "legitimate center" of the Colonial landscape, making that landscape yet another instance of errancy, another station on the errant itinerary of this family romance. "Only after independence did a *true picture* of the state of letters during the Colonial period begin to emerge," Rodríguez Monegal notes. An observation which obviously needs to be qualified. That qualification should stress that the character of this "true picture" is not an incontrovertible, apophantic truth which constitutes a more accurate picture of "how things really were." Rather, the significance of that revision, of that secondary insight which obtains in Romanticism's and our "ideologoical" perception is what renders that picture's eccentricity as truth. The "truth" in that "true picture," in other words, is entailed by our apprehension of the capacity of those works to become self-different, other than Colonial works, an apprehension whose own eccentricity cannot be denied unimpeachably. Equally significant in the discovery of eccentricity or errancy within those works is the discovery of a potential within them for reversibility, the Vichian convertibility of "truth" and "fabrication" within the historical *factum*. For if, as Rodríguez Monegal notes, the "true picture of the state of letters during the Colonial period begins to emerge" in the nineteenth century and continues to do so now, then the legitimacy, the sanctioned landscape of culture and its discourse was a fabrication which endured for more than three centuries. And if fabrication can endure as truth (provided of course that one believes in their alienability or otherness from each other), we cannot escape the haunting precognition that what the nineteenth century re-discovered and willed to us, and what readers such as Rodríguez Monegal continue to discover and hold up as a "true picture" may well comprise yet another fiction, communally sanctioned and legitimated, but whose efficacy, whose "centricity," may well lie in its eccentricity, in its potential to generate yet further self-differentiations within itself in some indeterminate time — in some uchronia — with an undecidable technique of fiction.

The reversibility of sanctioned fact and eccentric fiction discerned by nineteenth-century Romanticism entails a convertibility principle which violates, which ruptures, bursts open, in Lazama's words, all and any privileged center; in the process it undoes all sacrosanct dichotomies between norm and contingency, between structure and event; it opens up the structures of myth and myths of history, as well as the *imago* of textuality, of *incunabula*, to human event, to the repeated doing and undoing of poetics and poetization — to the *factum* of fabrication or *poesis*. This *making*, or "poetic history," this "making anew" without repeating, is the opening up to that perpetual "gnostic space" and the "technique of fiction" descried by nineteenth-century "historism" and refined by Curtius and Lezama Lima in our century. This process that I describe here evinces the internalization of the quest and its *errant* principle. A principle, or

Chapter 2
Borges's Ghost Writer

> Meanwhile do I talk to myself as one who hath time. No one
> telleth me anything new, so I tell myself mine own story.
> > Nietzsche, "Old and New Tables"

> Little by little the book will finish me.
> > Edmond Jabés, *L'espace blanc*

> No one is anyone, one single immortal man is all men. Like
> Cornelius Agrippa, I am God, I am hero, I am philosopher, I am
> demon and I am world, which is a tedious way of saying that I do
> not exist.
> > Borges, "The Immortal"

The itinerary of my tracking after Borges turns upon the epigrammatic triptych
I place at the head of this chapter. By "Borges" here I mean that measure of
interstitial space between the triptych's panels, the space where the pivoting
hinges at once join and separate its threesome tables. My object consists in trailing
that moot and problematic author — that inexistent speaker of this Borges epigraph
and its ghostly demarcations — deployed by Borges the writer; the authorial trace
that haunts as ghost, as spectral differential, that dwells in Borges the romancer's
obsession now as figure of ironic nostalgia, now as object of dispassionate
commemoration.

The form of appropriation which, in the previous chapter, we have seen
Borges exercise in "The Life of Tadeo Isidoro Cruz (1829-1874)" is typical of
his penchant for a certain kind of repetition and extenuation. I have in mind that
poetic topography which is simultaneously a scene of recognition, a recapitulation
of poetic inheritance, and a filial succession: A family romance that perseveres
at the concurrent planes of poetic tradition and of authorial self-inscription into
the "untimely" continuity or extension of textual space — the incunabula of
gnostic space, as Lezama Lima would have it. In this sense Borges's discourse
labors simultaneously in a redoubled project of extending literary tradition and
of extenuating (to the point of effacement) the authorial privilege of the writing
subject in the tale. What we conventionally call story, history, or poem, the
textual figuration, thus becomes "biography" in a plural, multivalent, and self-
disseminating sense. "La biografía de Tadeo Isidoro Cruz (1829-1874)" (I think
the original Spanish title is preferable for being more articulate in this regard)

does more than imply the mere dispersal of a national epic's hero into a further topography of textuality, into the "graphy" or *writing* of biography. It does the same for the authorial subject inscribed into the tale. Borges the author-biographer, as we have seen already, "biographizes" himself into that proliferating fiction. Ultimately, the authorial successor disappears into the graphic recesses of textual figuration, of topography or "negative, gnostic space," where he has already relegated the precursor author, José Hernandez, by appropriating his primacy and pre-empting his authorial privilege in a "biography" or poetic genealogy. The residual vestige, the surviving trace of this disappearing act, or authorial aphanisis, is writing itself — the story left "to tell myself mine own story," as our Nietzsche epigraph and its "Tables" would have it. Abandoned to itself, the "story" seeks to become self-same but ends in self-displacement. For in telling itself its own story, it becomes "another" to itself, in endless "self-repetition," and in becoming its own impossible self-identicalness, it mirrors the perpetual departure of authorial essences that wane into the phantomness of biography — ebbing essences whose traces perdure to haunt as telling ghost story. The "story" then extends itself into the "untimely" continuity, the perpetual timelessness of uchronic utterance ("Meanwhile do I talk to myself *as* one who hath time") in the utopic space of writing, a writing, that is, which does not originate in and can no longer be proper(ty) to a privileged locus or commonplace other than the topography of writing "itself." Authorial presence — José Hernandez and the biographer Borges — passes on to that baneful realm of the textual fabric; they become stitched into the texture of incunabula. No longer subjects of authority bearing the poem or story, they become objects of iconoclastic reading — or misreadings — borne by the textured space of incunabula as traces of what has been termed, by one of Borges's most astute students — Michel Foucault — "authorial function."[1] Borne unto the timelessness of uchronia and the placelessness of utopia, these authorial subjects become disseminated *à outrance* by the endless proliferation of the text into what one of Borges's unmistakable masters — Paul Valéry — called "immortality." This is not an immortality of transcendence, however; nor is it an infinitude/eternity of metaphysics, mathematical abstractions which the authorial and biographical Borges (if such a dichotomy could be maintained) dreads and is obsessed with. Rather, as characterized by Valéry, this is an immortality that "implies insignificance, indifference, perfect isolation — inexistence."[2]

I read in this authorial predicament the parable of Borges's unmistakable internalization (the problematic *sublation*, Hegel would say) of Lezama Lima's *landscape* into writing itself. In other words, the landscape that was incunabula — the topothesia that transformed nature into topography of culture, myth into multivocal image, geospatial history into "gnostic space" — as we have seen in the previous chapter, now in Borges becomes a process turned on itself. The poetic process, that is, becomes its own poetic object. The quest of this family romance, as a result, crosses yet another horizon in the perpetual endlessness of crossings, of imaginary horizons, of negative space (utopia) and "untimely adversity" (*destiempo, contretemps* — uchronia). That corpus of writing which our author-centered conventions make us wont to identify with the code-word Borges serves as demonstration of this unending process. The most tenaciously active element within this demonstration is the counter-self-directed authorial function or implied authorship itself. To elucidate this procedure I will allude to a number of pieces from the Borges codex, but focus primarily on that prodigious illustration entitled "The Immortal."[3]

Mortality/immortality, the verso and obverse of the same topical coin, emerge in Borges-writing as recurring obsession. In the commonplace topicality of this preoccupation, Borges, as always, pursues a problematization of the well-worn currency. Disbelieving in novelty[4] and, like the hero of his "Circular Ruins,"[5] dreading a predicament of derivative belatedness,[6] Borges deploys an ambivalent strategy whose overt, identifying signature consists in a deliberate and equivocal self-limitation to the topoi or commonplaces of originary inheritance; to the problematic foundations of literary heritage. As we have seen, however, topical appropriation in Borges becomes more than limitation. Yes, Borges does become a "paper author,"[7] weaving himself as authorial subject into the fabric of biography, of dynastic seriality — the legacy of a poetic tradition. And, yes, in this sense Borges fosters, through a taciturn quietism and studied attenuation of authorial self, a "phantomness," a mortality. But, and the equivoque of ironic ambivalence now comes to the fore, in insinuating that authorial self into the fabric of writing, he leaves behind a hedge, an untimely trace against the specter of mortal limitation. If mortality can be abetted, if authorial presence can negotiate the adversative *contretemps* of a disappearing act, the haunted space precipitated by such an absence endures and proliferates in the untimely, graphic quest as spectral visitation. And, as we have seen in our discussion of Lezama Lima, while the *imagines*, the *phantasmata*, may not cast an Eliotic shadow, their pullulation as negative presence (as absence), their untimely (uchronic) haunting in the gnostic space of incunabula leave the ghostly mark of the phantom's immortality. Absence, vacuity, disappearance can only have meaning as mnemonic and differential trace of a receded, effaced, defaced, and sublated presence. Borges's internalization of Valéry's equivalents *immortalité/inexistence* is itself a mark of the Argentine's ironic insight into this aphanisis paradox. That is why, I suspect, Borges displays such fondness for John Donne's *Biathanatos*, where it is said that "Homer, who had written a thousand things that no one else could understand . . . was said to have hanged himself."[8] Donne's "fabulous or authentic" exemplum of Homer's violent thanatopraxis, however, has not impeded Borges from pursuing and sublimating Homer as immortal phantom in the proliferating ghosts of incunabula. I am referring to the timelessly extended bloodline, the filiation of departed and departing authorial subjects that haunt as shadowless presence in the everextended deserts of "The Immortal." In the spirit of this ambivalent stance, of this equivocal posture of self-preservation in self-limitation struck by Borges, I am compelled to read the authorial, proprietary utterance in "The Immortal" as *apostrophe* — an apostrophic figuration in the dual sense of the Greek term: An exclamatory address that turns away from undifferentiated immortality and, simultaneously, an apostrophic, diacritical mark of the possessive that executes an elision, an omitted presence that haunts there in the elided spaces as genitive phantom. In other words, I read that apostrophe as enunciatory signature by which the Borges text turns the literary tradition, the archi-text, it appropriates into aleatory pretext, even while the apostrophe, the mark of elision, incrementally extends textuality, serves for further writing that augments and enlarges the inherited incunabula. I shall indicate the specific ploys of this program which justify my reading as outlined here.

Borges's presentation of this double-pronged strategy, literally a *discursus* (a duplicitous procedure, one has to say, since the characteristically ironic Borges is at work here), is mediated through the use of Sir Francis Bacon, author of the *Novum Organum* (1620) and of *The New Atlantis* (1627). Borges ironically re-presents this novelty-struck proto-scientist epigrammatically. He sets the tone of ironic duplicity, the redoubled strategy of his own authorial apostrophe, by epigraphizing a particular passage from Bacon that clearly undermines and contravenes the embattled "new scientist" in his own obsession with the "new." "Salomon saith, *There is no new thing upon the earth.* So that as Plato had an imagination, *that all knowledge was but remembrance*; so Salomon giveth his sentence, *that all novelty is but oblivion,*" *Essays*, LVIII (Borges's italics). Ironically, Borges, who proclaims elsewhere "One thing does not exist: Oblivion,"[9] rescues Bacon from the "oblivion" of his own *novelty* by inscribing him into the text as epigrammatic quotation; a mixed blessing, for while oblivion carries with it the redeeming virtue of the waters of Lethe, immortality stands for the perpetual precognition of self-loss, as this Borges story makes abundantly clear, as the "Biografía de Tadeo Isidoro Cruz" dramatically illustrates.

The authorial Borges's predicament is an oscillation, *ad hominem*, between epigraphs — Yeats and Francis Bacon. His is a voice of quotation in which authorial subject, authorial utterance (*apostrophe*), and textual discourse echo as desultory epiphenomena. The appropriated voices, in turn, hark back to authorial figures who are in themselves figurations of yearning, of nostalgia for augural initiations, for primal scenes long departed into the aphanisis of mnemonic phantomness. The presentation, the making present in remembrance, the seeking "the face I had/Before the world was made," suffers the mediations of what we recognize in that other American precursor of Borges, in Emerson, as "economy of compensation." For the attempt to present, to re-cognize a primal scene and a "transcendental signified" translates simultaneously as incremental accretion *and* as superannuation. "The Immortal," then, is the ghost story of a ghost made more ghostly in the incremental evocations of literature's self-history, in literature's "telling itself its own" differential story, a self-same utterance — illusorily believing itself to be so, at any rate — gazing at its specter since "No one telleth me anything new." Appropriately enough, arrogating to himself the Salomonic *sententia* by way of Bacon, "all novelty is but oblivion," Borges apostrophizes it in spectral mirror-inversion thus giving us its compensatory converse, "One thing does not exist: Oblivion." Borges inverts, too, that common ground shared by Yeats's and Bacon's Neo-Platonism. The One in Borges is not what is made present; it is not the One which infuses with its transcendental privilege the sundered and desultory fragments, the many. Rather, the One in Borges becomes exponentially fragmented, superannuated in augmentative refractions, hyper-extended in spectral, untimely perpetuity. Thus, in "The Immortal" Homer's avatar is Joseph Cartaphilus, is Marcus Flaminius Rufus, is the Warrior at Stamford Bridge in 1066, is the calligrapher amanuensis of Sinbad's adventures, is Borges, is Nahum Cordovero, is Ernesto Sábato — "a tedious way of saying" that the primal author devolves into "No One," i.e., the Immortal.

"The Immortal" has received its most extensive treatment in Ronald Christ's allusive *The Narrow Act*.[10] I detect in that conscientious effort a fundamental flaw, however. The shortcoming consists in reducing this ghost story to the figura of allusion. Within the Emersonian economy of compensation allusion becomes tantamount to superfluity, to pleonasm, to conspicuous abundance. For allusion, by definition, implies the multiplicity, the array of what are *res alienae*, an inflated economy of goods with discrete proprietorships. In short, allusion denotes allogenesis of "stories" or "histories," as opposed to what Borges's Emersonian economy places before us with the studied terseness of a self-problematizing story with an aphanitic author who eschews novelty and (ab)originality. The signatures appended to that story change and multiply, but only as allographs — the ghostly amanuensis displaced by his protean signature, an allonymy which screens out the aleatory signators by substituting itself in their vacated place. That allonymic trace configures simply the grapheme or "function" *author*, impersonal, undifferentiated, multiple, and immortal, i.e., inexistent as being, as *per* Valéry. Here a key distinction between "oblivion" and "inexistence" becomes imperative. The first, oblivion, is absolute indifference; the second, inexistence, is the difference which belies and spectrally haunts existence as critical or negative reflection. Immortality for Borges, as for Valéry, is entailed in the second. Immortality is what exacerbates existence into its differential supplement, into its converse or obverse ("L'immortalité . . . implique . . . l'inexistence," Valéry; "No one is anyone, one single immortal man is all men . . . a tedious way of saying that I do not exist," Borges). Like Marcus Flaminius Rufus, who *speaks* to us here and in our epigraph from the recesses of inexistence, Odysseus is, (in)existentially, *No one — Outys*. Polyphemus, however, can attest to his inconsonance with the bliss of oblivion. Immortality, then, stands for the inexistence which is born of inordinate extenuation, of the infinitely superannuated, of endless deferment and untimely extensibility. Borges's romance is a quest for oblivion that founders along the way on immortality. "The Immortal," as we shall now see, is a plaintive apostrophe, a self-conscious complaint, an aporia, an ironic lament against this insurmountable and self-perpetuating difficulty. I suspect this is why Borges's story opens with Bacon's Salomonic "oblivion" and "ends" with Homer's deathwish. Within each of these moments, and between them, we can now read the impossibility of either.

"The Immortal," the textual story, is well framed. It is sutured snugly between "bookends." At the opening paragraph we find Alexander Pope's *Iliad* (1715-1720). At the other end, we have Nahum Cordovero's *A Coat of Many Colors* (Manchester, 1948). That the first is an actual phenomenon — Pope's translation of the Homeric classic — and the second apocryphal, is moot. The significant fact remains that both container-frames are biblioform. What this frame-up encloses is also graphic — a manuscript found in the *last* volume of Pope's *Iliad* which was acquired by the Princess of Lucinge in June 1929 from the "antique dealer" Joseph Cartaphilus. "The orginal" of the manuscript "is written in English and abounds in Latinisms." The version offered us within the boundaries of this biblio-graphic framework "is literal," pleonastically enough.

One thing is self-evident in the ruse of this strategy, of this frame-up: Narrative voice and authorial privilege are one. What we read within this frame is what the narrator has authored. Authorial function and narrative utterance coalesce, become congruent and consonant. He who speaks is he who writes. We read and listen at once, we hear in reading, visually. We need, then, ask: Who is the provocateur of this ocular experience? Who is the author, the responsible subject with whom we find ourselves secreted within this frame, within this bookish cave? The responses to these queries are multiply duplicitous. They are a polymath's contestation who tells us he is "No one," who assures us, "I do not exist." And yet we must endure his graphic filament in our ocular center. Like Polyphemus, the questioning reader reads the voice of *Outys,* of "No one," even as he suffers the perduring scrawl. The scene of our predicament, beginning as it does where the *Iliad* ends, becomes a recognition scene. Our trial is not purely visual but re-visionary for we recognize the abyssal ground on which we read as the continuation of textual genealogy, an extended postscript of the Iliadic experience, i.e., *The Odyssey*. But this, the sequel in our manuscript, is no simple continuity for here, in this version, the authorial subject and the heroic deed are now become one, adjacent and supplementary. Homer *and* Odysseus have joined into *Outys*. Not only have narrating speaker and authoring writer fused in our manuscript, as already noted, but this linkage in turn becomes subsumed by the hero in a double bind. The *rhapsode*, the authorial voice and subject, has become stitched into the desultory fabric, the text, of the song. We might call this an economy of Emersonian compensation with a vengeance. Homer, the primal author, the transcendental subject, the mythical authority, the founding father, becomes woven as textual sign, as grapheme, as another untimely scribble or *garabato*, as mnemonic trace of textual space. He meets, etymologically, the fate spelled by his name: *Homeros* — to give as security, as hostage, as pledge; to accord, meet, join together, link in binding contract. (Borges, the perpetrator of this wily scheme, himself inexorably meets this same fate, as we shall see.) This authorial fate sunders the phenomenon "author" into his fragmented epiphenomena by which he is subsumed, *ad infinitum*, to become what Nahum Cordovero characterizes as "The Greek centos" and "the centos of late Latinity" (p. 118). The desultory paragraphing and endless resuturing of the authorial rhapsode is a fate overtly intimated in the second and concluding footnote of the story, where we read again ironically, of Giambattista Vico's defense of "the idea that Homer is a symbolic character, after the manner of Pluto or Achilles." From author to symbolic character, from rhapsode to a song's note, from arch-maker of structures of signification to a signifier, from signifier to phantom signified, this is the spectral destiny dealt to the "primal author": "It is not strange that time should have confused the words that once represented me with those that were symbols of the fate of he who accompanied me for so many centuries. I have been Homer; shortly, I shall be No One, like Ulysses; shortly, I shall be all men; I shall be dead." These are the concluding words of the Joseph Cartaphilus manuscript. The yearning of this Homeric epiphenomenon, of this Homeric pleonasm, resounds as mocking paradox, as insurmountable difficulty. The seeking after a "homing" in disappearance, in anonymity, in the oblivion of mortality serves, as it has done for over two millennia, to further the haunting immortality in the every-extended accretions of writing, of the *biographia literaria* and its self-perpetuating genealogy. That Homer/Joseph Cartaphilus should be pursuing this quest in our century, that Doctor Nahum Cordovero should be amplifying Joseph Cartaphilus, and that Borges should be, through us as accessories, supplementing this genealogical bloodline attests to the endless deferment, to the abiding postponement and ultimate subterfuge of that dynastic homecoming.

In this story, in this ghost history of incunabula, we can read the itinerary of a quest romance whose waylaying *contretemps* is an immortality endlessly perpetuated in the unflagging pursuit of mortality. "The Immortal" is a complex trope on and of this itinerary. It is a meta-trope really that at once dramatizes and compounds this unending project and its timeless difficulty. In this regard, the figment of fiction, the "symbolic character" we call "author" attains to the condition of Homer's epithet for his favorite hero, Odysseus, to whom Homer refers in the "Hymn to Hermes" as a *polytropos*. The wily prodigiousness of that *polytropic* hero has become the proper signature that identifies the author. Accordingly, Joseph Cartaphilus, the author in Borges's story, the author of our manuscript, the compounded Homeric avatar, the abyssal authorial Borges, displays his coat of many colors. To that end, Borges leaves little room for doubt. The paradigm "author" — Homer and the Homeridae — has been transfigured into the aphanisis of language, into the multitrope of writing and incunabula. Joseph Cartaphilus is a *homeros* — more a figure of language, a "hostage" or "security" of writing, a "pledge" of papyrus incunabula (a literal Carta-philus) than he is a writing/authoring subject. That he is from Smyrna, that he is an antique dealer, that he peddles another's (Pope's) intonation of the *Iliad*, that he appears as "a wasted and earthen man, with gray eyes and gray beard, of singularly vague features," that his mortal odyssey founders on immortality aboard a ship called Zeus, that his mortal body is beached on an island called Ios, are all desultory (co)incidents which, as mnemonic traces, commemorate, spectrally sublimate, and further timelessly his distant, immortal (and therefore inexistent, Valéry would say) prototype, Homer. In that subsuming or sublimation, the ghostly prototype also endures the passage into turns of language, into threads of the colorful coat's fabric, into stitchings of the text.

If as "homeros-cartaphilus" Joseph Cartaphilus extends the immortality of the paradigmatic author, he also attenuates the "essentialized" figure of the author as subject. That attenuation or diminishment is entailed by the emergence of the perpetuated Homer as spectral projection, as coeval image of the hero, Odysseus, a synergism that eventuates in our author. For Joseph Cartaphilus is at once Homer and cursed wanderer, i.e., Odysseus. Joseph's outer garment of many colors translates into the wandering hero of many turns, the *polytropic* man. The Autolycan Odysseus, the grandson of the wily schemer Autolicus who transferred the burden of odium borne toward him unto his grandson by giving him a name that signified his own "odious" fate, perforce emerges as the problematic progenitor and precursor of the Homeros-Cartaphilus. Thus, the author of our manuscript appropriates, internalizes the multiplicity, the many-sidedness of this polytropic fate. For in the name Joseph perdure not only the multiple and chameleonic vestments and the odium borne toward the biblical Joseph by his brethren but, also, the polyvalent and incremental ciphers which prodigiously augment and extend the economy of goods and tradition ("Joseph" has its root etymon in the Hebrew verb *yasaph*, meaning "to augment," "to add," "to increase"). "Joseph" and "Cartaphilus" then, as composite trope, augurs the unending incrementation, the perpetual deferment of totalization, or closure, in oblivion. It augurs the furthering of "immortality," and, semantically, of the graphic trace, the mnemonic cipher, the incunabula of that immortality. Accordingly, we should be less than surprised by the proemial line of the Cartaphilus manuscript: "As far as I can recall, my labors began in a garden of Thebes Hekatompylos, when Diocletian was emperor." Joseph Cartaphilus being epi-graphic cipher, an augural palimpsest, an epi-grammatic figure etched into the tables of writing, it follows naturally that a "garden of Thebes" with a myriad of apertures — hekatompylos, "a hundred-gated" — be the "original" locus, the inaugural station of his, our hero-author's, labors. Thebes, the Boeotian Thebes that supplementarily conflates with the Egyptian capital Thebes here, as the Greek epigrams teach us, is an originary site, a primal scene of writing; a point of transumption, where the Phoenician alphabet transmutes into the Greek, initiating thereby the variegated career of Greek writing and its palingeneses. In one of these avatars of Greek writing, in the *Phaedrus* of Plato, we read of a "great city in the upper region [of Egypt] which the Greeks call the Egyptian Thebes. It is here that the art of writing is first presented to Thamus the King by the divinity who is said to have invented the art, Theuth" (*Phaedrus* 274 c-e).[11] In this our Latinate avatar, our heroic-authorial figura that continues to "tell itself its own story" in the intoning of lines from the text of the *Iliad* — "the rich Trojans from Zelea who drink the black water of the Aisepus" — (from the end of Book II, the Catalogue of the Ships) goes by the suggestive name of Marcus Flaminius Rufus. We can read this code name as "the red trace," the filial blood-line whose timeless swell is to be read in the confluence of its streams beyond time and space (in utopia and uchronia), in the gnostic space of in-cunabula, in the spectral superscriptions and supplemental displacements of one epic palimpsest by another. Marcus's is a "new" Troy dance. Cartaphilus's a "new" Troy tale, where the adjective "new," as in Borges's Francis Bacon, must be bracketed or viewed as transparent, for what we read is both "another" *and* the self-same Troy tale, mediated by the diaphanous opacity of palimpsests and superscriptions which have accrued to it to extend its timeless perpetuity into unending *aristeia* and self-differentiating peregrination. As Iliadic hero, Marcus Flaminius Rufus's *aristeia*, a hero's attainment of honorable distinction in battle, is a pathetic failure whose anti-climax echoes with mocking incongruity and bitter irony in his exaggerated name, so cloyingly redolent with martial coloring and ferocity. The irony in this self-mocking pleonasm does not escape the hero. In this Sunburned (literally, "Iliadic," or "Aithiopian"), blood-colored battlefront on the Red Sea, Marcus contritely confesses, "I scarcely managed a glimpse of Mars' countenance. This privation pained me and perhaps caused me precipitously to undertake the discovery, through fearful and diffuse deserts, of the secret City of the Immortals" (p. 106).

In the apprehension of his own shortfall of heroic action, fame, and hero's immortality, Rufus seeks after a compensatory self-vindication. He transforms his self-deprecating difficulty, his *aporia* or self-questioning, into its synonym, into *zitisis* or a "questing after." In that transformation, in that figural transump-tion from *aporia* to *zitisis*, Rufus passes from being an Iliadic hero to being a wandering Ulysses, compelled, cursed, one should say, to wander in pursuit of an evanescent *nostos*, a homecoming, a self-absolution that may cleanse the curse, the "privation," as he calls it, which codemns him to wander through "fearful and diffuse deserts." As cursed wanderer, Rufus emerges as another form of pleonasm, as composite palingenesis of a filial genealogy which he perpetuates in himself — a lineage that extends from Odysseus through the Wandering Jew, the Flying Dutchman, and the Ancient Mariner. In this filial bloodline, we recognize that peculiar conflation of authorial subject — Joseph Cartaphilus — and symbolic personage — the character Marcus Flaminius Rufus. That *homeros*, or "linkage" literally, resonates in the suggestive lineaments of the gray and time-worn Joseph Cartaphilus, in his Salonika Spanish and Macao Portuguese, in his very name — an Old Testament cast-out, Joseph, and a New Testament fate, Cartaphilus, the porter in the service of Pontius Pilate whose abuse of Jesus condemns him to wander until the Second Coming. The thirteenth-century chronicler Roger Wendover (*Flores Historiaum*) identifies the Wandering Jew as a Cartaphilus[12] and Borges, in fact, has admitted to having drafted a story once on the Wandering Jew whom he called Cartaphilus.[13] (Further on, I shall return to the figura of Joseph Cartaphilus in that suggestive linkage that Borges intimates between this Jew/Homer/Odysseus and Flavius Josephus the Jew, whose apologia against Apion, the Greek grammarian and conjurer of Homer, adumbrates for us the "originary" authority of the "true" Homer.)

In this hypallage, this conflation of Rufus and Cartaphilus, *qua* schema of rhetorical trope, we recognize Rufus as the perduring and perennial quester of poetic invention, of literature, whose sought after *nostos*, his "homing," the "secret City of the Immortals" is the baneful ground of literature itself. The scene of the hero's wanderings in this written tale is itself a writing scene, as I shall amplify shortly. His itinerary is a passage from geography to geognosis, from the sunburned deserts and blood-hued plains into *topography* — the "written" topoi, the graphic scene and its polytropic labyrinths. We educe the forms of this transumption from Rufus's repeated declaration that his "labors began in a garden of Thebes," Plato's Egyptian cradle of writing, Ptolemy's belated reproduction in Egypt, once more, of that "other," and already secondary, Boeotian primal scene of writing. We suspect it, too, in Rufus's Homeric speech and idiolect. In short, we witness this passage, this transumption into incunabula, in that vast literary landscape which bewildered certain readers as a jungle of allusions, a landscape through which Rufus makes his pilgrim's way to his re-encounter with a troglodytic psychopompos he names Argos, "Ulysses' dog," who turns out to be Homer himself yearning for mortality.

The *zitisis*, the quest, of Marcus Flaminius Rufus has a negative origin. As I have pointed out, it is founded on a "privation," its inaugural point is a lack, an absence of the requisite ingredient for immortality: heroism. Like the Yeats epigraph ("I am looking for the face I had/Before the world was made") which articulates the fate of Tadeo Isidoro Cruz, Marcus's pursuit is a seeking after his own spectral reflection — his countenance suggested in eponymic and pronomial figures: "I scarcely managed a glimpse of Mars' countenance. This privation pained me." The hero's praenomen, Marcus, is traceable to Mars, the red planet (Rufus), and to Mawort, the Italic deity who became Rome's god of war. Marcus Flaminius Rufus is a "military tribune in one of Rome's legions." His tautological full name may be translated as "the red highpriest (*flaminius*) warrior god." Like Tadeo Isidoro Cruz, whose quest subsumes and is subsumed by a national epic, the *Martín Fierro*, "a poem which has come to mean 'all things to all men'," Marcus Flaminius Rufus is led by his pursuit to seek (and in the process carry on) a self-recognition scene, as already noted, in the abysmal space of writing, the topography of epic incunabula. His pursuit of the City of the Immortals translates into a questing after the *maximum bonum* of epic heroism and heroic action — immortality.

In this sense Rufus moves toward a locus of writing, a graphic topos, whose privilege is to privilege the heroic deed by redeeming the fallen hero from death, from oblivion. His sought-after object, in other words, becomes a privileged center, a writing scene, where death is transcended (timelessly) and immortality conferred. The Greek epic perpetuates in its narrative the immortality of the heroic dead. Life in the epic becomes consecrated and magnified by death. Death and immortality then are inextricably and paradoxically linked, as in Valéry's equation of immortality and inexistence. Epic narrative and writing are traditionally the privileged locus where the linkage takes place. The quest and vicissitudes of Marcus Flaminius Rufus become a vehicle through which Borges problematically explores and ironically explodes this topos, this traditional commonplace. Rufus's peregrination, his venture into the labyrinth of the City of the Immortals and his passage through its "center," emerge as a self-deconstructive reading and as demystification of a traditionally privileged scene of writing. His quest, then, becomes an irreverent allegory whose object is reading. What is unfolded on that itinerary divulges an insight into the problematic and self-problematizing nature of writing and the topical privilege, or centeredness, accorded to it by our literary tradition. We shall see how presently.

Homer, if he ever was, intones a narrative, the *Iliad*, into which he disappears to be displaced by Alexander Pope, who re-writes, in a modern language, the Troy tale into which he is subsumed as bookend for the manuscript of Joseph Cartaphilus, who, in turn, recedes into his writing so that Marcus Flaminius Rufus may etch himself into the script of his own adventures, into the "tables" of his own Troy dance. Rufus's writing, in turn, emerges as a differential re-writing, as mnemonic reading, where he reads himself as Iliadic hero, "lacerated," as he writes, "by a Cretan arrow," slouching toward dawn to be reborn, toward a landscape that "bristled up into pyramids and towers," to dream, intolerably, "of an exiguous and nitid labyrinth: in [whose] center was a water jar: my hands almost touched it, my eyes could see it, but so intricate and perplexed were the curves that I knew I would die before reaching it" (p. 107).

Beyond this death, a "sleep" in the presence of a "water jar" in the center of a labyrinth, a jar beyond reach but within view which tradition teaches us to identify as the jug of water fetched by Iris from the river Styx so that the gods may take their oath in its ablution, an oath which, if broken, the taker must be condemned to lie in a year-long coma and thereafter wander, ostracised for nine years more, beyond this "coma," when Rufus finally "became untangled from this nightmare," he finds himself "in an oblong niche no longer than a common grave, shallowly excavated into the sharp slope of a mountain." In this rite of passage from life, through death, to a transumption in which "on the opposite bank" of an impure and noiseless stream "(beneath the last sun or beneath the first) shone the evident City of the Immortals," Rufus drinks from the waters of the river of immortality. He discovers, however, that while granting immortality the waters grant not forgetfulness, not oblivion, but remembrance. And so, as he quenches his burning thirst, he finds himself *repeating* lines from the *Iliad's* catalogue of the ships — "I sank my bloody face into the dark water. I drank just as animals water themselves. Before losing myself again in sleep and delirium, I repeated, inexplicably, some words in Greek: 'the rich Trojans from Zelea who drink the black water of the Aisepos'."

Having drunk the waters of the river, crossed to the opposite bank, reached the City of the Immortals in commemorative utterance and painful peregrination, Rufus discovers, fortuitously, that the only access to the shining city, like the endless threshold of the labyrinth of writing in which he reads/writes himself, is abyssed, its central chamber multiplied, its centeredness abysmally repeated, the curse of nine years' wandering and ostracism transformed repeatedly into nine doors, of which the ninth repeats, *mise en abyme*, the passage to a center with nine doors: "The force of the sun obliged me to seek refuge in a cave; in the rear was a pit, in the pit a stairway which sank down abysmally into the darkness below. I went down; through a chaos of sordid galleries I reached a vast circular chamber, scarcely visible. There were nine doors in this cellar; eight led to a labyrinth that treacherously returned to the same chamber, the ninth (through another labyrinth) led to a second circular chamber equal to the first. I do not know the total number of these chambers; my misfortune and anxiety multiplied them" (p. 109).

One indeterminate day, again fortuitously, Rufus, wandering through this labyrinth of centers endlessly self-decentering in multiplicity, founders on another center, "a circle of sky so blue that it seemed purple," which suggests, with unmitigated irony, a path of transcendence. "Thus I was afforded this ascension from the blind region of dark interwoven labyrinths into the resplendent City" (p. 110). Having "ascended" to the yearned for City — the sought-after transcendental *ontos* of epic figuration — Rufus discovers the aberrant character, the mad structurality, and endless asymmetry of "structure." Far from a privileged center or a transcendental etymon, far from an ideal onto-telos or the richly structured intricacies of a labyrinth, the City proves a heterogeneous monstrosity. Its age is haunted by timeless antiquity, ''I felt that it was older than mankind, than the earth.'' Its fabrication is reminiscent of raving and departed deities, '''This place is a fabrication of the gods,' I thought at the beginning. I explored the uninhabited interiors and corrected myself: 'The gods who built it have died.' I noted its peculiarities and said: 'The gods who built it were mad''' (p. 110). Rufus finds himself before primordial, cosmic chaos: ''To the impression of enormous antiquity others were added: that of the interminable, that of the atrocious, that of the complexly senseless. I had crossed a labyrinth, but the nitid City of the Immortals filled me with fright and repugnance. A labyrinth is a structure compounded to confuse men; its architecture, rich in symmetries, is subordinate to that end. In the palace I imperfectly explored, the architecture lacked any such finality. It abounded in deadend corridors, high unattainable windows, portentous doors which led to a cell or pit, incredible inverted stairways whose steps and balustrades hung downwards. Other stairways, clinging airily to the side of a monumental wall, would die without leading anywhere, after making two or three turns in the lofty darkness of the cupolas'' (pp. 110-11).

In this profusion of chaos, we can read Rufus's own dissolution; the dissolving into aberrant undecidability of his own genealogy, of his own ontological anteriority as epic hero, as immortal cipher, as symbol of literature. His own writing, thus, becomes proleptic, augural, of his own diffusion into undecidable indeterminacy, into the fortuitous and heterogeneous centos of ''a coat of many colors.'' The object of his quest, once reached, divulges not a privileged center, not an order from which emanate the desultory fragments, the epiphenomena of a unitary and integral locus of origin, but an undecidable nightmare whose horrors afflict the quester with vertigo: ''I do not know if all the examples I have enumerated are literal; I know that for many years they infested my nightmares; I am no longer able to know if such and such detail is a transcription of reality or of the forms which unhinged my nights . . . I do not want to describe it; a chaos of heterogeneous words'' (p. 111).

Rufus's abandonment of this ''nefarious City'' translates into a process of self-demystification. His sought-after fountainhead proved not void (that would have been the supreme good of oblivion) but incomprehensible, beyond mastery. He encountered not a transcendental *primum mobile* but a senseless heterogeneity. Rufus does not, properly speaking, ''escape'' this aberration. Rather, he devises a ruse, a passage, yet another transumption into self-recognition where that insight means a perspicacity into the illusionary self. In that recognition, he problematizes his own ''naive'' quest by turning on the abysmal nightmare of literary historicity and translating the endless profusion into a game of which he partakes not only as pawn but as player, not only as deluded ''naive'' but as self-conscious, demystified participant. He extends that profusion, he augments the abyss by yet one more frame. He frames up the frame-up, as it were, by self-directed irony, by turning on *aporia*: He opts for voluntary forgetfulness — a self-engendered oblivion which foreswears to become oblivious to what it *knows* to have been relegated to oblivion, that is, *what it remembers to forget*: "I do not remember the stages of my return, amid the dusty and damp hypogea. I know I was not abandoned by the fear that, when I left the last labyrinth, I would again be surrounded by the nefarious City of the Immortals. I can remember nothing else. This oblivion, now insuperable, was perhaps voluntary; perhaps the circumstances of my escape were so unpleasant that, on some day no less forgotten as well, I swore to forget them" (p. 111).

The conjectural tone of Rufus's apostrophe ("perhaps . . . perhaps"), in view of what he still fears and what follows, serves to exacerbate self-irony. Having ventured into writing, into timeless and untimely textuality, he fears that on leaving its last labyrinth he may still be surrounded by it. Having transformed that fear into ominous precognition, into more than an apprehension, he *opts* to forget the chaos of a "primal" scene, of originary textuality and its history, so that he may go on writing, so that he may carry on the strategies of incunabula. His exploration and discovery prove untranslatable into statement, into cogent "meaning" or metaphysical "truth." His pursuit, as it happens, can only generate further writing, unending textuality, incontinent scenes of writing. At this juncture, what he recursively remembers to have proleptically written and what he self-consciously knows himself to be in the process of doing — writing — conflate. The momentary parabasis reads thus: "Those who have read the account of my labors with attention will recall . . ." (p. 111). What are we really to recall: that, as he writes, "a man from the tribe followed me as a dog might up to the irregular shadow of the walls"? Maybe so. But I suspect we are also being prompted to recall what we, along with Rufus, are remembering to forget: writing, the deluded history of writing, and the dreaded precognition that once "outside" of that writing scene, the City of the Immortals, we would again find ourselves surrounded. And so, having come out of the last cellar, at the mouth of the cave Rufus encounters the troglodyte of canine docility, "stretched out on the sand, where he was tracing clumsily and erasing a string of signs that, like the letters of our dreams, seem on the verge of being understood and then dissolve" (p. 111). That dissolution on the threshold, on the liminal border of decidability and mastery which Rufus experienced in the "nefarious City" plays itself out again on another frame of the abyss.

Thus, on that rudimentary threshold of the cave's mouth, we again encounter a writing scene which conflates the history of writing and the problematic process of a writing subject, of a beleaguered consciousness in the act of writing — an abysmal repetition of Rufus's parabasis. Only here the embattled co-incidence is more frenzied, more immediately counter-self-directed, more acutely aporetic, since in this scene anteriority or the history of writing and the writing process or act itself coalesce without any mediation. In the coalescence — the unwriting of anteriority in re-writing — there appears to be a privileged "present" where primal origin and its undoing, its demystification, become simultaneous: "At first, I thought it was some kind of primitive writing; then I saw it was absurd to imagine that men who have not attained to the spoken word could attain to writing. Besides, none of the forms was equal to another, which excluded or lessened the possibility that they were symbolic. The man would trace them, look at them and correct them. Suddenly, as if he were annoyed by this game, he erased them with his palm and forearm" (pp. 111-112).

At this juncture, *our* writing subject, Rufus, whose writing we are in the process of reading, finds himself "surrounded" once again (better yet, *still*) by the "nefarious City of the Immortals," as he well suspected and proleptically wrote earlier. He confronts on this threshold yet another spectral reflection of that abyssal, *eccentric* ground where writing, he would have hoped, originates but where, in fact, that origin is already a "figuration," the suggestion of a coming into being, which dissolves into monstrous heterogeneity, a desultoriness whose profusion proscribes, already and endlessly, the eventuation or actualization of any such privileged moment or occurrence. Thus, the possibility that this troglodyte's marks constituted writing, Rufus notes, is "excluded or lessened" since "none of the forms was equal to one another." In other words, the requisite element for "symbolic" figuration — the element of *identity* — is internally absent. What the troglodyte's graphic activity does suggest (and we may take this as emblematic suggestion or specular reflection for "The Immortal") is multiple or infinitely repeating substitutions, as opposed to symbolic or representational writing. That is, what Rufus de-scribes in his own scribing is not "writing" which can be reducible to representation, to symbol, but it is a process of tracing, effacing, and re-tracing, an open-ended play of displacements, free of referentiality or onto-teleological purpose — "The man would trace them, look at them and correct them. Suddenly, as if he were annoyed by this game, he erased them with his palm and forearm." The disembodied activity of the troglodyte, whose "humility and wretchedness . . . brought to my memory the image of Argos, the moribund old dog in the *Odyssey*, and so I gave him the name Argos and tried to teach it to him," incites Rufus to speculate "that perhaps there were no objects for him, only a vertiginous and continuous play of extremely brief impressions. I thought of a world without memory, without time; I considered the possibility of a language without nouns, a language of impersonal verbs or indeclinable epithets" (p. 112).

Thus, even as he *remembers* an arch-text, an epitome of originary "writing," the *Odyssey*, Rufus obliquely, ironically, beside himself in a literal sense, meditates on a pure, non-referential, anominalist discourse; on a textuality free from subjectivity, teleology, or transcendental historicity. His meditation becomes a spectral figure, a mirror image of the textual discourse he protagonizes and he himself a spectral shadow of the authorial ghost whose part he is deployed to dis-play or play out. In short, he becomes a mirror held up to himself. In the recognition of what he countenances he confronts yet another illusionary self and sees it as such, claiming, "everything was elucidated for me that day." The nature of that elucidation constitutes a demystification, a *desengaño*, which is rooted in further disconfirmation of his naive view, his historically preconditioned notion of representational writing. Rufus, we should recall, displays a traditional notion of writing when he observes, "it was absurd to imagine that men who have not attained to the spoken word could attain to writing" (p. 111). The elucidation which constitutes Rufus's corrective discovery comes with the realization that the abject troglodyte scribbling in the sand at the mouth of the cave, the humanoid whose wretchedness prompted Rufus to name him Argos, turns out to be Homer, the "primal author" himself: "Argos stammered these words: 'Argos, Ulysses' dog.' And then, also without looking at me: 'This dog lying in the manure.'

"We accept reality easily, perhaps because we intuit that nothing is real. I asked him what he knew of the *Odyssey*. The exercise of Greek was painful for him; I had to repeat the question.

"'Very little,' he said. 'Less than the poorest rhapsodist. It must be a thousand and one hundred years since I invented it'" (p. 113).

At this, one of an innumerable such pivotal points in the story, textuality turns on itself, repeats itself in an abyssed self-ostentation with the promise of endlessness and inexhaustability. Rufus's performance itself compounds, self-consciously, the unending "heterogeneity" that assails him repeatedly. I refer to Rufus's utterance in reaction to his discovery of the troglodyte's identity — "We accept reality easily, perhaps because we intuit that nothing is real" — in which he articulates his own self-recognition as "irreality," his own "reality" as cipher, as graphic trace, as ghostly character in the text he is "authoring" for us. That expressed precognition reverberates in his question to Argos and in Argos-Homer's response: "I asked him what he knew of the *Odyssey* . . . 'Very little,' he said. 'Less than the poorest rhapsodist'." If mastery of anteriority, of originary history, proves futile because that origin is a heterogeneous chimera, authorial self-mastery and mastery over one's "authored" text — authorial proprietorship in Vico's sense to be examined shortly — proves equally chimerical. The discovery of this futility entails the demystification of an evangelical (Flaminius — "high priest") quester who had naively sought after epic immortality where he believed it originates, in the heroic epic. Seeking after literature as embodiment of privileged, transcendental, and originary conteredness, he discovers, instead, textuality; that is, he discovers a decentered, self-problematizing, heterodox play of a writing scene; what he characterizes as "a kind of parody or inversion. . . . This establishment was the last symbol to which the Immortals condescended; it marks a stage at which, judging that all undertakings are in vain, they determined to live in pure thought, in pure speculation" (p. 113).

At this juncture also, the apostrophic quality of Rufus's discourse takes another turn. From the brazen tone of a quester seeking mastery over what he thought to have been a privileged origin and history, he passes to didactic speculation, to melancholy meditation, yet a contemplation which has a surfeit, a pleonastic self-consciousness that flows surreptitiously as self-irony: "These things were told me by Homer, as one would speak to a child" (pp. 113-14). In the same vein, Rufus sees Homer as one who was "like a god who might create the cosmos and then create a chaos," that is, as one who might have originated literature and then, or at once, precipitated textuality, the heterogeneous scene in which he (Homer) himself becomes another desultory fragment — a fate corroborated by Homer's own compliance with the prophesies of Tiresias whom Odysseus had consulted in the underworld: "He also related to me his old age and the last voyage he undertook, moved, as was Ulysses, by the purpose of reaching the men who do not know what the sea is nor eat meat with seasoned salt nor suspect what an oar is" (p. 114). This conflation of Homer with Odysseus adumbrates our earlier discussion of immortality as well as the moot presence of the authorial subject outside of the text, his impossible authority as privileged consciousness authoring from above or from a locus exterior to the scene of writing.

Rufus's meditations also harken to the Emersonian economy of compensation and to Valéry's insight on immortality I pointed to earlier. That is, authorship resides within discourse or a textual system; immortality is a condition of generality at its highest powers, a dissolution into insignificance, indifference, inexistence — an unending dissemination into inexhaustible multiplicity, a profusion into effacement which is never totalizable. This is how Rufus articulates immortality in this sea of indeterminacy: "The wheel of certain Hindustani religions seems more reasonable to me; *on this wheel, which has neither beginning nor end,* each life is the effect of the preceding and engenders the following, *but none determines the totality . . .* Indoctrined by a practice of centuries, the republic of immortal men had attained the perfection of tolerance and almost that of indifference. They knew that in an infinite period of time, all things happen to all men. . . . Seen in this manner, all our acts are just, but they are also indifferent" (p. 114). Hyper-extended to its logical exacerbation, the undecidability or indeterminacy of such a system reaches its supplementary obverse of necessity and inevitability, but an "inevitability" in which the authoring subject as privileged authority suffers no less diminishment and superannuation: "Homer composed the *Odyssey;* if we postulate an infinite period of time, with infinite circumstances and changes, the impossible thing is not to compose the *Odyssey,* at least once. No one is anyone, one single immortal man is all men. Like Cornelius Agrippa, I am god, I am hero, I am philosopher, I am demon and I am world, which is a tedious way of saying that I do not exist.

"The concept of the world as a system of precise compensation influenced the Immortals vastly" (pp. 114-15).

Rufus's peroration here on such a blatantly Emersonian note resonates too powerfully not to receive comment and, in our commenting, for us not to be remanded to his earlier apostrophe on the chimerical, primordial writing scene — the *history* and its slippery ground on which his quest founders and his naiveté dissipates: "'This City,' (I thought) 'is so horrible that its mere existence and perdurance, though in the midst of a secret desert, contaminates the past and the future and in some way even jeopardizes the stars. As long as it lasts, no one in the world can be strong or happy'" (p. 111). The unmistakable Emersonian echoes in both of these passages have never received comment, an oversight I hope can be remedied presently.

Borges has repeatedly invited and provoked comment on his work in the light, or shadow, of Emerson. His frequent citation of the New Englander speaks for itself and a good number of Borges's readers have followed the author's prompting. These include Ronald Christ to whose discussion of "The Immortal" I have referred earlier. Inevitably, however, a monadic and transcendental Emersonian *figura* is invoked in these discussions — "genius is all," the Over Soul with literature as its record, the single author who penned all literature, all called up at one time or another by Borges. Invariably this type of referral takes Borges at his word and his word at face value, avowing a parasitic reliance on a naively privileged author rather than offering a reading that derives its strength from self-reliance. These eulogistic allusions pay homage to "the lengthened shadow of one man," in Emerson's own words. Yet, Emerson himself decries such servility when he observes that in this sort of sacralization of literary history "Our reading is mendicant and sychophantic. In history our imagination makes fools of us, plays us false."[14] Indeed, the assiduous quest of Marcus Flaminius Rufus and his insight into the nefarious and aberrant character of the "institution" and its history, his demystified discernment, echoes Emerson's own brazen inveighing against the privileging of anteriority's penumbra and his invenerate attempts at displacing history's shadows rather than extending them. I cite from the introductory lines of his essay on "Nature" (1836 version): "Our age is retrospective. It builds the sepulchres of the fathers. It writes biographies, histories, and criticism. . . . Why should not we also enjoy an original relation to the universe? Why should not we have a poetry and philosophy of insight and not of tradition, and a religion by revelation to us, and not the history of theirs? . . . [W]hy should we grope among the dry bones of the past, or put the living generation into masquerade out of its faded wardrobe? The sun shines today also."[15]

Herein lies the iliadic "shining" and its unending Troy dance. Herein lies, too, the incitation to a "coat of many colors." Most blatantly we find resonances of this Emersonian "self-reliance" in Marcus Flaminius Rufus's ironic discernment and self-recognition, as well as in his didactic apostrophe on immortality as "indifference." Rufus notes of that baneful and chimerical locus of anteriority that "its mere existence and perdurance, though in the midst of a secret desert, contaminates the past and the future and in some way even jeopardizes the stars. *As long as it lasts, no one in the world can be strong or happy*" (p. 111, emphasis added). In "Self-Reliance" we read, and the reverberations are self-evident, "man postpones or remembers; he does not live in the present, but with reverted eye laments the past, or, heedless of the riches that surround him, stands on tiptoe to foresee the future. *He cannot be happy and strong until he too lives with nature in the present, above time*" (p. 76, emphases added).

In the American context of both Emerson and Borges to "live with nature" has a purely etymological connotation, meaning to live with constant "birth," which points to that timeless, or uchronic self-regeneration that characterizes America's family romance and its unending quest: A tireless errand internalized by our fictions' textuality and manifested in Borges's text, as we are in the process of seeing. Thus, living "in the present, above time" does not mean the venerate privileging of presence, authorial or temporal. It implies the strength to move in transitoriness, to remember to forget, like "Homer" and the Homeridae in "The Immortal," to displace and self-displace. Such strength translates into the capacity to quest exhaustlessly and inexhaustibly, to transgress even in repeating transgression, to "play" freely in the undecidable heterodoxy of "landscape" and textuality, to exercise the power of what Emerson called "shooting of the gulf": "Power ceases in the instant of repose; it resides in the moment of transition from a past to a new state, the shooting of the gulf, in the darting to an aim" ("Self-Reliance," p. 77). What I earlier characterized as Borges's quest for oblivion foundering on immortality is an ironic "foundering" of this untimely, or counter-timely (contretemps) order — a perpetual leap into the infinite, a seeking after a zero point, an ab-original anteriority, but only encountering the unending displacements which constitute the vertiginous pursuit itself. "Death (or its illusion)," Rufus tells us, "makes men precious and pathetic. They are moving because of their phantom condition; every act they execute may be their last; there is not a face that is not on the verge of dissolving like a face in a dream. Everything among the mortals has the value of the irretrievable and the perilous. Among the Immortals, on the other hand, every act (and every thought) is the echo of others that preceded it in the past, with no visible beginning, or the faithful presage of others that in the future will repeat it to a vertiginous degree. There is nothing that is not as if lost in a maze of indefatigable mirrors" (p. 115-16). Borges, like Emerson, is a textual illustration of this power of abandon in the maze of mirrors and the perils of their "randomness." As a consequence, he turns from brooding, cataleptically, on the "precious and pathetic condition" which the "timely" arrogates to man.

An indispensible distinction needs be made at this juncture, before we go on to witness Rufus's own dissolution into the vertiginous "maze of indefatigable mirrors." Emerson postulates a program, a propaedeutics, in his essays which he attempts to exemplify in his own poetry. Borges, on the other hand, deploys that program self-consciously and problematically, often ironically, as textual strategy. This is why I "cite" Rufus, a figural ploy of that strategy — the authorial character, the scriptor-scripture — here and not Boges; or I cite Borges only through the obliquity of a Cartaphilus, a misdirection of "vertiginous mirrors." Any attempt to read, in view of this distinction, "The Immortal" as completion, "totalization," or concretion of the Emersonian program (or even as "culmination of Borges' art" itself, as Ronald Christ would have it)[16] would be nothing short of naive and deluded mystification, a "mendicant and sychophantic" reading. Emerson is many things but, least of all, an ironist. Borges, the abysmal Borges of mazes and indefatigable mirrors, is foremost an irionic and wily romancer, a significant datum which, in his zeal for a literary poetics and politics of dynastic and oedipal succession, Harold Bloom overlooks in his perspicacious but otherwise *weak* "misreading" of Borges.[17]

Emerson's self-reliance is a god-hood of the "I," a brazen disdain of the "secondary man," an impatient quest and assertion of the primal selfhood. Borges, the wily, polytropic Borges of "The Immortal," sublimates the Emersonian ferocity with reticent persiflage, subverting its rage, subsuming its determination and determinacy into ironic ploy, into self-consuming stratagem, into textual ruse. We witness that subterfuge in the dispersal of selfhood, in the proliferation of the "I" into scattered refractions, where anteriorities conflate as pleonastic, distended selfhood whose very prodigiousness divests it of individuality, of primacy of being-in-itself. Borges, we might say, exacerbates Emerson's anxious "compensation" for the dread of dynastic succession, for the mere possibility of belated secondariness. In the ironic subterfuge of Emerson's dynastic anxieties and their shrill programmatics, Borges, as I will show more explicitly in short order, strikes a dual blow at the mystification of privileged centeredness. First, he subverts the notion of an illusionary, primal self — a privileged subject, authorial or otherwise. Second, he undermines the notion of an equally illusionary primal origin — a locus of pre-scriptive ontos, a Pascalian, ubiquitous center at a transcendental point of "zero" which authorized subsequent desultory discourse and textuality. As we have seen, Rufus's quest in this regard reaches *not* an aboriginal center or transcendental etymon, but founders on the indeterminacies and mad diffusions of heterogeneity. Analogously, or homologously we could say in terms of structure, this problematic non-origin and non-originary historicity has its correlative in a hyperextended, superannuated Emersonian anti-dynasticism: Cartaphilus/Rufus is *not* a belated figure, a latter-day Odysseus or Homer. Rather, the pleonastic synergism Cartaphilus/Rufus (and we have seen and shall see again how they conflate) *is* Homer and Odysseus, and much more. Appropriation, in other words, as already discussed with respect to "Tadeo Isidoro Cruz," ceases to be serial, successive, dynastic, and emerges as displacing adjacency, differentially supplemental, at once "self-same" as and also different from the appropriated; a situation in which priority or anteriority becomes moot and, therefore, dynastic succession, or earliness and secondariness, becomes concomitantly etiolated, faded out, diminished.

The conflation of Rufus and Cartaphilus, on the one hand, and the process of counter-seriality or the exacerbation of dynasticism into adjacency and supplemental simultaneity, on the other, occur concurrently in "The Immortal" and they must be examined together. That turning point in the story pivots on the separation between Rufus and Homer at the end of the story's fourth part and our passage into the fifth. Ironically enough, Rufus's separation from Homer is followed immediately by his fusion into Cartaphilus, who, in the conclusion of this fifth part of the story, will have written, "I have been Homer; shortly, I shall be No One, like Ulysses." Just as ironically, the grammatical means for bringing about that turn at this pivotal point is the subject pronoun "I." A clearly ironic turn since the outcome of the process consists in the unmitigated attenuation, the eradication through over-exposure, of the subject and of privileged subjectivity. The closing lines of part four prepare us for the decrement of the timely, for the ebbing of any possibility for unique eventuality, the effacement of subjectivity, the fading out of any nostalgically guarded or evoked presence. Simultaneously, those lines open up the textual field to play, to "non-seriousness," to "serious non-sense": "There is nothing that is not as if lost in a maze of indefatigable mirrors. Nothing can happen only once, nothing is preciously precarious. The elegiac, the serious, the ceremonial, do not hold for the Immortals. Homer and I separated at the gates of Tangier; I think we did not even say goodbye." The essential question "who is this I?" or the performative query "who is speaking here?" becomes altogether specious and, in view of what follows, downright irrelevant. Since we are stalking that shadowless figure, for exegetic purposes we can identify the first person subject pronoun with Rufus — the Rufus we have been following in his peregrination which culminates in his dialogue with the troglodyte who turns out to be Homer. Now, on taking his leave of Homer, without goodbyes (wholly unnecessary since here there is no "first" or "last" or "once" for such encounters and departures), the "I" transits to part five which opens with "I travelled over many kingdoms, new empires." With rare exception, each sentence in the next two paragraphs (about a page) has the first person singular pronoun as its subject. The following page also abounds in the subjective, though less so. I have pointed to the irony of this procedure. What may be just as significant, however, is what the text itself problematically sunders, or dis-articulates, and that is the *unreality* issuing from a certain ungrammaticality, an anacoluthon, or *the confusion of subject*, to the unquestionable detriment and loss of a speaking or authoring subject — a ghostly "I" who at one point cloyingly, ironically, with phantasmal perspicacity mutters, *sub rosa*, an unflagging determination to go on writing, "no matter if I am judged fantastic."

In a sweep which sees the individual "I," the jealously narcissistic Emersonian selfhood, scattered, disseminated timelessly through a history whose historicity is neither unique nor precious, neither new nor self-same, but sundry, simultaneous, and refracted in the "maze of indefatigable mirrors," this "I" courses indefatigably from Stamford Bridge in 1066, to "the seventh century of the Hegira, in a suburb of Bulaq," transcribing "with measured calligraphy" the adventures of "Sinbad and the history of the City of Bronze [read: Ilium, or Troy]," professing the science of astrology in Bikaner and Bohemia. "In Aberdeen, in 1714, I subscribed to the six volumes of Pope's *Iliad*; I know that I frequented its pages with delight. About 1729 I discussed the origin of that poem with a professor of rhetoric named, I think, Giambattista; his arguments seemed to me irrefutable. On the fourth of October, 1921, the *Patna*, which was taking me to Bombay, had cast anchor in a port on the Eritrean coast. I went ashore; I recalled other very ancient mornings, also facing the Red Sea, when I was a tribune of Rome and fever and magic and idleness consumed the soldiers" (p. 116). In this multitudinous dispersal of the subject over the disparate space, the desultory "landscape" of incunabula, of historical and marvelous textuality as homologated space — from the historical field of the Norman Conquest, through the abysally compounded frames of the *Arabian Nights* to the Vichian *New Sciences* and the steamer *Patna* of Joseph Conrad's *Lord Jim* — we witnessed at once the profuse dissipation of hero into textual cipher (in the sense of the term's Arabic root etymon *sifir*, meaning "zero," and the Odysseyian *Outys* ("No One") and the conjunctive agrammaticality, the rhetorical *anacoluthon*, which (con)fuses, conflates, Rufus the Roman tribune and Joseph Cartaphilus, the peddler of Pope's *Iliad* in our opening frame, who subscribed to the six-volume translation of Pope in Aberdeen in 1714 and who had occasion to discuss its origin with a professor of rhetoric — Giambattista (Vico). In this maze of convergence and dispersal, the spectral tirelessness of non-mimetic, echoing mirrors, of disseminated and disseminating textuality, we witness, too, an implosion, a caving in of the opening frame, the prefatory threshold of the text. The text, that is, recapitulates its container-frame, its bookend — Pope's *Iliad* that contained *our* manuscript — into itself. The degree of ironic chastisement endured by Emersonian subjectivity in the strategy outlined thus far should be readily apparent. Ironically, however, what may not be so obvious is a peculiar dilation or magnification of selfhood, of a "primal" I, in being subjected to the desultoriness and intense dispersal which vitiates it. I place "primal" as modifier in quotes since in these vicissitudes serial or dynastic primacy and secondariness become moot and are displaced by an "I" which repeatedly re-capitulates, an "I" that now and again "heads" or "moves to the head" to subsume and internalize as pre-dicant and predicate the spectral or ghostly subjectivities and their "anterior-ity," their authorial power and proprietorship, their *auctoritas*. In this "odd" deployment of the economy of compensation, more becomes less and less becomes more. Borges's Emersonian striving suffers subterfuge and chastisement but finds its "self" ironically vindicated in being vitiated by dispersal.

In "Guayaquil" (August, 1970), a story that comes nearly two decades after "The Immortal," the authorial Borges offers an exordium with a singularly suggestive confession that helps elucidate this ironic stratagem. In a poem entitled "Emerson," which dates from Borges's visit to New England in 1962 he offers another, equally suggestive adumbration. I shall take these in turn. We read in the opening gambit, the second paragraph, of "Guayaquil," "My opening paragraph, I suspect, was prompted by the unconscious need to infuse a note of pathos into a slightly painful and rather trivial episode. I shall with all probity recount what happened and this may enable me to understand it. Furthermore, to confess to a thing is to leave off being an actor in it and to become an onlooker — to become somebody who has seen it and tells it and is no longer the doer."[18] As prefatory ploy, Borges's cloying ruse of self-effacement has a feint and a surfeit to it. The recounted episode of the story is clearly not a "trivial episode," and it is obviously more than "slightly painful," and the "note of pathos" infused into the proemial paragraph is by no means countermanded or proscribed from the rest of the story by virtue of being relegated to the purported marginality of prefatory strategy. What does fade out is authorial presence and immediacy, now mediated by authorial trace become spectacle to itself. That spectacle or mirror-object watched constitutes the surfeit of the feint, the authorial self become a guest in the text, hosted by the self-effacing, faded-out author-prefator now haunting as remainder in his own story; the precipitator-doer turned onlooker, now watching his own surfeit, the remainder-doer in spectacular performance. In this sense, the proemial confession of the exordium belies its own marginality. It betrays the self-effacement of the "diminished" authorial self. For to "leave off being an actor" by means of confession in order "to become an onlooker" is tantamount to looking on the self as *acting*. In that redoubling, far from ceasing to be an actor, the subjective self (the authorial subject) becomes the performer acting the role of actor, being a "someone else" that founders on the self, on one's own ghost, on one's own mirror specter. The "confessor," the authoring subject that seeks to cast itself out as ratiocinating exteriority, implodes from the peripheries and enters (falls) into literature, into abyssal textuality. That is the fate of "Borges" in "Guayaquil"; that too is the fate of Rufus and of Joseph Cartaphilus in "The Immortal." That is, as well, the supremely ironic fate reserved for Emerson himself by Borges in the poem "Emerson," where we read of the brazen high priest of the self and of self-reliance:

He thinks: I have read the essential books
and written others which oblivion
will not efface. I have been allowed
that which is given mortal man to know.
The whole continent knows my name.
I have not lived. *I want to be someone else.*[19]

The ironic exacerbation wrought upon the Emersonian "self" consists here in an etymological and literal overdetermination of self-reliance as a re-alignment or re-assembling of self, a redoubled bind (*re-ligare, reliance*), as in a confession, where the subject becomes an onlooking spectator of the self as "someone else." The strategy displayed through authorial self-dramatization in "Guayaquil" and dramatized at Emerson's expense in this poem is the same operative principle deployed in "The Immortal." In this sense "The Immortal" could be read as Hermetic parable of a textual economy and politics (Hermetic in the sense of Hermes's role as god of property and thievery); that is, the economy of appropriation and divestment of texts which authorize authorial selfhood — in the Vichian sense of a synonymy between property and *au(c)toritas*, where author means property, and authorial status is defined by ownership (*autos; proprius; suus ipsius*).[20] The *text* of "The Immortal," the Joseph Cartaphilus manuscript we read, is predicated on such economy: Pope's *Iliad* is acquired from Joseph Cartaphilus the "dealer," the manuscript-text is found in the last volume and becomes "*literal* offering" of an authorial persona, Borges, who, in making the offer, divests himself of the appropriation. This is the opening frame, the proemial gambit of the story. That prefatory propriety becomes subsumed, or reclaimed, by the text it frames when the text itself adumbrates the feint of that ploy; when it discloses the frame-up. And at this juncture our text, the Cartaphilus manuscript, authorizes its own readability as Hermetic economy, as compensatory linkage or contractual dealing which is "binding."

At this critical point we glean, as well, the spectral adjacency between the over-wrought Emersonian *re-liance* and the Homeric/Cartaphilusian *auctoritas*. I refer to the already cited passage in the text where we read that our synergetic "subject" Rufus/Joseph Cartaphilus *writes*: "In Aberdeen, in 1714, I subscribed to the six volumes of Pope's *Iliad*. . . . About 1729 I discussed the origin of that poem with a professor of rhetoric named, I think, Giambattista; his arguments seemed to me irrefutable" (p. 116). In another of the text's putative peripheries, in the supposed exteriority of a footnote, *our* "dealer," the authorial Borges (parading as broker, in dealership of Cartaphilus' the dealer's property, his manuscript), would have us understand unmistakably, by way of another obliquity of attribution, that the mentioned "Giambattista" is none other than Giambattista Vico. Borges attributes the "suggestion" to one of his contemporary compatriots and his frequent antagonist: "Ernesto Sábato suggests that the 'Giambattista' who discussed the formation of the *Iliad* with the antique dealer Cartaphilus is Giambattista Vico; this Italian defended the idea that Homer is a symbolic character, after the manner of Pluto or Achilles.'' The effect of such a stratagem that attempts to delinate liminal lines, thresholds between textuality and the peripheries of textuality, is to co-opt any and all privileged ''beyondness'' of authorial subjectivity as the text's shaping agent from above or from the outside. We can attribute that ''unexpected'' outcome to the fact that the text recapitulates into itself, sucks in, and thereby pre-empts any extra-textuality, eradicating in the process any ideological differentiation between a biographical (in the ''real life'' sense) author with his contemporary-world writing scene (Ernesto Sábato being an index here) and the authorial persona, the ''broker,'' in this case the ''wheeler dealer'' who delivers the goods, offering them to us ''literally.'' As with Homer and Emerson, Borges suffers a re-alignment, an entry *into* literature which is ''binding.'' The ''linkage'' here could be outlined in the following compensatory and mirrored spectrum: What Vico (basing himself on, in collusion with, Flavius Josephus the Jew) does with Homer, is what Borges does with Emerson, is, in turn, the fate of Borges, and, no less so, becomes the fate of Giambattista Vico. In this regard, ''The Immortal'' could be read, and I opt here for reading it as such, as Vichian enterprise that turns on Vico his own method, dramatically fulminating and extending, in the process, that ambiguous and equivocal project in *The New Science* which announces itself as the ''Discovery of the True Homer'' (Book III).

Short of converting Vico's method in *The New Science* into overdetermining principle for ''The Immortal,'' one must remark the distinctly Vichian procedure entailed in the text's strategy for inter-dicting frames, peripheral liminality, exteriority, and onlooking or ratiocinating subjectivity (authorial or remarking, i.e., Borges, Sábato, this or any other reader) and, by that inter-dicting, suturing these would-be peripheries into itself.[21] That ploy, which problematizes Vico himself by turning his ''method'' on the Giambattista whose arguments on the origin of the *Iliad* ''seemed to me irrefutable,'' appropriates the methodological axiom that serves as controlling postulate in *The New Science*: ''Doctrines [Theories] must take their beginning from that of the matters of which they treat'' (paragraph 314); and ''It [The New Science] must begin where its subject matter began'' (paragraph 338). The *principle* (*principium*) of procedure, in other words, must be of the essence of that which it treats. Thus, the deployed stratagems must be *of* the text; textualizing strategies with a text as their object must be *proper* to, must *pertain* to, their putative mark, to their considered matter, i.e., to the text itself. Such a principle of filiation, then, permits no exclusivity, liminality, or periphery. All that is about the text (all that ''surrounds'' it) becomes a filiate part of its constellation, of its textuality. The ''author,'' the ''authorial subject,'' the ''proprietor'' (*auctos/proprius*), the economic dealer of this *appurtenance* is neither excepted nor excludable from the binding snare of this entanglement. Thus, in the bindery of texts and textuality the weavers and their weaving appertain to the fabric of their labor. In this simultaneous adjacency and filiation, *self-reliance* entails and is entailed by a *self-re-linkage*, a re-binding of self, an economic re-alignment to and within the web of fabrication, the texture of the text — a (re)entry into literature and literature's textuality. While Homer may not have *written* the *Iliad*, as rhapsode he wove its desultory fragments where, in turn, through etymology, homonymy, and compensatory economy, he himself, as *homeros*, has been stitched into its maze of links, into its macula. The Vichian postulates, in this regard, extend with firm constancy as method of *The New Science*; they also dramatize and display the *principii*, the "beginnings" which Vico's project subsumed, appropriated, internalized into itself as method:

> Homer left none of his poems in writing, according to the firm assertion of Flavius Josephus the Jew against Apion the Greek grammarian. The rhapsodes went about the cities of Greece singing the books of Homer at the fairs and festivals, some singing one of them, others another. By the etymology of their name from the two words which compose it, rhapsodes were stitchers-together of songs, and these songs they must certainly have collected from none other than their own peoples. Similarly [the common noun] *homeros* is said to come from *homou*, together, and *eirein*, to link; thus signifying guarantor, as being one who binds creditor and debtor together. This derivation is as farfetched and forced [when applied to a guarantor] as it is natural and proper when applied to our Homer as a binder or compiler of fables (paragraphs 850-52, brackets in the translation.)

Within the Vichian schema method and matter become so integral, so inextricably interwoven that one can no longer speak of their duality. We have in Vico more than adjacency, more than supplementarity, with the logical consequence of an impossibility of "beginning at the beginning" or taking our *principii* from the *principium* of our subject matter since we ourselves cannot (could not) be an external element of that matter, just as Homer is not. In the Vichian procedure the *method* (literally the "way" — from the Greek *hodós*), the *pursuit* of *scienza*, of knowledge, is the knowledge itself; the path of wisdom is itself wisdom and all wisdom for Vico is "poetic wisdom." It is what one achieves in the *poesis*, in the "making," or fabrication, on the "way," in the pursuit itself: "Indeed, we make bold to affirm that he who mediates this Science narrates to himself this ideal eternal history so far as he himself makes it for himself. . . . For the first indubitable principle posited above is that this world of nations has certainly been made by men, and its guise must therefore be found within the modification of our own human mind. And history cannot be more certain than when he who creates the things also narrates them" (paragraph 349). Emerson has his own intⅬnation of this Vichian principle and its consonance with Vico's *verum ipsum factum* is unmistakable. In "Nature" we read, aphoristically,

"Every man's condition is a solution in hieroglyphic to those inquiries he would put. He acts it as life, before he apprehends it as truth."[22] Under, within, these circumstances, a *procedure* necessarily devolves upon its poetic etymology, upon its paleonymy. It literally becomes a *ceding* (*cedere*) "before" or in favor of, a yielding to a going before. Concomitantly, Emersonian "self-reliance" as pursuit of primacy, of "beginning" or *principium*, connotes a self-re-adjustment by which the self surrenders in order to re-capitulate, move to the fore — a compensatory economy of reciprocity whereby the self seeks to recoup the loss sustained in ceding, in yielding up of self so that its re-aligned remainder could attain to the sought after primacy or anteriority.

There is, we could say, an inescapable measure of capitulation in any re-capitulation. The duality or dialecticality of a self in a reciprocal, compensatory transaction with itself is a false duality or dialectic, Vico and Emerson seem to be telling us. For certainty in history, as far as Vico is concerned, resides in the mutuality, more accurately, the congruity of deeds, of things created, and of their narration. As for Emerson, our life is a rebus whose shape we live and what we live figures as that shape which we apprehend as our "truth." While a redoubled subject or a dialectical self seems to be a figure with one term too many for Vico and Emerson, the "truth" of our fictions, the narration of our fabrications, of our history, require this superfluity at least as ploy, as feint so that the subject, authorial or otherwise, may *act* as onlooker, as outsider to his own actions, as exteriorty to the fabric his actions weave as web, as text or incunabula which figures as the "actor's" historical truth. If, as Vico tells us, man cannot comprehend anything outside of what he himself has made, and, as Emerson would have it, if man's actions are themselves the questions to which the human condition is a solution, which man "apprehends as truth," that discernment both for Vico and for Emerson is itself an act and resides within the web of man's deeds, fabrications, procedures. The posture of self-distancing from the performance of this "drama" is more properly an "imposture." In other words, authorial activity, just as acts of confessing, of onlooking which would have the self divide into spectator and spectacle, carries with it a necessary falsity — necessary in the sense that the feint is inherent, but also necessary in the sense that such play-acting is an indispensable element which infuses these human activities with an *aporia*, a difficulty.

Emerson contends with such difficulty by turning it into impetus, into energizing source which he terms our necessary "poverty." Vico, descrying the necessity of such a predicament, tells us that there can be no outside guarantors and, thus, an etymology which would link such a privileged, overriding status to *homeros* is, as he notes, "farfetched." For Vico there are only "creditors/debtors" who are at once both creditor *and* debtor, who "bind" and 'compile' and who are also bound and compiled into the fabric of the compilation. Borges conflates Vico and Emerson, contending with this difficulty by treating its predicament as irony. Accordingly, he exacerbates the feint, the ploy, the "falsity" inherent in a strategy of self-re-gathering, of re-collection, of a subjectivity bound into, entangled by, the textual economy we call (so cavalierly at times) literature and literary history. In the light of this "exacerbation," of this highlighting of *aporia*, we read Joseph Cartaphilus, the Borgesian avatar of Vico's Flavius Josephus the Jew, as he engages in the gymnastic performance of this playacting in order to recall and recollect the self as authorial subject severed from the synergesis Cartaphilus/Rufus; so that he may cogitate from a (feigned) exteriority, self-aware and cognizant of the feint and conscious, too, that his feint yields a surfeit, is a yield(ing) of an irony which produces a remainder, an alterity as spectacle, an "other" as, or in, self-reflection, i.e., his own authorial specter:

> After a year's time, I have inspected these pages. I am certain they reflect the truth, but in the first chapters, and even in certain paragraphs of the others, I seem to perceive something false. This is perhaps produced by the abuse of circumstantial details, a procedure I learned from the poets and which contaminates everything with falsity, since those details can abound in the realities but not in their recollection. . . . I believe, however, that I have discovered a more intimate reason. I shall write it; no matter if I am judged fantastic.
>
> The story I have narrated seems unreal because in it are mixed the events of two different men (pp. 116-17).

Cartaphilus' ruse aims at disarming and, in disarming the reader, diffusing the aporia, the predicament of ironic difficulty. His ploy consists in rendering his insight as having the appearance of, as *seeming* to be "unreal." He betrays his own awareness of the fact that he is engaged in an *extra-vagant* act here. He displays a precognition of not only being "judged" *as* but *being fantastic* by dint of "walking out on himself" — of extra-vagance. He engages in a procedure by which he yields as subject in favor of "another" who is not "another" but is a yielded or produced self out of an act of self-deflection. We may call this act a differential simulacrum, the simulation of specular reflection, a ghostly visitation, by means of which he feigns to be an on-looker looking on himself, as in an act of confession, and yielding in deference to Homer. The feint betrays itself, however, when in the next paragraph he tells us "I have been Homer." For the moment, he descries not only his own "fantastic" nature born of extravagance — or the attempt to extricate himself or drift from inside the web of the textus to the periphery — but he beholds as well that the story, under these circumstances, "seems unreal because in it are mixed the events of two different men." Only, and here is the surfeit, the ironic superfluity, if you will, the second of the "two different men" is not rendered from the terms of the synergism Rufus/Cartaphilus. Rather, it is deflected to read Rufus/Homer with Cartaphilus as the aspiring yield, the "third man" as remainder, as surfeit, as ratiocinating-narrating subject in authorial and authoritative exteriority: "Flaminius Rufus, who before has applied to the city the epithet of Hekatompylos, says that the river is the Egypt; none of these locutions are proper to him but rather to Homer. . . . Spoken by the Roman Flaminius Rufus, they are not. They are spoken by Homer; it is strange that the latter should copy in the thirteenth century the adventures of Sinbad, another Ulysses, and should discover after many centuries, in a northern kingdom and a barbarous tongue [Pope's English], the forms of the *Iliad*" (p. 117).

We recall, of course, that the grey and wasted antique dealer peddling Pope's *Iliad* is Cartaphilus, the dealer who subscribed to the six-volume translation in Aberdeen in 1714, and who "discussed the origin of that poem with a professor of rhetoric named . . . Giambattista." But so does Cartaphilus, in spite of the "falsities" which contaminate "recollection" of "details [which] can abound in the realities." And in trying to mediate which words are proper to whom, in attempting, that is, to delineate an economy of proprietorship, of authority, of *authorship*, his "confusion" betrays that no such privileged status obtains within this economy (whether it be the status of guarantor, *homeros*, or the status of ownership, *proprius*). "When the end draws near," he *confesses*, "there no longer remain any remembered images; only words remain" (p. 118). Reflecting on (and compounding) his own extravagant status as "fantastic" and on the con-fusion his earlier procedure perpetrated, he writes, "It is not strange that time should have confused the words that once represented me with those that were symbols of the fate of he who accompanied me for so many centuries. I have been Homer; shortly I shall be No One, like Ulysses; shortly, I shall be all men; I shall be dead" (p. 118). The quietus, the ultimacy of that wishful peroration, however, becomes interdicted. Having woven his own aphanisis, his own re-ceding (or yielding up of self) into the text, having become text by "exiting" *into* textuality, now that very text pro-scribes its own closure. That pro-scription, with ironic consistency, takes on the form of "Post-script," clearly a chiasmus, our rhetor Gimabattista would interdict. Thus, far from an expiration in ultimacy, in clausura, the text runs its course only to run "out" of that course, to work itself out into literature, into landscape of incunabula; a course not unlike Cartaphilus' re-ceding into words, into textuality disseminated and self-dis-seminating, scattered into desultoriness — the heterogeneous centoism, the monstrous heterogeneity of abysmal decenteredness where Rufus's quest foundered vertiginously.

I shall be taking up the nature of "Post-script" in its relations to script shortly. For now, I should like to focus on this trailing opuscule in relation to itself, as its own pleonasm or inflated economy which superannuates into its own ironic "poverty" of disseminated desultoriness. The procedure in this "Post-script" should be familiar to us by now. It consists in the Vichian *method* postulated as axiom for the *New Science*, in the Emersonian questioning self as hieroglyphic solution for the question posed — a self-gain in capitulation, or moving toward subsuming all in order to eradicate all anteriority. The "Post-script" is concerned with the question of a "most curious" commentary elicited by the publication of the Joseph Cartaphilus manuscript, if we can still call it that. This curiosity is a cento, a patchwork quilt of "some one hundred pages" that speaks of "the Greek centos, of the centos of Latinity," among other fractions. It is biblically entitled *A Coat of Many Colors* and emanates from "the most tenacious pen" of a Doctor Nahum Cordovero,[23] yet one "more" palingenesis of Flavius Josephus the Jew and of Joseph Cartaphilus. What this "most curious" commentary expatiates is nothing more and nothing less than its own cento of Joseph's coat of many colors. Its biblical title remains consonant and, thereby, one with its biblioform, its "biblical" interiority. The fabric, the text(ure) of its Cordoban vellum, stitches its own incunabulistic "consolation" ("Nahum" has precisely this literal meaning in the Hebrew). In its one hundred pages resonates a reminiscence of Homer's myriad "Thebes Hekatompylos," the hundred-gated Theban writing scene. Far from a post-script, an addendum of clausura, an after-mathemata, this supposed appendix *recapitulates* the preceding textual corpus *but not* as synthesis. Rather, it subsumes its graphic antecedent so that it may move to the head of the process. For it is clearly apparent that in this purported after-word we have not an ending but a beginning. The textual poetics of an "epic" quest, the family romance of textuality of incunabula, sally forth for the innumerable first time. The textual *nostos*, the homing or home-coming anticipated in a "post-script" ends up as *zitisis*, as renewed quest.

Like Marcus Flaminius Rufus, whose peregrination founders on a problematic locus where synthesis is impossible, where heterogeneous desultoriness interdicts cogency and the centeredness of transcendental origin or privileged *principium*, Nahum Cordovero's "commentary" must confront the insurmountable diffuseness of a mad structurality. Thus, his own enterprise can only manage a ragtag patchwork. Like the Homeroid troglodyte whose scribbles in the sand at the mouth of the cave lack internal identity, Cordovero's project can muster no "commonality" or internal consistency in these "Greek centos," these "centos of Latinity" that might enable him to martial this scattered fragmentariness into coherent transformation. In the face of this predicament and its impossibility, Cordovero contends with his *aporia* by subsuming its difficulty into his enterprise thereby making his own project of one piece with its subject matter. True to the Vichian axiom that theories must take their *principii*, their principles or beginnings, from the *principium* of the matters which they treat, Cordovero can do nothing but compound inaugural actions since his subject-matter — the "Cartaphilus manuscript" — consists in repeated and self-compounding beginnings. Like the authorial ghost emanating from the synergism Homer/Cartaphilus/Rufus, Nahum Cordovero devises his own self-conscious ruse, his self-ironic strategy which he deploys against the difficulty of his predicament. Faced with the desultoriness of multivalence, of polysemia disseminated into uncontrolled structurality, like the spectral heroes and authorial subjects *on* whose manuscript he pens his own palimpsest-like commentary, Cordovero devises a spectral space for his own ghostliness from where he can look on his predicament as spectacle. We are told that in the face of this heterogeneity "he infers from these intrusions or thefts that the whole document is apocryphal" (p. 118). In view of his perspicacity into that Vichian filiation between his commentary and the document he comments on, Cordovero infers that his own performance is of the essence of its treated object. His inference thus betrays the insight that his own commentary, *A Coat of Many Colors*, must be *apocryphal* as well, if its re-marked object is indeed apocryphal, with the concomitant realization that he himself is an apocryphal figure, a polytropic fiction. Here we embark, more explicitly, on the relation between the "Post-script" and the "script."

We can read Nahum Cordovero's performance as commentator as a Borges parable on commentary and on self-extending textuality. Put into the form of "Post-script," Cordovero's commentary displays its palimpsest relation to its object betraying and subverting, thereby, the liminal median between "script" (object of commentary) and "Post-script" (the commentary). That subterfuge of divisory liminality, as we have seen already in the case of the manuscript itself, eradicates once more the dichotomy of an inside and an outside space of the text. Deployed in the guise of "commentary," the "Post-script" undermines the finality or concluding end it was devised to carry out. In that guise, in that ruse, the "Post-script" becomes an inter-diction, a dilatory *dictation between* continuity and discontinuity of the text, of the quest inscribed therein, of textuality's family romance in other words. Ironically, then, the "Post-script" assures unmitigated pursuit, continuity, textual peregrination by endlessly "pro-scribing" an ending of the script. In this sense "Post-script" becomes an extension and integral part of the script. In Vichian/Emersonian terms we could say that the *theoros* — the on-looker — falls into the *hodós*, the path, the way of *method* (into the "midst" of pursuit — *mid-hodós*, literally).

Thus even to the last structural unit, the last mark on the page of "The Immortal" becomes an extended con-versation, a pivotal path, a pursuit that *turns* on itself for its own perpetuation. In that conflation the onlooking commentator, the conversant authorial subject, like his utterance or scribing activity, also becomes sublimated, subsumed into the endless self-perpetuation of the script as well, as we have seen in the case of Homer, Cartaphilus, Rufus, Cordovero, and, of course, Borges. "When the end draws near . . . only words remain," writes Cartaphilus. "It is not strange that time should have confused the words which represented me with those that were symbols . . . ." he continues. Thus he himself passes into the realm of textuality's graphic figuration. In that coalescence, the *nostos,* the homing, of our questing subject — authorial and heroic — becomes the script itself, never "already written," but endlessly in the making, its pilgrimage become its own shrine in unending peregrination.

Chapter 3
Erotomania:
Mexico's Gothic Family Romance

Bodies are visible hieroglyphs. Every body is an erotic metaphor
and the meaning of all these metaphors is always the same: death.
Octavio Paz, "Mask and Transparency"

Octavio Paz's statement in our epigraph refers to the work of a fellow Mexican,
Carlos Fuentes's *The Death of Artemio Cruz*.[1] Another Mexican novel, Juan
Rulfo's *Pedro Páramo*,[2] proves a justifiable companion to the context of Paz's
assertion. I aim here to focus on these two works and on the Paz apothegm
through that dark glass which tradition has willed to us as the Gothic romance — a
haunting pleonasm whose redundancy resides in the eros, or questing desire,
inherent in both terms. I shall pursue specifically the Mexican figuration of this
topos.

As poet and erudite essayist, as a self-consciously Mexican poet (meaning,
a poet of the New World and its attendant secondariness, anxiously awake to
his ambivalent relationship to tradition), Octavio Paz is not naive to the cultural
mediations underlying his premise. Accordingly, his terms must be read in the
light, and shadow, of their etymons. The statement that "bodies are visible
hieroglyphs" clearly implies its differential supplement, that is, the hieratic
quality of bodies as signs of an *invisible reality*. Plato's hierarchies resonate
sharply in that implication. Just as emphatically, one senses in Paz's pithy
assertion the ghost of those early Christian Platonists who saw the sensuous in
an analogous relationship to the divine, a view in which Gothic art would find
its genesis. That momentous occasion, according to the plots of art history, takes
place at the turn of the first millennium as Abbot Suger of Saint Denis communed
alternately with architect and Architect to construct the first Gothic cathedral not
far from Paris.[3]

With its conclusion, our epigraph implies a transition from an analogical to a metaphorical relationship in which body, the visible sign, turns from sign rendering a service to (being a sign for) a transcendental signified to being a metaphor with its own *raison d'être*. The body, the visible sign, that is, no longer seves as substitute or as "stand-in" for an invisible transcendent reality. The body, the sign, is now itself, for itself, as *res ipsa loquitur* signifying its own invisibility, its own "absence," its own death. As metaphor, the body is the "presence" of its own "non-being," or the specter of its own "being." As "erotic metaphor," however, it haunts, unrequited, as force of desire, questing after its own life after life. We shall see how shortly in the specific instance of these two novels.

In its dénouement, Paz's affirmation sublimates the developmental process of the Gothic as artistic figuration, as landscape or textual topography. In its anagogic stage — as analogue — the sacred sign (hieroglyph) stands as image, as representation. The transmutation of that image, its transumption from hieratic symbol to thanatos, is a function of the changes that befall Gothic art, displacing it from celestial firmament to profane and temporal condition of human contingency. That displacement may be summed up as a passage from *imago dei* to *imago regis* to *imago mei*. In its geometric configuration the process resembles a vertiginous motion, a funnel with a movement toward the narrower dimension, in short, a vortex. As erotic metaphor, the tansition could be seen as moving from the eros, or questing, for the divinity, to a desire for the King, to a love of self — a questing love's body — in short, a narcissism. Topo-graphically speaking, the process could be characterized as a *décalage*, a shift or falling into topothesia — the landscape as echo chamber where incunabula's textuality (in the Lezamaesque sense already discussed in our first chapter) becomes its own sound box, the murmuring voice become its own echo.

Viewed in this manner, the Gothic image passes from sacral, mystified Schema to manneristic figure. Geometry as antechamber of horror reveals its fearful figuration in this transitional process. What spirals heavenward in its *embodiment* of the infinite, moves to a diametrical inversion, the *disembodiment* of (as) itself. The sacred edifice, the anagogic body, no longer reaches upward. Gothic by virtue of *representing* the infinite on Earth, that body strove in its sublimity to undo through mystical union, through immediacy, the analogous relationship between itself and the divinity. Now, the gaze has turned, autoscopically, inward and the heavenly spiral has become a vortex, the acentric geometry of an all-devouring maelstrom. The mystic, the poet, the architect in this process realize that infinity is not transcendental but descendental, that it does not reside, or preside, as privilege in an ontological anteriority — the One — but that infinity lies in the infinite desultoriness of vertigo. As a result, the privileged analogy between the sensuous and the divine becomes obliterated. The undoing of that analogous relationship may have meant, at one time, the consummation of mystical immediacy, of the mystic's impatient quest. We now know, however, that such fulfillment implies as well the dissolution of hierarchy. In that demystification of the hieratic image, metaphor, Paz's "erotic metaphor," connotes not correspondence but questing transumption and, consequently, the infinite capacity of "bodies," of signs, as metaphorical shifters to substitute each other endlessly; an irrepressible interchange, an erotomania, whose yield, whose surfeit is open-ended, infinite figuration. The erotic metaphor, like analogy, strives to become its object. Mataphor, however, becomes its own object. It is narcissism become autoscopy, a textual self-knowledge in the "biblical" or bookish sense. Thus, that the diametrical inversion of the sublime, twelveth-century Gothic spiral into vortex should come about as a culmination of the "age of reason," the self-reflexive and hyper-self-conscious eighteenth century, should not surprise us. In that mirror-image rebirth the doctrine of analogy cedes to self-reflexive metaphor. Herein lies the difference between the Cathedral of Abbot Suger and Mary Shelley's Promethean creation.

The fictions of our literary history trace the itinerary of the Gothic as we know it — its passage from the sublime to the plutonic, from diaphaneity to dungeon — dating its literary beginning to Horace Walpole's *Castle of Otranto* (1764). The attendant arbitrariness in such datings is inevitable; so are the debates about whether such a genre as the Gothic could still be said legitimately to persist beyond the eighteenth century. In his *After the Lost Generation*,[4] for example, John W. Aldridge rejects the notion of a new Anglo-American Gothic. Irving Malin, on the other hand, argues for its existence in his *New American Gothic*.[5] Theirs is a family quarrel from which I prefer to abstain. At the risk of compromising neutrality, however, I should point out the *topoi* which Malin delineates as "themes" and "images" whose interaction characterizes what he considers the new Gothic in fiction. These images consist of the *room*, the *voyage*, and the *mirror*. The corresponding themes are *confinement, flight* and *narcissism*. The usefulness of these categories cannot be disputed. Whether Malin's discussion of Truman Capote, Carson McCullers, J. D. Salinger, Flannery O'Connor, John Hawkes, and James Purdy proves the case for the new American Gothic, however, I prefer to leave to the Anglo branch of the American family to ascertain. In a subsequent article entitled "Gothic as Vortex: The Form of Horror in Capote, Faulkner, and Styron,"[6] J. Douglas Perry adds *structure* as category to Malin's theme and image. Those corresponding structures supplied by Perry consist of concentricity, predetermined sequence, and character repetition. In an earlier published version of the present chapter I introduced a series of diachronic coordinates and synchronic correlatives corresponding to theme, image, and structure which I gleaned from Mexican narratives ("historical" and "fictional") in order to adumbrate the Gothic mode in Mexico's literature.[7] Rather than rehearse that earlier endeavor here, I shall redirect my efforts toward tracing the itinerary of the Gothic's erotic metaphor. I shall attempt, that is, to chart the map of a quest for the eye of a maelstrom, where "eye" becomes the synonymy of its homonym — the "Narcissistic" ego, the self-destructive subject, the "I" as its own ghost that haunts as questing passion where maelstrom is the frenzied, conflictive, and deleterious process of Mexico's violent history, an incubistic family romance bent on self-destruction.

Fruit of a utopian quest turned dystopian Conquest, the Mexican sublimates, internalizes, the violent eros of his own conception in history, inverting its energy into erotomania which seeks not after self-completion but after the realization of self in self-denial — a self-affirmation through self-negation, or the disfiguration, the vengeful desecration of history. The itinerary of this family romance, then is a flight toward self-disembodiment. Quest, whether Telemachiad (as in Rulfo's *Pedro Páramo*) or Narcissistic (as in Fuentes's *Artemio Cruz*) undergoes an inversion, as with the Gothic spiral, whose object and ultimacy figure not as plenitude of self-possession but as the violent effacement which figures in self-dispossession. In the obstinacy of that reversal, of that compensatory venegeance in re-turn, nothing escapes the rancorous violence of contrariety. As we shall see presently in these two works, landscape reverts to shimmering desolation, to arid wasteland; body turns into phantom; language becomes muted into murmur or incubistic soliloquy; sign yields to ominous silence; power becomes the power of impotence or of its victim; ritual gives way to chaos; memory turns into anachronous prophecy, paternity to patricide, and history becomes woven as plot of adversity, as sought-after fatal *contretemps*, or *destiempo*.

Critics and observers of Mexican culture have repeatedly noted that the Mexican is engaged in an obsessive dialectic with death.[8] As Octavio Paz observes, "death and birth are solitary experiences."[9] For the Mexican those polar points of the life cycle spectrally converge into that mirror of the self, the battle ground of a ceaseless dialogue between body and death articulated in a rhetoric of silence and haunted space. The muted voice deepens the tomb of taciturnity, transforming it into a metaphor of/for death and its solitude. Birth, the other pole of the solitary experience, is shrouded in a penumbra of shame and imputative secrecy; a furtive attempt to veil, to screen out a conception through violent conquest. The Mexican, as Paz reminds us, sees himself as the illegitimate progeny of that violent union between the conquering European and the violated indigenous Mexican mother. The hermetic taciturnity, the self-effacement into mystery, becomes the measure of desire for the concealment and ultimate eradication of that originary history, of that primal scene of falling into history. The rhetoric of mutism, then, represents the Mexican's ambiguous attempt to muffle, to skew, and screen out his own inescapable history — inescapable because it is embodied by him in his very existence, in his corporeality; and ambiguous because, in the very attempt at self-denial, that history becomes re-affirmed. Death, as mechanism for existential disembodiment and for effacement of the body's historicity, means eternal freedom from history (from the self as history). That self-divestment into absence stands for ultimate timelessness — an anachronous *uchronia* — and a state without want, a state in which all necessity, including the primal flaw of paternity as history and history as violent paternity, becomes eradicated. But, while death may be the ultimate meaning of Paz's "erotic metaphor," death is not an end. Rather, it is part of the process, a station on the pilgrim's way, within the anxious quest of this Mexican Gothic. As geometric configuration that spirals inversely, concentrically downward, trapping the self in its vortex of solitude and silence, death has no finality. In its uchronic timelessness it becomes infinite. History which traps and confines the Mexican in time, simply metamorphoses into ahistoricity, or, more accurately, into the meta-historicity of the timeless. History's masks and plots, as Juan Rulfo's work clearly shows, become transposed with it into death's infinite mirror to haunt there as muted utterance, as spectral bodies, as ghosts of presence. Displaced by its own phantomness toward an ahistoricity, a uchronic incubism, where the ghosts of time (timelessness) and of language (murmur and mutism) become, respectively, a perpetual spectral present and a re-sounding echo, history itself along with its revenants becomes transumpted into myth, if we can legitimately consider the suppression of the *mythos* (the word, the ancient Greek's performative speech) into mutedness as "myth." Clearly, this has to be a problematic myth of inversion, the paradoxical mirror image of what we normally understand as myth. In this world of spectral contrarieties, we should not be surprised to encounter yet another reversal. Accordingly, the myth of quest, too, as plotted by the works of Rulfo and Fuentes, becomes inverted. The Telemachiad in *Pedro Páramo* figures as search for the father *not* for the purpose of delivering the ancestral home, the *patria*, from the depravities and depredations of usurpers in the father's absence, but for demanding accountability of the father for his violent spoliation of a maternal paradise — the edenic *mneme*, or living memory, of the cast-out mother willed to the abandoned son as future ("Green fields. You can see the horizon rise and fall when the wind moves in the wheat, or when the rain ruffles it in the afternoon. The color of the earth, the smell of alfalfa and bread. A village that smells of new honey. . . . And everything had the flavor of orange-blossoms in the warmth of the season. . . . But make him pay . . ." [pp. 16-27]). The Narcissus in Fuentes's *The Death of Artemio Cruz* also figures as abiding inversion. While Narcissus was not aware that the image he contemplated in the fatal pool was his own, the supremely Mexican Artemio Cruz, assailed by his own hyper-self-consciousness, is acutely cognizant that the ghastly present which reflects his own image at the threshold of phantomness is the culmination of his entire history in this intermediacy, this liminality, of the self and of the moment. "Man . . . is not *in* history: he is history," notes Octavio Paz,[10] and this embattled figure of man/history, now on the verge of death, seeks total transparency. He yearns for the divestment of the spectral mask which is the self questing after disembodiment. If man *is* history and if his transumption into specter effaces history's baneful historicity into a ghost as well, then on that liminal ground, that desolate threshold between "mask" and "transparency," nothing is left but the permeable fabric of the tale — the history's ghost story. In that haunted space, even the impatient dialectic of an "erotic metaphor" itself figures as transparent mask of a dialectic between body and specter, between historical presence and timeless absence. These observations will become clearer as we turn to the specific phantasmal traces of that liminality.

Pedro Páramo is narrated and overheard from the grave; Artemio Cruz from a deathbed. In both novels diachrony collapses, not into synchrony, but into a timeless adjacency. In Pedro Páramo that contiguity of emptied out or voided historical time dimensions occurs when we realize that all the events of the novel, which span many years, reduce to and emanate from the subterranean uchronia of a "posthumous" conversation. Likewise, the narrative of Artemio Cruz consists in simultaneous rather than sequential revelations as the hero "re-lives" in simultaneity the events of his biography during the final hours of his life. In both instances, historical and biographical incident becomes the cipher of a threshold, an enigma which haunts the hero (and the reader) begging to be de-ciphered. In that timeless instant death and birth — the embodiment and disembodiment of history — converge. The apotheosis of solitude (the mask) and the rhetoric of silence (tranparency) become sublimated into ominous emptiness where narrative "ceases" and communication (mythos) becomes mute. There the Gothic irony surfaces, grinning in its death-skull: Perception of one's image (self-recognition) proves tantamount to self-negation, self-gain equals self-loss in perverse apotheosis of the Romantic and of our post-Romantic quests. This structural culmination in silence and immobility serves to accentuate the indefatigable celerity of the maelstrom, whose furious motion gives the impression of perfect immobility and silence, but whose whirlpool sucks the characters into its inescapable void.

J. Douglas Perry observes that while the maelstrom of Edgar Allen Poe regurgitates its victim, there can be no re-surfacing from the modern Gothic vortex. Georges Poulet notes that "A sort of temporal circle surrounds Poe's characters. A whirlpool envelops them, which, like that of the maelstrom, disposes its funnel by degrees from the past in which one has been caught to the future in which one will be dead."[11] That "closed time," Perry points out, can be applied to modern Gothic with slight modifications. The modifications necessary for its application to Mexico's Gothic family romance are even less than slight. One need only substitute history for maelstrom and Poulet's statement speaks the predicament of the Mexican with canny accuracy. The "past" is sealed and, in the process, undone. Self-history feverishly seeks to seal — to mask and cancel — the "future" as well. The obsessive and unremitting itinerary of that pursuit traces the graphic map of Mexico's Gothic landscape and its violent family romance.

Like Robin Molineux of Hawthorne's "My Kinsman, Major Molineux" before him, and Joel Harrison Knox of Truman Capote's *Other Voices, Other Rooms* after him, Juan Preciado, the hero of Rulfo's *Pedro Páramo* is a young man in pursuit of self-knowledge. His search, as already noted, is a skewed, inverted Telemachiad quest, which, like that of his counterparts to the north, converges on the family history. He seeks out his father whom he has never known except for the man in the ambivalent (now paradisiacal, now acrid) recollections of his now dead mother. Juan Preciado's quest leads him, rather precipitously, into a forebodingly enchanted geography, the infernal town of Comala where "The heat shimmered on the plain like a transparent lake" (p. 2). That abysmal geography, soon to become geognosis, a mirror for autoscopy, lies at the end of a long and tortuous descent: "We left the warm air up there and walked down into pure heat without a breath of air in it. Everything looked as if it were waiting for something" (p. 3). The plunge downward is also a voyage back which undoes time, back to a "primal scene" of transgression, into history's baneful conception where Juan Preciado will encounter his identity wrapped in the haunting and violent past of his parents. Time and geography close in when Juan discovers that his arrival has been anticipated and the inhabitants of Comala who receive him are ghastly phantoms. The identity quest and the descent into the hell hole are closely linked from the very beginning; the Gothic vortex which will deepen even further confronts the young man from the outset. Those who lead and receive him in Comala are asphixiatingly close to him by dint of violent filiation and will emerge as beacons, as haunted mirrors, to his search for identity. That recognition scene, thus, becomes tantamount to spectral apprehension, his self-discernment a haunted image in this ghastly topography's shimmering phantomness. Abundio, that aberration of Eumeus, Mentor, and Virgil, who leads him down, is his half-brother. He eventually proves to be more than that. He has already accomplished Juan's goal well beyond the latter's expectations of assuaging the bitterness of his abandoned mother. Abundio, as we discover in the final pages, is a parricide; as the murderer of Pedro Páramo, their father, he has avenged every woman wronged by the violence of the patriarch. Juan's mother had extracted a promise from him on her deathbed that he would avenge the treatment accorded them by his father. Thus, Abundio haunts as Juan's alter-ego. This enigmatic incubus opens the circle of the novel. He will also close it with the bloody dagger still in his hand.

The woman who receives Juan into Comala (as Juan discovers, actually the ghost of a woman) is Eduviges who, by all rights, according to her account, should have been his mother. (She substituted for his actual mother in his father's bed on their wedding night since the moon did not favor the bride that night. Pedro Páramo was too drunk to even attempt to notice the substitution.) Juan, then, is taken back to his pre-conception, to the violent conquest and despoliation of his mother by the machismo and raw power of his father; back to his conception and its supplement, his should-have-been conception; back in time and down in geography to what could be that enchanted landscape which James Joyce, in another context — the "Proteus" episode of *Ulysses* — called the "all wombing tomb."

Juan Preciado's incursion into history and into the ominous time and geography of Comala is reflected, refracted, and repeated in the mirror of filial characters and in the structure and *topoi* of the narrative with such rapidity that the concentric effect seals, irrevocably, all possibility of flight from the Gothic maelstrom. His identity crisis is reflected in the obsessed soliloquy of his father which becomes recurring leitmotif, as do the lyrical recollections of his mother, the restless soul of Eduviges, which can find no solace in having arrived at this underworld through suicide, and in the disquieting "innocence" of Dorotea. A series of spectral, of mutually reflecting dualities, furthermore, scatter through the novel: Juan Preciado's descent into Comala is mirrored in the lowering of Susana San Juan by *her* father into the pit of a mine shaft to search for gold, here, as in Mexico's ambiguous history, the earth's other prized subterranean excrescency. She finds only a death skull and its disembodied skeleton. Juan's quest has its echo in the ideal dream and delirious pursuit of Dorotea, with whom he now shares a tomb. Pedro Páramo's lyrical recollections of his adolescence and his unrequited love for Susana San Juan are echoed in the lyricism of Dolorita's memories and Susana's eroticism. Dorotea, in her role as procuress of women and young girls for Miguel Páramo, has her counterpart in Filotea, who fulfills the same function for his father. The novel itself is in fact divisible into two spectrally complementary parts, as a few critics have already pointed out.[12]

The pullulation of solitudes and masked specters, each trapped in the unfulfilled yearnings of its own and, literally, in the tomb of its individual "inexistence" is augmented at each turn of narrative incident. All these creatures partake of the same congenital crisis and grotesque disfiguration. They are all bound in an organic chain, linked in a mutually destructive need for each other. And each in some way elucidates the story of Juan Preciado's past and the character of his father; each contributes to the reformation of his ghostly identity and to the mnemonic edification of Pedro Páramo, a contrite memory whose aridity reverberates in his very name, literally, "barren plain" — a not so subtle coincidence of a landscape and a paranomasia of emptiness. Every one of these ghosts "embodies" to some measure the essence of Pedro Páramo. To that extent, Rulfo's protagonist is not merely an individual figure but a collective, family hero. He finds himself reflected, as in refractory fragments, in the totality of all those under his domination. While he exercises the violence and prerogatives of power over them, he also mirrors their unfulfilled yearnings which become transformed from hope to grotesque spiritual mutations. Susana San Juan, the only woman Pedro Páramo had desired in vain, emerges as his true antagonist. Insofar as she too is an embodiment of the vulnerable, the open and the collective womanhood of Mexico, she becomes his true counterpart. While she remains unreachable, she does not, she cannot, escape the need to be desired by Páramo. Her eroticism and earthiness is as narcissistic as the power and machismo of Pedro Páramo. Disembodied of her love's body, she now can only "embody" the revenant of bodily desire in her voice of phantom succubus, her language of passion ever-flowing with incontinent yearning.

Irving Malin views the family unit as the microcosm of new American Gothic.[13] The aberrations created by the monstrous there, he claims, are more readily evident and shocking. In *Pedro Páramo* these disfigured relationships are no less powerful. Susana San Juan's relationship to her father is menacingly unclear, his paternity ambiguous. She always addresses him as Bartolomé, his first name. The incestuous brother and sister, condemned to wallow in the mire of their sin, turn slowly into mud and slime, becoming bodily undone, so to speak, into the innocence of clay. The murder of Pedro Páramo by his son, Abundio, marks the culmination of family disintegration in a world where filiation has violence as its rubric and blood as its baptismal unction.

Violence is the only flight from confinement. As Paz reminds us, the Mexican tears off his mask and hermetic shell like a volcanic eruption. The revolt is a disclosure, a baring of self, a frenetic *fiesta*, a blood bath. Pedro Páramo and Abundio simply play out that ritual. Páramo's father fell a victim to violence; so did his favorite son, Miguel. In the fury of that revolt and eruption, the repressed energies break loose. The powers of darkness explode and the Mexican finds a momentary transcendence in the frenzy of *ekstasis*, of chaos and its destructive energies. And here, too, the novel's narrative structure follows suite: it becomes enthymemic — only one of the premises of normal behavior's syllogism becomes operative here. Repression and the reality principle are muted, suppressed into inexistence. Accordingly, in the final part of the novel the aberrant world of this desolate landscape is seen through the crazed eyes and distorted mind of Abundio. With alcohol gnawing at his brain and years of repressed rancor flashing in his eyes and on his dagger, he stumbles into the ignominious act. His perspective becomes ours in those moments of hallucination in which all order breaks down, time becomes confused and undone, and the individual is transformed into blind, irrepressible force that signifies death.

The structure of Juan Rulfo's novel bespeaks Octavio Paz's assertion that the meaning of the body as erotic metaphor is ultimately death. The bi-partite construction of the novel elucidates the dialogue between the two terms of the metaphor. In the first part of the work the reader "accompanies" Juan Preciado in a descent which leads to the grave. The transit within that journey is, in fact, illusory and a function of the narrative, for the reader, as already noted, becomes aware that the voices and narrated events have originated there, in the grave, all along. Once the geometric spiral downward has reached the irrevocable abyss and all exits have been sealed ("Yes, Dorotea, the murmurs killed me"), the narrative voice and point of view change. The hermetic echoes and murmurs of conscience become subsumed by an omniscient, third-person narrative voice. Now that the whirlpool has reached its culmination by inexorably enveloping the hero in its maelstrom, there, in the timelessness of death, in death's spectral recognition scene, the meaning of the entire process can be revealed; the disparate stations along the pilgrim's journey, the concentric and centripetal circles of history which have disposed the hero from past to future into a peroration of timeless ahistoricity and death can now be uncovered as post-historical layers in desedimentation.

The second part of the novel draws a ''new'' narrative circle, setting into motion an ''other'' concentric circle in which the reader, along with Juan Preciado, witnesses the dis-play of spiraling events that culminate in the novel's narrative present. By the end of the first part, the work achieves a reverie of silence, ''an incommunicable state of consciousness,'' to use Frye's term.[14] For what we have *listened to* (not ''read,'' for this part of the novel is muted utterance, murmured and not ''written'') is a series of echoes, of haunting voices, uttered not for communicating but for carrying on their incubistic soliloquy. The two parts of the novel join as concentric and as mutually reflecting circles. The questing hero finds the desolate fragments of the self-knowledge he seeks in the first part within the history which is revealed by the ahistorical, untimely (or timeless) disclosures of the second part. Like the two terms of a metaphor, the two parts of Juan Rulfo's work mutually, supplementally reflect to produce the yield, the spectral surfeit of a Mexican rebus, skewed as inverted Gothic paradigm.

Equally haunting in this respect is Carlos Fuentes's *The Death of Artemio Cruz*. ''I must have white water to navigate,'' its hero exclaims, ''distant targets, enemies to repel. Ah, yes. In the eye of the whirlwind. No: calm doesn't interest me'' (p. 80). Artemio Cruz himself marks the frenzied epicenter of this whirlwind whose eye is none other than the hero's own shattered consciousness and its febrile gyrations. The frenetic celerity of self-cognizance and fragmentary reflections maintain the concentric motion, its revolutionary gyrations preventing, deflecting, the imminent dive into the ultimate abyss, the plunge into the bottom of the whirlpool which is forever impending. Fuentes's novel begins with a shattered world whose hero lies in a catatonic state. From this prismatically refracted recognition scene, Cruz looks on the desultory fragments of himself and of his life as they spin through the mind-eye of memory and futile re-collection. As the circle closes in with the convergence of birth and death, the fragments of time and becoming flow into each other to reconstitute a biography whose specter nosedives into the maelstrom, never to resurface: ''The three, we . . . will die. You . . . die, have died . . . I will die'' (p. 306).

One of the epigraphs Fuentes appropriates for his novel is from the *Essays* of Montaigne: ''The premeditation of death is the premeditation of freedom.''

Montaigne's statement anticipates the quest metaphor of eros in the work. The world of the novel and its hero are the "hieroglyph," the metaphor itself. Artemio Cruz premeditates not death, but being, albeit not a consummate being but a liminal one on the threshold between existence and inexistence: his corporeal being and its historicity, his bodily and spiritual self whose ultimate and unknowable meaning as erotic metaphor signifies death. Cruz's "premeditation" is a process of the vortex and its "whirlwind," as he calls it. His bodily sensations cede to desultory mental images and reflections: mirror images as well as history's spectral, reversed, "pre-meditations" as mnemonic recollection. What Artemio Cruz experiences in the hours before his death is a chapter of Mexican family history and the biography of one man become one with it. In a significant sense, the hero's liminal life becomes a poetic revenant of a ghost biography, of that family history made spectrally "incarnate," the transparent opacity of a ghost metaphor seen through its own glass darkly. In this process Artemio Cruz becomes more than an individual facing death; he emerges as figura of a synecdochal typology within Mexico's family romance. The images, themes, structures employed by Fuentes to achieve this darkly transparent metaphor constitute those elements which we have already delineated as characteristic ciphers of a Mexican Gothic. I shall refer to the most salient of those ciphers in what follows.

Disintegration of the individual and his world is a requisite of the Gothic romance just as the unhinged destructurations of language into fragments of mutism, catachreses, and stressed figures of utterance emerge as textual signatures in the literary fabric of Gothic metaphor. The Gothic quest is a wayward path, its pilgrimage composed of the aberrations self-identity and human filiations are made to endure. The anomalies and marvelous distortions among different spheres of experience, the grotesque and the heteroclite stem from the attempts at re-integrating a fragmented cosmos and dismembered identity — an identity of self and (or *as*) an identity of language. Such disordered heterogeneity and the futile attempt at reconstitution mark the itinerary of the hero in Fuentes's novel and, within the novelistic plot, mark, as well, the rhetorical fragmentation, the agrammaticality, the anacoluthons of the text itself. The confusion of identity, in other words, has its counterpart in the grammatical confusion and diffusion of subject. In his catatonic state Artemio Cruz physically perceives the shattered and refracted image of himself and of his world: "I am this, this I am: old man with his face reflected in pieces by different-sized squares of glass. . . . I try to remember my reflection: face cut up by unsymmetrical facets of glass, the eye very near the ear and very far from its mate: a face distributed among shimmering mirrors" (pp. 4-5).

Time and identity, so problematically and inextricably interrelated, lose all sense of unity as well. The hero experiences his life not in any "logical" order but in a frenzied isochronism in which all time and incidents co-exist as chaotic heterocosm of language and body: "No: someone else, someone different, someone in a mirror in front of his sick bed, the bed of someone else. Artemio Cruz: his twin. Artemio Cruz is sick, he does not live. No, he lives! Artemio Cruz did live once. He lived several years. Years, not yearns. No he lived several days. Days, not daze. His twin, Artemio Cruz, his double. Yesterday Artemio Cruz, he lived only a few days before dying, yesterday Artemio Cruz, who is I am I, and yesterday'' (p. 7). In his scrambled world, Cruz plunges into the confines of an unhinged time and solitude, a phantasmagoria, a space and temporality emptied out, made ghostly but raging. What he articulates, what he *re-members*, from there in incubistic monologue is our only access, our only means of delineating the configurations of a man, of a history and the features of its masks. As the protagonist affirms in his raving soliloquy: "You will become the images of your imagination, like an empty wrinkled wineskin . . . insisting on remembering what will happen yesterday'' (pp. 9-10). Within this confused time, historical events become inevitable and, therefore, meaningless certainties, just as the acts and fate of the hero become predictable. In their predictability and recurrence, all deeds acquire the character of a disfiguring ritual. The life of Artemio Cruz enacts one complete cycle within that predetermined sequence of recurring events whose accretion configures the map of this Mexican family history. That history becomes dis-covered in the novel as isomorphism of timeless repetition, exposed, desedimented through the metaphor of a frenzied language. In his clairvoyant hallucinations, the protagonist perceives Mexico as the baneful superimposition of embattled cultural layers: Amerindian, Christian-European, and African. This recognition, too, is self-recognition. For Cruz, son of a mulatto peasant woman and a white *hacendado* is himself a genetic syncretism; a spectral embodiment of that cyclical process of violent conquest and despoliation, fated to re-enact the disfiguring cycle of violating and ravishing others.

Just as the maelstrom of Mexico's history produces an enclosed phantom world, so the individual experience results in a self-encased, protective, or defensive solitude that hides behind a mask of invulnerability and hermeticism, a facade hiding phantasmal necessity and the insecurity of insufficiency.[15] When all enemies have been repelled, and the fortress of the self has been "secured," then the true battle begins and there the white water and its accompanying whirlwind crest. On this score, Carlos Fuentes evinces a significant affinity for one of the great masters of inner darkness and demoniacal cruelty, Henry James, who, Martha Banta observes, "knew the traditions of the Gothic novel well."[16] To those traditions James added "the terrors of a new Gothicism which — like the new psychology of the period — revealed the self as victim of its own self-villainy."[17] Artemio Cruz shrilly articulates his author's furious Gothicism as he perceives in a fit of clairvoyance his final self-begotten predicament: "taking the risk successfully until no enemies are left: and then you will become your own enemy, that the proud battle may go on: all others conquered, there will remain only yourself to be conquered: you will step from the looking-glass of still water and lead your last attack against the enemy nymph, the nymph of passion and sobs who is daughter of gods and mother of goatlike seducer, mother of the only god that has died in man's time: from the looking-glass she will step too, mother of Great God Pan, nymph of pride and again your double, your double, your last enemy in the depopulated land of the victims of your pride" (p. 86). Thus, after everything and everyone have been razed, the hero turns on the only presence — his own phantom specter, his mirror image — which inhabits the ghostscape of his own history.

The clammy, haunted underworld elaborated by Juan Rulfo in *Pedro Páramo* has given way in Fuentes's novel to a more elaborate horror: the dark, necromantic and menacing chambers of the psyche. While the outward trappings of Gothic romance yield to a psychological Gothicism, bringing Fuentes into closer affinity with what Irving Malin and J. Douglas Perry delineate as new American Gothic, the basic tenets of this other American, the Mexican, Gothic persist. Unlike the mythological prototype, the specter of Mexican Narcissus retains his acutely menacing self-consciousness. Thus, Artemio Cruz as perilous, as self-destructive *persona* is made cognizant of the potential connotations of his own name, as the passage just cited clearly indicates. His identification with the *hubris* of his mythological namesake, Artemis, as well as the link to the Christ King (Cruz — Cross — Christ: "the only god that has died in man's time") are unmistakable. The consciousness of his own villainy is in direct relation to his spirituality. In this sense Cruz seems to understand his own Gothic nature as a grotesque aberration of the sublime. Beyond identifying Cruz as an epitome of the neo-Gothic, his self-awareness, his self-menacing perspicacity, would indicate that Fuentes, knowingly or not, depicts his hero with the adumbration implicit in an insight of Henry James's father: "Our experience of the spiritual world," writes the elder James, "dates in truth only from our first unaffected shiver at guilt."[18] Such an experience in the life of Artemio Cruz will become admissible in recollection alone; in those moments before his death in which the mask too is shattered, and memory, on the threshold of oblivion, lays bare the solitude, power, and impregnability of the hero. Only when death becomes a mirror for life, like all mirrors, an unforgiving and mockingly equivocal eye, will the hero and the reader glimpse the disfigurations of what has lain hidden behind the impenetrable mask that good Mexican form demands of the virile: The guilt choked by Artemio Cruz when, as a thirteen-year-old boy, he shattered his uncle's face with the blast of a double-barreled shotgun trying to protect Lunero — another mirrored face of Artemis-Artemio; the hero's other specter — and the paradise of childhood ("Your innocence will die, not at the hands of your guilt, but before your enormous surprise" [p. 295]); the guilt muted upon abandoning a comrade to die on the battlefield, at negotiating his own life with that of a cell-mate whose inheritance and sister he would appropriate; the guilt suppressed at seeing the only woman he ever loved dangling from a hangman's noose will suddenly overtake Cruz mercilessly. In each instance he feels ire and rancor that nourish his frenzied sallies in the face of incalculable odds, that same fury which he first experienced behind the weight and power of the exploding shotgun ("Fury because now he knew that life had enemies and was no longer the smooth flow of the river" [p. 295]). Now, after all battles have been won and enemies have been silenced, when he gazes into the rancor of the ambivalent mirror, the resolve of his fury becomes its own object and, as it devours itself, Artemio Cruz, its battlefield, looks on as contrite conscience: "You will bequeath the futile dead names, the names of so many who fell that your name might stand: men despoiled of their names that you might possess yours: names forgotten that yours might be remembered" (p. 269); "those dead names: Regina . . . Tobias . . . Páez . . . Gonzalo . . . Zagal . . . Laura, Laura . . . Lorenzo . . . I think about it and ask myself . . . without knowing . . . so that they may not forget me" (p. 263).

In the Mexican syllogism the two premises for machismo are the stoic suffocation of sentiment and the mask of unvulnerability. The second premise becomes inoperative here, giving way to an enthymeme in which the poignant self-identity of the hero breaks through as the hermetic mask is rent. Like the characters of Rulfo's *Pedro Páramo*, in the ensuing, spectral transparency Artemio Cruz finds the menacing reflection of his life in his death. The obsessive preoccupation of Fuentes's hero with the hitherto masked, solitary self and its deformed interiority in the face of death, on the liminal threshold of existence, may be understood in part through Octavio Paz's insight that "Our deaths illuminate our lives. If our deaths lack meaning, our lives also lacked it."[19] The second epigraph from Calderón's *The Great Theater of the World* which Fuentes adapts for his novel reveals as much:

> Men who come to the surface
> Cradled by ice
> Who return through graves
> See what you are . . .

Accordingly, Artemio Cruz, the bastion of power, must extend the domination he exercised over others in life into his death. Power must also find its reflection in death if it is to have "meaning." Thus, as he endures the physical pain of his collapse, he does so mutely, without the slightest response to those around him. In fact, he taunts their altruistic as well as selfish preoccupations. He does not reveal whether he has left a *will*. When he finally implies something to that effect, he diabolically sends his wife and daughter scurrying to search in the wrong place. His only "diversion" from pain and recollection in those final hours consists of listening to the taped recordings, another form of self-mastery in remembrance, of his business dealings and political machinations — a dissonant record of discord and barren conquest. Nothing of what is, has been, will be Artemio Cruz must be left out as the many fractions of his life complete the aberrant hieroglyph. Above all, the desultory and multiple faces of Narcissus and those in whom he found the spectral echo of his character must come into their disconcerted sharp focus. The result is a legion of repeated characters reflected in a gallery of multi-faceted mirrors — the hero's memory — all of which reflect and circumscribe the protagonist. The most striking of these is his son Lorenzo who dies in a Spanish Civil War battle, a death Artemio Cruz thinks he himself should have died many years earlier. Lorenzo's memory, along with that of Regina, evokes the most poignant leitmotifs in Cruz's recollection. Each of these images becomes an inheritance of life passed on to Cruz in the death of others. They range from his father, Atanasio, who was hacked to death with machetes on the day of Artemio's birth, to the comrade in whom he saw himself but whom he abandoned to die on the field ("He tried to push away that pain-twisted face with open mouth and closed eyes, tangled mustache and beard no longer than his own. With green eyes, the man could be his twin" [p. 69]). Teresa, Artemio's daughter, emerges as his own inheritor, his unmistakable successor. Although a woman in a family romance with a premium on virility and the masculine ethos, Teresa comes forth as the aggressor rather than the victim, the "closed" rather than the "open"; despoiler rather than the despoiled. She manifests the intrepidity of her paternal grandmother who spent the last thirteen years of her life shut up in the delusion of her private world of past glory and power rather than admit defeat; the grandmother whose last utterance as she collapsed under the weight of her hundred years and the slash of a whip was a rancorous: "Chingao!"[20]

As the cycle closes, Artemio Cruz sees himself as "animal who foreseeing your death, sings your death, talks it, dances it, paints it, remembering before you die your death" (p. 270). He thus arrives at that primal scene of recognition, back and forward, at once, where the two extremes of solitude — birth and death — converge: "You will be the boy-child who goes to the land and finds the land, who leaves his beginnings and encounters his destiny, *today when death is the same as beginning and ending and between the two, in spite of everything, is strung the thread of freedom*" (pp. 271-72; emphases added). In that interstitial space between beginning and ending as self-same, the "thread of freedom," "in spite of everything," is the Ariadne's thread, not out of the labyrinth, but into repeated peregrinations through its timeless byways, the repetitions which undo time and history but which cannot eradicate the congenital necessity to retrace the steps, to thread through the haunted course of a filial blood line. As the novel's narrative thread takes us to that timeless moment and geography where beginning and end are equally inevitable, we are given to understand what Artemio Cruz's centenarian grandmother knew all along by "the reason of blood." The boy-child Artemio Cruz, whom she saw only through her window for thirteen years, would carry on the specters' dance of Mexico's family history: "his flesh, my flesh, moving about, another life like Ireneo and Atanasio, another Mancheca, another man like the men they were. . . . I have known that he is mine when you have not even seen him. Blood understands . . without eyes, touch" (p. 289).

Like the fated men of the darkest Gothicism, Artemio Cruz was marked from birth, destined for the irrevocable whirlwind and its devouring white water. In the final hour of dissolution where all gets undone only to be spectrally repeated, blood, like the liquid mercury of the mirror, becomes hermetic menstruum, transmuting all peremptory potency and dominion into haunted quest, the revenant's hapless yearning.

Chapter 4
Baroque, or the Untenable Ground: Quest as Self-Reminiscence

> — baroque, language takes pleasure in the supplement, in the
> excess, and in the partial loss of its object. Or rather, in the search,
> by definition frustrated, for the *partial object.*
>
> Severo Sarduy, "Baroque and Neo-Baroque"

Partial by definition, flawed of necessity, tautological as insufficiency, the baroque is the surfeit of e*cc*entric fragmentation. Pearl with a bias, *ostracized* semi-preciosity, it seeks after the other half, striving for the bivalve, the vacated space, the home of pre-excrescency. In compensatory self-indulgence the baroque proliferates its cloying mannerism, substituting redolent paraphrase as hedge against primogenial emptiness become abysmal void: *horror vacui.*

Art of compensation for an originary and perpetual exclusion, the baroque is the language of prodigal and prodigious substitution. Nostalgic for a *nostos*, yearning for a homing, the trajectory of its quest is rendered as its own spectral impossibility, moving in mirror reflection and inverted telos inexorably away from, rather than toward, its longed-for destination. Partial object seeking after its supplementary alterities, it manages not plenitude or integral refusion into its illusionist, prelapsarian ethos, but oversees the diffusion of its partialities into supernumerary displacements of ever-questing pathos. Counter-self-directed aim, darting toward futurity through mnemonic illusion, the baroque discourse sublimates its difficulty of pilgrimage into eccentric figure — asyndeton, enjambment, catachresis, chiasmus, oxymoron — an equivocal language of conceits in which mutually displacing terms insist on being remembered, persist as reminiscence, simply, as paratactic contiguities, and as condensed accretions: "marvelous reality," *The Kingdom of this World* — a language of heterogeneity where the disparities "marvelous" and "real" clash as a dysfunction and condense in interchange, in affiliate third term; a language of alterity where *The Kingdom of this World* becomes mnemonic yield, reminiscent as surfeit of "another" world which resonates in the demonstrative but which remains equally elided with transcendental presence, reverberating only as suggestion.

The itinerary of these shifts and their textured multivalences find their adumbration in Lezama Lima's condensed metaphor, "the American era of the image": "the American era of the image has its most evident expression in the new meanings of the chronicler of the Indies, the baroque dominion, the rebellion of romanticism. . . . The chronicler of the Indies brings his already-formed images, and the new landscape bursts them open. The baroque seigneur begins his contortions and repolishings anchored in fable tradition and Greco-Latin myths, but very soon the incorporation of the phytomorphic and zoomorphic elements which waylay him . . . create new collections of fables which grant a new center of gravity."[1] Those heterogeneities constitute the ever-shifting foundations of a discursive praxis, a heterotopia of poetic language, a sanctioning discourse whose paramount characteristics are ex-centricity, diffusion, random accretion, and prodigal agglomeration: a sea of language turned loose by the undoing of similitude, the shattering of a one-to-one correspondence in representation, the depletion in the "naive" adequacy of language to orderly resemblance between world and symbol, history and nature, the visible and the invisible, space and image, sign and meaning, signature and signator. While for some (Eliot, Foucault) this rupture signals in Europe a historical discontinuity, or paradigm shift, a discursive transformation, in America it is "a natural principle," that is, a factitious originary discourse inaugurated as fiction in October of 1492 when Columbus hears the "May nightingales of Castille" in tropical *terra incognita.* Initiated as figura of exclusionary discourse, as *mundus alterius*, as "New World," as cosmic supplement, as antipode, America still persists as primogenial alterity, as eccentric satellite. America as baroque discourse, one might say, is tautologically synonymous to itself. By virtue of that tropical tautology, of being its own synonymic reflection, the American image is always "other" to itself, it is its own differential, its own supplement. Its quest for self-presence through prodigiously compounded figures of language manages to configure nothing more than self-absence in self-deferral. With the accrued figurations tracing ever more intricate byways of peregrination, those language figurations themselves become supplementary filigree whose intercession as excess introduces mediating *impedimenta* that waylay and perpetually interdict the *nostos*, the arrival of the image into its mnemonic self-presence, and proscribe its becoming self-same in self-similitude. With specific reference to Alejo Carpentier, on whom the focus of the present chapter will narrow shortly, Roberto González Echevarría makes the following pertinent observation, itself problematic as we shall see: "The plot of Carpentier's stories always moves *from exile and fragmentation toward return and restoration*, and the overall movement of each text is away from literature into immediacy, whether by a claim to be integrated within a larger context, Latin American reality or history or by an invocation of the empirical author. *But . . . the voyage always winds up in literature and remains as the reason for yet another journey.*"[2]

From T. S. Eliot to Michel Foucault, observers of this periphrastic predicament in the history of European culture speak of a peripeteia in Europe's cultural horizon. Foucault, in a work which, he admits, derives its incitation from the slippery ground of an American discourse — Borges's — views that shift, or *décalage*, as the "discovery of language" that precipitates the passage from the sixteenth to the seventeenth centuries — from Renaissance to the Baroque.[3] T. S. Eliot, working out of the same chronological framework as Foucault, some forty-five years earlier had made a parallel observation in the form of a plaintive monody he called "The Metaphysical Poets" (1921).[4] The Anglo-American's term for that shift is "the dissociation of sensibility." In the case of America, as I already noted, the peripeteia is simultaneous with the eruption of the New World into European historical consciousness. Columbus himself is jolted into the insight that what figures and what is figured are disparate and contiguous rather than congruent similitudes. The discovery of the New World is unexpected (a happenstance), although sought after. As Lezama Lima reminds us, the *nature* (meaning both nascence and ecology) of that world is much less expected and far beyond the purview of the European's modes of knowing. The system of discourse and ways of representation at the disposal of the discoverers and their chroniclers prove less than adequate. The New World, then, at the gates of Europe's Renaissance precipitates, necessarily, an epistemological and discursive crisis which exacerbates consciousness and modes of articulation. The first Latinate Europeans who forcibly become Latin-Americans by dint of having endured the chastisement and baptism of the New World experience, are compelled to examine the very bases of language and its structures of representation. Their narrative discourse, as a result, becomes unavoidably self-conscious. In that self-consciousness they discover linguistic inadequacy, a shortfall of discursive praxis. We are constantly made mindful of these inadequacies by Columbus, Ramón Pané, Hernando Cortés, and many who followed them as chroniclers. Their hesitations, circumlocutions, apologies, become the inaugural epistemes of an American discourse troubled with its own dilemmas, a language whose bold and profuse figurations both assert and belie its self-confidence. Just as significantly, or perhaps even more so, the first scriptors in America discover the potential power of language as authoritative performance, freed from imperative similitude to its object, capable of being self-serving as system. The momentousness of this redoubled discovery may be appreciated best when we recall that Europe's three-hundred-year colonial rule in America is a reaction formation to that peripeteia. The Spanish imperial administration, for example, saw fit to extend medieval, monadic normativity and its discourse, something akin to T. S. Eliot's nostalgic "unified sensibility," in the New World well beyond Europe's

Renaissance, Reformation, Baroque, and Enlightenment. Or at least that was the official program of the sanctioning institutional order. The result, however, from the very beginning has been just the opposite. What was in fact established was a differential schism, the interstitial space wherein sanctioned discourse attains to semantic signification in its own elisions, in what it absents from itself, or in what it shrouds with a veil of suggestive connotation, in what becomes its force of desire, its ever-errant — in erring's double sense — quest. In other words, baroque language, which, as our Sarduy epigraph notes, is "the search, by definition frustrated, for the *partial object.*" Having discovered its own density, its own quality of being more than transparent medium for representation, baroque language undermines its originary inauguration in the New World by pointing to the necessary fictionality of its founding *arches* as the poetic operation of a supplemental, "antipodal" language. Thus, freeing itself from the weighty center of an overdetermining origin, the American baroque frees itself too from the nostalgia for that inaugural, necessary fiction now become sublimated, internalized, as we shall see in the case of Carpentier shortly. Baroque discourse, then, becomes its own object of reminiscence, without any *telos*, any shrine at the "end" of its peregrination other than itself as its own supplement, its own prodigious self-difference. The end of the quest, that is, becomes the endless quest itself through *terra incognita*, what Lezama calls the "gnostic space" of incunabula. In this sense, the American baroque evinces a kinship with the febrile twists and turns, the irrepressible dynamism of Europe's "baroque prose style," descried by the keen critical eye of Morris W. Croll. The "baroque style," Croll tells us, "preferred the forms that express the energy and labor of minds seeking the truth, not without dust and heat, to the forms that express a contented sense of the enjoyment and passion of it. In a single word, the motions of souls, not their states of rest, had become themes of art."[5] That liminality, that ever-extended errand which characterizes the baroque enterprise as perpetual mobility and displacement is diagnosed as well by Wölfflin in his differentiating study entitled *Renaissance and Baroque*: "The Baroque never offers us perfection and fulfillment, or the static calm of 'being,' only unrest of change and the tension of transience."[6]

Alejo Carpentier, whose novel *The Kingdom of this World* I shall refer to in this chapter to illustrate my reflections on the American baroque, echoes both Croll and Wölfflin. Here is Carpentier, mediated by the Mexican novelist Carlos Fuentes in the latter's brief reflection on Faulkner's *The Vanquished:*

> The Baroque, Alejo Carpentier at one time was telling me, is the language of peoples, who, ignoring truth, seek after it eagerly. Góngora, like Picasso, Buñuel, Carpentier, or Faulkner, *did not know: he encountered.* The Baroque, language of abundance, is also *the language of insufficiency*: only those who possess nothing include everything. Their horror of vacuity is not gratuitous; it is due to the certainty of the fact that

one is in emptiness, that one lacks security. The verbal abundance in *The Kingdom of this World* or in *Absalom, Absalom!* signifies the desperate invocation of a language that is to fill the absences of reason and of faith. It is not for any other reason that post-Renaissance, Baroque art rushed to fill the abysses opened up by the Copernican revolution.[7]

My aim in this chapter is limited. I shall attempt a glimpse of the baroque as erring and errant operation in the text of *The Kingdom of this World*.[8] The choice of proof-text from the Carpentier *oeuvre* may be questioned since this particular work of the Cuban author is, more than his other novels, ideologically programmatic, mired in a metaphysics of authenticity, in a myth of history and historical consciousness. Given my foregoing observations on the baroque, some might say that other Carpentier texts, such as *Concierto barroco* or *Reasons of State*, might have been more natural choices. I opt for *The Kingdom of this World*, however, precisely because of this apparent difficulty and because of the very problematics inherent between the novel's predicative program and its errant praxis. I believe my case for the baroque as a natural principle of, indeed as synonymous with, the American sensibility will be stronger as a result, the novel's programmatics notwithstanding.

The baroque as acentric (or eccentric) and frenzied proliferation, as subversive and ever-errant deflector bent on de-authorizing all privileged programs and centeredness — metaphysics, orthodoxy, myth, authenticity, primogenial acts, hieratic monads, transcendental signifieds, mnemonic determinacies, and mystified historicities — manifests an inexorable gravitation toward its illusionary antitheses. It persistently insinuates itself and its operation, like a magnetic pole, into its contrary field of self-centered and mystified puissance. One thinks inevitably of the baroque's propinquity to Europe's Counter-Reformation (in Europe and in America); the filial space of language and image which they co-inhabit, the intimate commonality in discourse of which contrite orthodoxy and hedonistic conceits collaterally partake. One cannot help but recall, as well, the Metaphysical poets in whom the baroque *figurae* and transcendental ontology, much to T. S. Eliot's chagrin, strive and play in symbiosis.[9] Little should be our surprise, then, at finding the positivities of an irrepressible baroque undermining declared solemnity, unmasking as error the self-mystification of a project which seeks to privilege a historical field as authentic, originary, and ontologically transcendent, beyond reflexivity and beyond the artifices of literary discourse. I am referring to Alejo Carpentier's programmatic enterprise in *The Kingdom of this World* and to the author's prologue-essay to the original 1949 edition of that work where Carpentier proposes such a program. He first announces the outlines of this project in an article of April 8, 1948 in the periodical *El Nacional*, a year before it prefaces the novel. The author's code term for what he seeks is "lo real maravilloso," a "marvelous reality," which is authentically American and perceivable only through an element of "faith," capable of leading one to a "liminal state," a pre-reflective, pre-discursive revelation: "The marvelous begins to be such, unequivocally, when it emanates from an unexpected alteration of reality (miracle), of a privileged revelation of reality. . . . To begin with, the sensation of the marvelous presupposes a faith. . . . This became particularly evident to me during my stay in Haiti, on finding myself in daily contact with something which we could call marvelous reality. . . . But, I thought, as well, that presence and force of the *marvelous reality* was not a unique privilege of Haiti, but inheritance of America as a whole, where, as yet, the establishing of an inventory of its cosmogonies, for example, has not been completed.''[10] In its actual execution, the novel, as intended enterprise, suffers the chastisements of its own errancy at the hands of a baroque mediation that disposes the praxis from solemn earnestness toward one more instance, one more station of the baroque's perpetual peregrination, the text become transformed into yet another pretext of ever-errant textuality.

We have already seen in an earlier chapter how an analogous enterprise in Borges (Marcus Flaminius Rufus's pursuit of a primogenial, privileged center and a transcendental history) founders on the slippery ground of heterogeneity, desultoriness, raving polysemia, and unmitigated dissemination. One key difference between Borges and Carpentier must be noted — a moot difference, in the final analysis, since the outcome in both projects is not essentially different: whereas Borges betrays a complicitous perspicacity into the equivocal fate of his text and its personae, Carpentier sets out blind to the vicissitudes and chastisements his enterprise ultimately must endure. In imputing such an illusionary itinerary to Carpentier's point of departure, I obviously insist on the fact that the novel's prologue-essay forms an integral and constitutive part of the novel, even if the author has excised the prologue from subsequent reprintings of the work. I view that after-the-fact excision itself as evidentiary sign that Carpentier has, in fact, endured the unmasking, attained an insight into his announced project's errancy in the act of writing, in the chastising praxis of an illusionary, predetermined program.

Roberto González Echevarría, an astute and informed student of Carpentier's *oeuvre*, grants as much in the third chapter of his already cited book on Carpentier, even though González Echevarría, as noted above, privileges an ontological ethos, "a lost unity," as transcendental signified in the enterprise of Latin American culture and its history. In the passage already cited in chapter 1, he speaks of "a desire for communion, or, in a Hegelian sense, for totality through reintegration with a lost unity" (p. 21). In discussing *The Kingdom of this World*, however, González Echevarría, with characteristic acumen, is forced into hesitant recanting. He writes, "Carpentier's text would constitute only a fragment of that immense book which would include in its dense and complex concordance the total design of the universe. But Carpentier's hand has already been shown in the act of violating that assumed harmony between history and nature in order to force history into the design of its own text, into the itinerary of his own writing" (p. 146). And yet, González Echevarría cannot divest himself of his tenacious nostalgia for ontology. He privileges a substitute *ontos*, albeit a playful one, Carnival, for the displaced transcendental signified unmasked as error, and he impugns Carpentier's ontology not as essential error or as ontic falsity but as a "false formulation"; further, González Echevarría abets the secret ("apocryphal") presence of a privileged *ontos*, echoing, how consciously I cannot tell, the commentators at the end of Borges's "The Immortal": "The prologue-epilogue to *The Kingdom of this World* is also part of the fiction, of the baroque masquerade. It is Carpentier's first/last mask in the text. *The affirmation of a presence* which simultaneously denies and affirms itself, it is the Carnival. His prologue is the *false formulation of an American ontology*, of *the apocryphal presence* of a marvelous reality" (p. 146. Emphases added).

The pertinence of Hegel to American culture and history in general and to the Carpentier under discussion in particular is unquestionable. In noting the inalienability of prologue and novel, González Echevarría is clearly mindful of Hegel's *The Phenomenology of Mind* and its equivocal, self-problematizing "Preface." I suspect he is party, as well, and his references would indicate as much, to the insightful cogitations on textuality and its inside/outside dimensions sparked by Hegel in contemporary philosophy.[11] Where González Echevarría allows Hegel (as well as Spengler, whom he relates to Carpentier in an informed manner) to overdetermine the itinerary of Latin American culture, and of Carpentier's baroque enterprise in particular, is in the notion of a plausible synthesis or reduction, an ontological "unity" which is retrievable provided the *right* combination could be struck (as opposed to Carpentier's "false formulation"). If Carpentier errs where González Echevarría acutely notes that he does, i.e., in presupposing a harmony between history and nature and setting out to partake of that privileged integrity, only to end up "violating that assumed harmony of history and nature in order to force history into the design of its [the novel's] text, into the itinerary of his own writing," González Echevarría himself falls into error in imputing to *history* a transcendental status, or, at least, an independent status (akin to Hegel's "spirit of history") *outside* the text, beyond textuality, beyond incunabula, extraneous to the fabric of writing, so extraneous that its incorporation "into the design" of textuality entails a studied intentionality galvanized with "force." Clearly, however, one can only arrive at such a dialecticality by blinking the geognostics taught us by José Lezama Lima, one of the most self-consciously baroque sensibilities in America's *landscape*, as we have seen in our opening chapter. Through Lezama Lima and what he descries as the participatory weaving of the American image, the hermeneutics which makes, *fabricates*, history in the interpretation,we can refocus the Vichian *verum ipsum factum* principle upon Hegel himself, where Hegel is most sympathetic to such a focus — in the *Phenomenology* and the *Logic,* where conceptualization and concept, philosophizing and philosophy cannot be extraneous alterities to each other — to appreciate thereby the possibility that American writing and American history are not disparate or discrete one from the other. I shall explore the possibilities of a Hegelian reading in the manner suggested here when dealing with Carlos Fuentes and his novel *Terra Nostra* in our next chapter.

In juxtaposing "history" to Carpentier's enterprise, in positing a historicity as presence of a discrete and prior entity to be deployed by Carpentier and, subsequently, pointing to and expatiating that author's *ad hominem* errancy in the deployment of that project in writing, González Echevarría reproves one "false" dialectic (nature/history) only to introduce another — history and writing. Lezama Lima, we have seen, had already unmasked the speciousness of such a binarism as dialectic, eschewing it in Pater as "criticism of evocation," and espousing, instead, the "difficulty" of a "technique of fiction," a "form of becoming in which a landscape [read 'culture'] moves toward a direction, an interpretation, or a simple hermeneutics, in order to move toward its reconstruction." More recently, in a perhaps unrelated but relevant context, Paul de Man echoes Lezama Lima's American-based insight when he observes: "To become good literary historians, we must remember that what we usually call literary history has little or nothing to do with what we usually call literature and what we call literary interpretation — provided only it is good interpretation — is in fact literary history. If we extend this notion beyond literature, it merely confirms that the bases for historical knowledge are not empirical facts but written texts, even if these texts masquerade in the guise of wars or revolutions."[12]

Alejo Carpentier presumes an anterior ontological presence, the transcendental "marvelous reality," and privileges its historicity. He sublimates the itinerary of that "history" into his own project, into his text. The history of that sublimation has been thoroughly delineated by González Echevarría, an accomplishment admirable for its conscientious detail, painstaking tracking after sources, tracing correspondences, and lines of intertextuality. In spite of his following Carpentier into illusionary historicism, González Echevarría perceives that author's mystification, even if in methodological procedure only. The task I set for myself here consists in moving two steps further, or closer, than an intertextual source study by first cursorily examining the textualizing process itself, the weaving of its fabric, and then examining how that praxis becomes contiguous with and, thereby, contagious to the adjacencies of a textual *bricolage*[13] that comprises nothing less than the baroque landscape itself, the topography of textuality. In other words, I shall comment on how a "technique of fiction" in the sense of Curtius and Lezama becomes paratactic adjacency to and a displacement of what Carpentier, in the manner of dynastic or serial succession, considers to be beyond and prior to literature. Only by understanding that process, can we appreciate the paradoxical impasse of Carpentier, his problematic dialectics polarized as "marvelous reality" and "marvelous literature" (the latter being a derisive term he applies to the productions of the Surrealists);[14] a dialectic which proves to be false and whose terms refuse to be made mutually exclusive, as he sets out to demonstrate. We can appreciate, especially, how the work itself in which he undertakes this enterprise becomes a self-defeating illustration of his task's impossibility. A clear demonstration, that is, that literature is literature and there can be nothing *outside* literature where literature is concerned. Or, to recast the tautology in Lezamaesque paraphrase, "the fictions of myths are myths of new fictions." As in the best tradition of the Baroque (one thinks of Cervantes, for example, or of Quevedo, or, even of the interstices of Calderonian plots), the fictionality of these fictions and the literariness of literature are not grounded on unshakable certainty. Rather, they derive and generate their energy from a precognition of the problematic nature of any privileged ontology or from an insecurity about any transcendental firmness anchored in an immutable center. Such a resolute steadfastness lingers only as reminiscence, that is, as fiction's force of desire, as insufficiency, as impetus of necessity ceaselessly generative of desiring, of questing fictions.

The very title of Carpentier's novel, with its nostalgic resonance in a biblical topos, as already noted, evinces that force of desire in its pointed equivocality. The epigraph of the work, an appropriation from one of the most imposing voices of the Baroque, Lope de Vega, is itself equivocally articulate. It masquerades the Devil ("The King of the West") in dialogue with Providence, speaking in the Old World of the other, the New World, over which the Demon ("we are legion") already claims sovereignty. The kingdom(s) of Carpentier's novel, *The Kingdom of this World*, finds itself already as legion, disseminated to desultoriness, fragmented *à outrance* into untotalizability, where any project, even Carpentier's, can "achieve" its realization only in illusionary error, or alternately partake of that fragmented proliferation as prodigious fiction, as imaginative figure of prodigality. Carpentier purports, in his prologue-essay, to do the first, without anticipating the derision of self-mystification. In practice, however, he accomplishes the latter, in spite of his programmatic pronouncements. Accordingly, from the outset of *The Kingdom of this World* we encounter what Carpentier, in his waylaid intentions, had to fall into: antithesis, metonymic tropes, contrapuntal adjacencies, interlaced contiguities, contentious juxtapositions, deflective substitutions, chiastic heterogeneities, disparate accretions, catachrestic displacements, in short, a baroque *tropo-gráphia*.

The novel's opening chapter, "The Wax heads," tropes, syntagmatically, the metonymies of heads, allegorized by Ti Noël's stream of consciousness to the point of catachresis; metaphorized, one could say in baroque terms, into rhetorical conceit. In a morning replete with heads ("The morning was rampant with heads" [p. 11]), Ti Noël transforms these visual contiguities into violent substitutions, into contrapuntal "historical" realities.

While Ti Noël's master, M. Lenormand de Mézy, is being shaved, the Negro slave gazes at the four waxed heads, their expressionless countenances framed by the curly wigs the barber is displaying on his window counter. With amusement Ti Noël notes the coincidence by which the adjacent window of the tripe shop displays skinned calves' heads, with a sprig of parsley across each of their tongues and of the same waxy quality as the heads in the barber shop. When his master finally emerges from the barber's, Ti Noël observes the striking resemblance of his face to the lifeless heads ("His face bore a startling resemblance to the four dull wax faces that stood in a row along the counter smiling stupidly" [p. 15]). When on his way out M. Lenormand de Mézy buys a calf's head in the tripe shop, which Ti Noël has to carry home, the Negro slave cannot help musing on the head's resemblance to his master's bald pate ("Ti Noël clasped the white, chill skull under his arm, thinking how much it probably resembled the bald head of his master hidden beneath his wig" [p. 15]). Ti Noël's ruminations, however, go beyond the playfully analogical association of these heady contiguities. The sudden vision of an abominable feast ("un abominable convite") transforms these metaphoric contiguities into metonymic contingencies where Ti Noël's mental projections become a *manteia*, a prophecy, proleptic of the rolling of countless heads in subsequent, cataclysmic events of the novel. With ambivalent jocosity and amusement Ti Noël speaks of these coincidences and of an abominable feast at the hands of some experienced, macabre cook: "Only a wooden wall separated the two counters, and it amused Ti Noël to think that alongside the pale calve's heads, heads of white men were served on the same tablecloth. Just as fowl for a banquet are adorned with their feathers, so some experienced, macabre cook might have trimmed the heads with their best wigs" (p. 11). The expert cook whom Ti Noël anticipates in this ominous hypallage will emerge as the master and chef of Auberge de la Couronne, Henri Christophe, whose renowned dishes were widely praised for their perfect seasoning and whose *olla podrida* was famous for its varied and interesting ingredients (pp. 47-48). The same Henri Christophe becomes the *macabre cook* when he takes down the tin crown, long an emblem of the inn, puts on the uniform of the Colonial artillery, and marches toward becoming the first "Crown Monarch of the New World" and mastermind of Citadel La Ferrière, the fortress above the clouds whose walls are raised by drinking to saturation the blood of men and brave bulls.

Ti Noël also goes beyond the physical syntagma which stimulate his associations. He tropes, contrapuntally, realities of other worlds whose signs provoke a European-colonial actuality *vis-à-vis* a mnemonic world that stirs a generic memory within him. The latest prints from Paris, hung with clothespins by the bookseller next to the tripe shop, depict the bewigged head of the King of France and of other nobility. There is also a copper engraving in which a French nobleman is being received by a Negro sitting on an elaborately carved throne. When Ti Noël musters the courage to ask the bookseller what kind of people those might be, he states, "That is a king of your country" (p. 12). That hypomnesic confirmation incites a mental juxtaposition of the powdered, effeminate kings of Europe with the "true kings" of Africa, of Back There ("El Gran Allá"), kings of a mythological past and idealized world which, Carpentier's intent as declared in his prologue-essay notwithstanding, must always dwell Back There, screened through and by the mediations of mnemonic artifice. There is no question in Ti Noël's mind that in this antithesis the kings of the colonial masters do not measure up to the former kings of the slaves. The chapter closes with Ti Noël vituperating the European kings and superstitious practices of their ladies and fulfilling, in the process, the expository proclamations of Carpentier's prologue by reviling those formulaic marvels easily identifiable as the rites of that black Romanticism known as Gothic: "he had little esteem for the King of England, or the King of France, or of Spain, who ruled the other half of the Island, and whose wives, according to Macandal, tinted their cheeks with oxblood and buried foetuses in a convent whose cellars were filled with skeletons that had been rejected by the true heaven, which wanted nothing to do with those who died ignoring the true gods" (pp. 16-17).

Far from serving as entry into the marvels of an ontology, the baroque mediations — rhetorical and mnemonic — of this opening chapter displace any privileged *ontos,* foregrounding in the process an ambivalent, sensuous reality. Physical appearances and their rhetorical depiction substitute their artifice for the mythopoeic reality of Ti Noël's mnemonic cosmos. With ineluctable immediacy, the concrete phenomena of sensorial experience are *already artificial,* even before their rhetorical depiction, by virtue of their contrivance as ornamental displays in shop windows. Aesthetically, that is, in terms of the sensuously perceivable, the world of a transcendental sensibility, filtered through Ti Noël's associative consciousness, becomes even less substantial and more derogated in being reduced to metonymy for rhetorical troping, in being rendered a figurative *schema* of dialectical counterpoint, mnemonic paradigm of *bricolage,* dramatic antithesis, playful juxtaposition or hypallage. In the troping gamesmanship of Ti Noël (of Carpentier through his personage), in this play, one can read the spuriousness of this reality as the "bad faith of art" (albeit "good art"), as against the announced transcendental faith of the "marvelous reality" and its putative ontology. In subsequent chapters of *The Kingdom of this World,* in which we are presented with the marvelous Nature of Macandal, the Metamorphoses, Henri Christophe's architectonic madness, and the compounded interstices of history, we see the accentuation and intensification of the Carpentierian project's self-difference — an exacerbated internal disparity between aim and praxis, the depletion of the project's announced metaphysics, the deauthorization of its ontological determination — so that the baroque enterprise may carry on its "subversive" *métier.*

If in the first chapter the juxtaposition of a historical actuality — the "here and now" of late eighteenth-, early nineteenth-century colonial Haiti — with an eidetic leftover of Ti Noël's mnemonic past renders all presence (worldly, historical, and ideal reality) spurious and insubstantial, the second chapter points to an outright ahistorical, timeless cosmos, a mnemonic utopia/uchronia which only dwells as trace, as faded suggestion. The phenomenal world of the concrete gives way to a transitional process, one which aims at tropically trans-substantiating itself as ritualistic, playful impulse in the putative name of the marvelous. Accordingly, there is a shift in focus from the physical contiguities of the first chapter to a synecdochal apprehension of mnemonically *re-presented* "unities" *circling back*, in revolutionary fervor, upon "themselves." Carpentier's rhetorical *schemas*, the figurative, symbolic, and metaphorical tropes emerge as a function of this transition. The signs and geometry of these figures are unmistakably clear: the wheel, the body, blood, and the heavenly city. The setting is the sugar-cane mill, where the horse *circles* mechanically, out of habit. Macandal shoves cane sheaves into iron *rollers* as he speaks of *cupolas of red clay*, giant *drums*, the mothers of drums, with *red-painted* legs, feasts of *circumcision*, when youths danced with *bloodstained* legs. He speaks of *Widah, the holy city*, where the *cobra* was worshiped and the *eternal wheel* was mystically *represented*. Through Ti Noël's fascination, we witness Macandal's *bloodshot eyes*, his incredibly slender-waisted *torso* whose powerful and terrible gestures are spellbinding; the *torso* whose left hand is mangled by the *rollers* as he speaks, from which an *eye of blood* begins to widen in the pan of sugar juices: the arm that is amputated on the spot with a machete. The chapter is entitled "La poda," The Pruning, whose affirmative, open-ended, generative possibilities are foreclosed in the English translation when the chapter title is misrendered as "The Amputation." The title of the next chapter, as we shall see, is equally suggestive in view of this manual severance: "Lo que hallaba la mano" ("What the hand Found").

The novel's first and second chapters counterpose the antithetical terms of a typically baroque dialectic: the obsessive concern for appearance and a sensuous texture interfaced with the concerns of a return to/of transcendental, ontological numinosity. What follows the two initial chapters is *not* a reduction into synthesis, but a synaesthetic transumption of this dialectic; an antithetical sublation embodied in Macandal's metamorphosis into a high priest of the Gods of Widah, the holy city, who ruled the vegetable kingdom (we are back to Pan and pantheism), and his discovery of a deadly life and potent pharmacy in the many species of flora. (The systematic and "mysterious" death of colonial masters and of their chattel ensues, along with the surreptitious mobilization of all the Negro slaves). Macandal's animistic prosopopeia discovers a primogenial schema within the heart of Nature itself. In the sensorial texture (in what the hand finds) inheres a mnemonic figuration, a repetition of a primal scene — not a primal scene but, again, its conscious repetition — from Back There.

As textual strategy, this synaesthetic compounding harks back to the Metaphysicals of the early Baroque, whose literary ambit, as Frank Warnke observes with particular reference to Crashaw, consists of an "imaginary world which insists on its difference from ordinary life, even while, at the same time, both utilizing the sense data of that life and claiming an ontological status superior to it."[15] The antitheses descried by Warnke underlie, as dialectical paradox, the self-denying enterprise of Carpentier, giving that enterprise an ironic twist which textualization — his own rhetorical stratagems — turns against the illusionary intentions of the author. The same *décalage*, the same deflective shift, in a manner reminiscent of Ovid, becomes operative in Macandal's metamorphoses, as well as in the transformations of Ti Noël at the end of the novel; not to mention, of course, the transmutation of the Venus of Canova into Pauline Bonaparte in the tactile reveries of Soliman the masseur (in the fourth and final part of Carpentier's work). In this respect, Warnke's characterization of the seventeenth-century Baroque becomes wholly relevant to Carpentier's project and its neo-baroque aesthetics. Warnke observes that "the Baroque conception of reality as transcendent underlies two prominent features of seventeenth-century literature — the paradoxical and the phantasmagoric."[16] The hallucinatory world of Macandal, the nightmarish existence of Ti Noël, and the cataclysmic state of colonial society at the hands of "incomprehensible" but artfully manipulated forces; the theatrical world of Henri Christophe, and the lamentable "theater" of Mademoiselle Floridor ("The Daughter of Minos and Pasiphaë," Chapter 1, Part II) clearly point to the Baroque phantasmagoria of "a world gone mad."

The greatest paradox in Carpentier's work is textual in the broadest sense, that is, contextual, topographic, and is perpetrated within history. Its deployment, whether Carpentier consciously intended it or not, unmasks history's ironies, the nightmares of Heraclitus, the antinomies of his *Logos*: "the discourse of Nature." The narrative events of the text, so true to Herodotus in their exegesis, so documentary,[17] are rendered as the historical climax of the Age of Reason: the Enlightenment, whose political pinnacle would be the guillotine, and whose decorous aesthetics would metamorphose into the lugubrious sensuality, the preternatural *tranches de vie* epitomized in the dark, "elective affinities" of the early Romantics.

Paradox, however, whether gleaned in a novel or in the (con)texts of Heraclitan "discourse of Nature" (the embattled Greek's term for self-reflexive history), is a trope, a contrivance, an artifice and, Carpentier, like any contriver, intends particular significance, mystified or not, in his stratagems. Suggestively, and problematically, in this case, those intentions are set forth by the work's original "Prologue" and we can proceed accordingly to read, to decipher Carpentier's trope — itself a baroque conceit recursively become counter-self-directed. What Carpentier (through Ti Noël) does imagistically in the juxtapositions of the novel's first chapter, he achieves intellectually in the whole work by decentering, by turning loose the ahistorical rhetoricity of a "primordial world" within the time-space frame of an elaborately reflexive, self-conscious, and thoroughly "un-natural" historical period — the eighteenth century. The baroque conceit, in this case truly unnatural, a game with time, in the characteristically Carpentierian manner, consists in juxtaposing the acolytes of the naive and utopian Philosophes of the French Enlightenment with the eudemonic culture embodied in Macandal and in the revolutionary ("repeating"), syncretic reality of the Afro-Antillean slaves. This contrapuntal antithesis becomes yet one more point of confluence in Carpentier's problematic dialectic.

Considered as trope, as "Metaphysical" conceit, *The Kingdom of this World* clearly manifests Carpentier's preoccupation with the baroque as timeless, self-conscious, and continually self-mediated genre. In this sense we can appreciate some of the novel's studied accouterments which function in a way so characteristically reminiscent of what our historical plots designate as the Baroque tradition. The fifth chapter, Part II, of Carpentier's work is particularly telling in this regard. Entitled "Santiago de Cuba," it presents, contrapuntally, the Hispanic colony, which is the patrimony of seventeenth-century Counter-Reformation, *vis-à-vis* the French colony of Cap Haitienne, now in the throes of political holocaust, suffering the consequences of liberalism in Paris and under constant siege from revolted slaves who find solace and support in the fervor with which certain humanitarian Jacobins were beginning to defend their cause. Devastated by these slave uprisings, M. Lenormand de Mézy and a handful of survivors take refuge in Santiago. After a carnivalesque binge, an abandonment to the earthly pleasures of flesh and fantasy — erotomania and theater — so characteristically baroque, M. Lenormand de Mézy, in this his final appearance alive within the novel, is overcome by the contrition, also baroque par excellence, of *vanitas vanitatum et omnia vanitas*. In the company of Ti Noël, he takes "to spending long hours groaning and rasping out ejaculatories in Santiago Cathedral" (p. 85). Meanwhile, Ti Noël listens, bemused, to the discordant symphonies of a Christmas cantata in rehearsal. Like his master, Ti Noël finds a peculiar comfort, an ataractic refuge, we could say, in this Baroque Hispanic setting and its elaborate heterotopia, which is so unlike the French Cap: "the Negro found in the Spanish churches a Voodoo warmth he had never encountered in the Sulpician churches of the Cap. The baroque golds, the human hair of the Christs, the mystery of the richly carved confessionals . . . the dubious color of St. Benedict, the black Virgins . . . had an attraction, a power of seduction in presence, symbols, attributes, and signs similar to those of the altars of *houmforts* consecrated to Damballah, the Snake god. Besides, St. James is Ogoun Faï, marshal of the storms, under whose spell Bouchman's followers had risen. For that reason Ti Noël, by way of prayer, often chanted to him an old song he had learned from Macandal:

Santiago, I am the son of war:
Santiago,
Can't you see I am the son of war? (pp. 86-87)

As González Echevarría accurately notes, counting consecutively without regard for the novel's division into parts, this fifth chapter of Part II falls into the numerical center of the novel, thirteenth of twenty-six chapters. We could add that it is also the embattled and problematic epicenter of the text as rhetorical trope. For here the reader encounters the crux of what Carpentier himself has delineated as his own dialectic of sensibility: a putative "marvelous syncretism" whose numinosity and ontological privilege irrevocably founders on the decentering, deauthorizing heterocosm of baroque prodigality. This is the "syncretism" which, according to the program of Carpentier's prologue-essay, was to have "unified" sensibility; an intended project that endures, as we have seen, the subterfuge and artifices of a most neo-baroque deflection.

In one of his latest novels, *El recurso del método* (1974), from a period in his career which sees the author confronting, now self-consciously, the paradoxical difficulties in his illusionary itinerary of the 1940s, Carpentier suggestively broaches the antithetical terms of this dialectic. That reconsideration retrospectively elucidates the self-subverted delusion of his earlier mystified enterprise. In this 1974 Cartesian parody, itself a baroque trope, a figure of irony, Carpentier, recursively at his best, re-evokes the dialectic whose contrapuntal terms emerge, once again, as the French culture, for him a paradigm of a hopelessly Cartesian "dissociated sensibility" of European civilization and, on the other hand, the polyvalent, heterocosmic Hispano-African-American culture, paradigm of a pluralist and many-centered and, therefore, endlessly decentered or eccentric "syncretism." In this avatar, however, the dialectic is rendered satire by dint of self-irony. By virtue of the exaggerated emphases which satirical figures require, the terms of the dialectic become more readily apparent. In one of the numerous repartees that fly between the baroquely sybaritic protagonist of *El rucurso del método* — a Latin American satrap — and his friend, the Illustrious Academician, the latter, with his Cartesian éclat, French self-righteousness, and air of superiority (airs which always border on rekindling the Thirty Years War) observes that, "L'Afrique commence aux Pyrénées."[18] The Academician's quip, reminiscent of Ortega y Gasset's ruminations in *España invertebrada* (1921), points to a pluralistic complex of cultural confluence in which the likelihood of syncretism within the Hispanic world is infinitely greater than in the culturally individuated contexts east of the Pyrenees. This type of cultural reductionism, however, borders on caricature and it bears the brunt of Carpentier's own (now) conscious self-parody. The differentiation is, nonetheless, fruitful in view of the distinct types of "naive" *pathos* the French Cap and Spanish Santiago elicit from Ti Noël.

The religious iconography encountered by the black slave in the Cathedral of Santiago, and the magnetism it holds for him emanate an almost heretical polysemia alien to the world of his French masters. The catholicity of this iconography, racially ambiguous, sensuously polychromatic, paradigmatically pluralistic, symbolically syncretic, becomes hermeneutically substantiated before Ti Noël's eyes as the altar of Damballah, the god-Serpent of his African forefathers. In this play of substitutions, Santiago, the patron saint of Hispania Magna emerges as Ogoun Faï, patron of war and tempests in whose name Bouckman's enslaved African host rises against the colonial masters. Far from the achievement of a "unified syncretism," the cultural multiplicity, which Carpentier assumed to be the foundation of a "marvelous reality" and its syncretism, proves to be an uncontrolled polysemy, a baroque heterotopia whose weave, whose macula, cannot integrate the sundry threads, cannot synthesize its variability into transcendent "unity." The polysemic baroqueness of this American imagery, as noted earlier, ironically enough, dates to the monadic and "homogenizing" efforts of the sixteenth century's Counter-Reformation, particularly to that momentous and prolonged occasion which stands as the apotheosis and bathos of that Movement: the Council of Trent (1545-1563). For some, the event represents the moment of conception of the Baroque. A number of scholars of varying critical persuasion (Heinrich Wölfflin, Helmut Hatzfeld, José Antonio Maravall) link, in broader terms, the Baroque aesthetics to that momentous occasion of the Counter- Reformation. Wylie Sypher, another scholar of similar bent, takes the historical connection between the religious movement and the Baroque most literally. The Council of Trent, he argues, gave the Baroque a degree of legitimacy and impetus when, in trying to counter the secularizing influence of the Renaissance, it baptized the numinous energy of sensory experience, notably, the religious iconography of the Roman church. Sypher observes, furthermore, that "By [its] sanctioning [of] the veneration of images and its emphasis upon transubstantiation, the Council, in effect, gave the pious confidence in sensory experience and offered a means of reducing the anxiety in mannerist consciousness, relaxing the tension between body and soul."[19] But unlike the "mannerist consciousness" of the pious and the "dissociated sensibility" of Eliot's Mataphysicals, Ti Noël knows no "tension between body and soul," and he playfully conjugates the "two," as we have already seen in Carpentier's first chapter. For Ti Noël, the first, the body, is made *insubstantial* by the many and repeated metamorphoses (Macandal's as well as Ti Noël's); the second, the soul, becomes transubstantial by virtue of its polyvalent inconstancy, its uncanny ability for repeated metempsychoses in the face of mutability. If the Baroque as sanctioned mechanism or aesthetic for the diffusion and easing of that "tension" achieves that aim imputed to it by Sypher, then we can speak of a *rapprochement* on the scene of American landscape between the Hispanic and African *imagines*. And, perhaps, herein lies the crossing point of Carpentier's "marvelous syncretism" — the point at which the self-consciousness of the tirelessly prodigious baroque and the multifarious élan of the Afro-American reality coalesce.

That coalescence, however, figures *not* as marvelous "reality," as ontology or *ontic* transubstantiation of disparate elements into *ontos* of "syncretism" or reductive synthesis. Rather, it figures as the conflation of discrete interpretive processes become affiliated into what Lezama, after Curtius, called "a hermeneutics," a way of *figuring*, a "technique of fiction" that weaves and unweaves its own "reality" and knows itself to be doing so. If there is anything "marvelous" in this, it is the marvel of fabrication, of a baroque process infused with the prodigious energy of multifarious American circumstances which intensify eccentric proliferation, galvanize its plutonic flight to a new extreme. Far from being a transcendental metaphysics of primogenial authenticity, a pre-discursive and pre-reflective emanation revealed through faith's privileged alteration of reality (as Carpentier's program assumed), this "syncretism" proves, in Carpentier's own novel, an endlessly momentary, contingent co-incidence of factitious practices whose process deflects, endlessly, any privileged stasis, or pause, that might eventuate in a transcendental ontology. Alejo Carpentier, at times in spite of his declared intentions, has inextricably figured as itinerant sensibility in the restless quest of this cultural pilgrimage. The revolutionary (playfully repeating) métier of the sensory, of the aesthetic (the sensuously perceivable), I believe, is that quality which makes for an ultimately subverts the oxymoron "marvelous reality." It is also what links Carpentier to the Baroque and the Metaphysicals in their "sensuous apprehension of thought," as T. S. Eliot says of John Donne.

Insofar as Carpentier is as much a progeny of Cartesian and Newtonian Europe as he is of Henri Christophe's Antilles (even if it be through the artifice of a self-consciously willed affiliation, or precisely because of it), his literary world, the textual map of "the marvelous reality," is afflicted with the dialectical antitheses Ti Noël gleans between Cap Haitienne and Santiago de Cuba. The sensorial experience and its polyvalent syncretism perdure in the cultural landscape for which the latter, Santiago, stands as paradigm. The first, the French Cap, on the other hand, stands for a world in which reflexivity and individuation have all but obliterated even the possibility of tension by reducing to an institutional arithmetic all mediate relation between body and soul — in rendering the first a pure "thought," or Reason (Cartesianism) and the second a machine (Newton). This contrapuntal schema, caricaturesque because rendered as a parodically Cartesian mathematical reduction, forms the ironic underpinning of Carpentier's *El recurso del método*. The dialectic between the American and the European (French) worlds simmers unabated, as one can see in the protagonist-narrator's self-justification before the Illustrious Academician: "And so, according to him, because of the lack of Cartesian spirit (it's true: carnivorous plants do not grow, toucans don't fly, nor are hurricanes possible in *The Discourse on*

Method) we are all too fond of boundless eloquence.''[20] Taken recursively, as almost everything in Carpentier inevitably must be taken, such an affirmation continues to reiterate the pluralistic fabric of reality and palpable American topography, the "landscape," as Carpentier's 1949 prologue-essay nostalgically posited.

While Carpentier's recursiveness makes him a Cartesian in method, he continues to yearn for and to harken to a pre-Cartesian apperception much like the Afro-Antillean sensibility of Ti Noël, and not unlike the "unified sensibility" the Council of Trent sought to recoup, managing only its monadic caricature. I am not equating these modes of apprehension categorically; for the implicit pluralism of the Afro-Antillean *élan* would be a heretical nightmare to the retrenched orthodoxy of the Council of Trent, while the "sensuous apprehension of thought" (or Pascal's "la peinture de la pensée") evinces an intellectual and imagistic figurativeness on the part of Donne and of the Metaphysicals. I only wish to highlight the significance of sensory experience and its rhetorical conceits which are common to all these modes of sensibility, a significance largely obliterated by Cartesian and Newtonian epistemology by which all "knowing" and apprehension have been rendered ideational, abstract, mathematical. In the enlightened mode of consciousness which begins with Cartesian rationalism, "primal ideas are not built upon evidence from the senses; for whether we wake or sleep, Descartes assures us, a square has only four sides: 'truth so clear and apparent' we cannot question it. . . . Descartes seemed to prove that reality is not the physical world but our notion of what that world is. . . . Newton completed the reconstruction of the world upon the basis of abstract ideas by making the universe a mathematical system governed by gravitational laws. He located all bodies within an ideational framework . . . like a conceptual envelope for all things existing here or there, now or then."[21]

Insofar as Carpentier presents us with a polyvalent "reality" transubstantiated as text, the marvelous *élan* and its requisite faith (even if it be the "bad faith" of art) continue to dwell in the sensoriality and free play of the textual *imagines*. Insofar as the textuality of this scriptural substantiation stands as *discourse*, that faith, which Carpentier saw as a prerequisite, and its object (the "marvelous reality") devolve into figurative schema, into rhetorical trope of baroque textuality and its filigree. In other words, Carpentier's supposed pre-rational ontology becomes contaminated by the Cartesian *cogito* and its ideational, abstract, and unhappy consciousness (in the Hegelian sense of the term, which we shall be examining shortly in our next chapter). Carpentier has obviously become acutely aware of the dialectical dilemma in his own circumstance as mediator between the nostalgia for a world of "faith" with its own logos which, as he desired in his 1949 prologue, pre-exists rational discourse, and a world of language whose articulation renders the object of its parlance a subversive and self-deflecting schema of textuality. The baroque ebullience of sensory imagery and linguistic deluge, as Carlos Fuentes observes in the passage cited earlier, may be a form of compensation for the dialectical predicament and the threatening imminence of a *horror vacui* which may await at that equivocal and ambivalent threshold.

This predicament, as I have pointed out already, is essentially no different from the one which Baroque sensibility, particularly in its Metaphysical discernment, had to confront, *mutatis mutandis*, within the context of the late sixteenth and most of the seventeenth centuries. In his *El recurso del método*, where the dialectic is dramatically and ironically played out by the narrator-protagonist, Carpentier's ruse and subterfuge of this bipolarity consists in rendering Cartesianism sensorial with a vengeance. He seeks to accomplish that *décalage* through a transanimation, a baroque metalepsis of the *cogito* as "Siento luego soy," "I feel, therefore I am" (p. 309). This critical point of crossing, of conjunction and disjunction, replete with its historical mediations, comes (as a second coming, one might say) a full quarter of a century after *The Kingdom of this World* and its "naive" prologue. Novel and prologue, by virtue of their contiguous appearance in the same volume, stand as binary terms of a dialectic of a nostalgia for *being*, for ontology, and its problematic contravention in the praxis of *discourse*. This textual quest and its baroque accretions continued to haunt Carpentier and, as we have already observed, have haunted every American writer since the earliest chroniclers put pen to paper to chart the incunabula of the New World.

Chapter 5
The Quest's Impossible Self-Seeking

> . . . criticism determines the causes and structures of things and
> is such a delicate instrument of mediation that it has made
> indetermination itself a principle of physics.
> Octavio Paz, "The Liberated Man and Liberators"

It is a commonplace that Latin American literature, like its Anglo-American counterpart to the north, is a belated literature with an acute awareness of its own belated status. Since the earliest chroniclers of the late fifteenth and early sixteenth centuries, as we have already seen in our opening chapter, writing in Latin America manifests a self-conscious insight into its own belatedness. It is, after all, a writing whose problematic "beginnings" are contemporaneous with a self-dubbed secondary birth, the Renaissance, and, just as significantly, it is the discourse of a "voyage of discovery" which, for those errant questers who endured the baptism of a *New* World, becomes an *autobiographical* voyage of discovery. As a consequence of re-discovering itself in the nineteenth century, the century of nationalist revolutions and movements of liberation, modern Latin American literature, as we have seen, compounds secondariness with an attendant intensification of self-conscious belatedness. In the "revolutionary" repetitions of "inaugural" acts that know themselves to be secondary and belated, the anxious quest after novelty and originality has become itself the topical commonplace. The result is a literary tradition whose salient topos is the vehemence with which *topoi* are evoked and problematized, a tradition whose literature becomes the object of its own critical consciousness. Latin American writers, such as Octavio Paz, have edified this critical enterprise into a cultural landscape, a landscape of unremitting self-chastisement, in an anxious attempt to keep the critical project from becoming mystified by its own vocation. Accordingly, the cry that the shibboleth of criticism as self-mystification may have already overtaken the critical enterprise has been resounding, for some years now, as apostrophic jeremiad.[1] In fact, before Franco-American critics, such as Paul de Man, anxiously and symptomatically diagnosed in this country the pleonastic binomial of "criticism and crisis," Latin American writers, such as Paz and others we have discussed in this study, had faced the ironic difficulties of this predicament.[2]

The Mexican Carlos Fuentes, whose particular case will serve as our proof-text in this chapter, figures as hyper-self-conscious sensibility in the critical project of Latin America, and one of the most influential contemporaries in Fuentes's formation is none other than his older compatriot Octavio Paz. I shall not rehearse Paz's own critical itinerary here. That has been done already by a number of critics, most succinctly by Enrico Mario Santí.[3] I invoke Paz as threshold to my discussion of Carlos Fuentes primarily because Paz, as Fuentes concedes, does in fact figure as mediating force in Fuentes's own self-conscious enterprise. And my primary concern here *is none other than mediation* — the sort implied by Paz's discussion of self-conscious secondariness as critical (as self-critical) dialectic. Thus, I shall be dealing with that problematic ground where, in our own critical enterprise, we often, all too often, grant unquestioned and privileged immediacy. My discussion of Fuentes's undertaking, then, will focus on the self-mediations an author's enterprise deploys against and for itself. In dealing with Fuentes, and generally with hyper-self-conscious writers like him, we are always faced with the problematics of an authorial authority which compounds its power play by arrogating critical authority to itself as well. In both of the Fuentes texts I shall be examining (*Terra Nostra* [1975], *Don Quixote, or the Critique of Reading* [1976]/*Cervantes o la crítica de la lectura* [1976]) the discerning reader must deal with this compounding. In the manner through which these texts interrelate, there figures yet an additional self-mediation whose ploy must be scrutinized and whose innocence, or innocuous neutrality, we obviously need to suspect.

Suspicion is a form of denial, which is another way of saying criticism. What an author's enterprise denies or arrogates to itself in its autoexegesis becomes, in turn, the object of our own suspicion or critical reading. What we question through our critical activity (if our reading truly be such) are the determinacies wrought by the author's self-corrective (or self-serving) exercise. In suspecting, denying, or de-authorizing those *determinacies* we move toward making *indetermination* itself an operating principle — a working-point of departure — as Octavio Paz aphoristically suggests in our epigraph. However, as Paz also reminds us, the negation involved here is a creative moment which ultimately affirms. And what becomes affirmed, above all, is a supposed "mastery," a power play over what is appropriated through negation or denial. From the broader context of Paz's observation, it is clear that Hegel and his dialectics of creative negation underwrite in large measure Paz's and, through him, Feuntes's critical modernity, if I may venture that pleonasm. Paz reminds us in this same essay that in "Hegel's dialectic, negation is a creative moment within the process and negativity the road to Being."[4] He characterizes that "creative negation" as "revolutionary criticism, the contradiction that affirms the very thing it denies." The practitioner of this repetitive turning ("revolutionary") on novelty, of this creative criticism, Paz continues, views his critical practice "as a way of appropriating the world: through negation, the concept changes the world and makes him its master."[5] That "mastery" through the Hegelian concept, however, is itself subject to innumerable critical mediations and "revolutionary" assaults in turn, leading Paz to observe that our "criticism . . . has made indetermination itself a principle of physics." What Paz aims to do with this delimitation of mastery, or with its perpetual sundering into innumerable indeterminacy, is to bracket, to check, to deflect the ultimate mastery and the programmatic totalizability as Being or Absolute Knowledge that awaits as finality in the Hegelian project. We could say then that Paz's thwarting or checking of such final completion guarantees that the achievement of absolute mastery impending in the Hegel project always remains impending. Thus, its attainment may not foreclose or interdict the revolutionary quest and its creative spirit of negation.

Within this critical context and its corrective indeterminacies as "determined" by Paz, I should like to consider Carlos Fuentes's itinerary in *Terra Nostra* and its self-critical supplements as Hegelian enterprise. I am prompted to do so not only by Paz's self-problematizing, Hegel-inspired mediation in Fuentes but, as well, because of the direct and problematic concessions Fuentes makes to Hegel's haunting and haunted presence within the texts we are about to examine. The measure of those concessions will become self-evident as we proceed. Of course, in my plotting of Fuentes's itinerary I shall endeavor to guard against granting the privilege of overdetermination to Hegel, as well as exercise the obviously necessary caution toward conceding unconditional immediacy and unquestioned authority to Fuentes's own corrective dialectic. But, as the case of Carpentier discussed in our last chapter illustrates, we must remain mindful of the fact that authors in general are far from immune to the phantoms of self-delusion.

Terra Nostra[6] stands as the most elaborate and most extensive (some seven hundred and eighty pages) novel of the Fuentes *oeuvre* to date. It is an "omnivorous" text whose voraciousness for inclusion is matched only by the ferocity with which it safeguards against its own textual closure and satiation. The tenacious force of the possessive adjective in its title is jealously guarded, lest its desire become fulfilled. The object of its possessive energy is the endless process of metamorphoses as landscape of culture: the history of textuality and the textuality of history extended and maintained, unremittingly, as *untenable* ground. In the process, the possessive "Nostra" haunts as the perpetual force of desire, "contained" by the text, but only as incontinent passion which endlessly proscribes the possession, or mastery, of its object: the *terrae*, the topo-graphies of cultured landscape, the incunabula, as Lezama would say, of Western and New World civilization. As a result, desire, in its possessive form, becomes the object of its own force, converting its putative object from *terra firma* to haunted *speculum*, phantasmal space reflecting the very force of desire.

Lest we overlook the mercurial furtiveness of that mirror's glance or the unrequited spectral transformations — the *espejismos*, or mirages — that pullulate in that space, the novel's epigraphs unmistakably turn our gaze to that abysmal landscape: "What does that old spook want?" Goya, *Los caprichos*; "Fervid in her fetid rags. It is she, the first/False mother of many, like you, aggrieved/By her, and for her, grieving," Cernuda, *Ser de Sansueño*; "Transformed utterly: A terrible beauty is born," Yeats, *Easter, 1916*. Once the ardor of appropriation implodes these spectral figures into the abyss of the text, there we see them reflected in the phantasmal mnemonics of Thomistic parable: "Nihil potest homo intelligere sine phantasmata," whose economy Fuentes amplifies into, "Man can understand nothing without images. And images are phantoms" (p. 555). Our world, *terra nostra*, then, is emplotted by Fuentes as erotic phantasmagoria — erotic in the Classical sense of unending quest; phantasmagoric in the imagistic sense of *mneme*, or living memory, and in the reflective or spectral sense of carnivalesque inversion. As such, the force of eros and the reversed, "negative" (creative) image deployed by Fuentes perpetrate a décalage, a shifting, which severs all firm mooring, subverts all steadfast centeredness, releasing the *terra firma* to float. In floating that *terra* becomes identical with the performative acts, the interventionist consciousness, the dialectical flight of self-critical writing/reading. In this strategy, negative reflection bridges the phantasmal world of *terra nostra* and the spectral (speculative) activity of self-consciousness. In other words, the ground of *terra nostra* as our cultural history — our incunabula — and as this particular novel, this particular incunabulum-*Terra Nostra*, become breached (mutually *sublated*, Hegel would say) by/as critical acts and specular reflections of abyssed self-consciousness.

In the "Preface" to *The Phenomenology of Mind*, itself a hyper-self-conscious meditation of self-consciousness, Hegel obviates the strategy I proleptically outline here when he writes, "mediating is nothing but self-identity working itself out through an active self-directed process; or, in other words, it is reflection into self, the aspect in which the ego [read: text/novelist] is for itself, objective to itself. It is pure negativity, or, reduced to its utmost abstraction, the process of bare and simple becoming. . . . We misconceive therefore the nature of reason [read: writing] if we exclude reflection or mediation from ultimate truth, and do not take it to be a positive moment of the Absolute. It is reflection which constitutes truth the final process, and yet at the same time does away with the contrast between result and the process of arriving at it."[7] In addition to what I have bracketed already in the citation itself, when dealing with Fuentes and his plots we should bracket, as well, the programmatic teleology of the Hegelian project — "ultimate truth," "the Absolute," "truth the final result." In doing so we qualify Hegel's relevancy to Fuentes by circumscribing the purposive

ultimacy toward which the described process serves as peregrination. By inter-
dicting that privileged teleology, we see *Terra Nostra* as "result and the process
of arriving at it." Just as significantly, however, we can appreciate that the
"result" in this case is not a transcendental figuration (Absolute knowledge,
Being, truth) which lies beyond the process of this "working-itself-out." Rather,
in bridging "result and process" the "result," the novel as in the making, mirrors and elucidates the dynamic process of its own becoming. The novel, "the
result," never achieves static completion or a state of *being* as such. Process itself emerges as perpetual becoming, capable of displacing, substituting, sublimating (capable of becoming *aufgehoben*, in Hegelian parlance), in other words,
capable of supplementing the mirror reflection, the spectral negative, the critical
perspicuity of itself: the novel as its self-differential image. Moreover, the process
not only of becoming, but also the "surfeit," or "yield" of that process (that
is, the enabling supplement, or the becoming-process's supplemental capability),
is endlessly self-empowering, perpetually self-displacing, ever-errant as questing
force that privileges no single moment or event within its mirror image, within
the novel. For this reason, any specific instances I may "freeze" or evoke for
the sake of argument should be taken only as illustrative indices rather than as
privileged centralities around which the rest of the work's working-itself-out
pivots. (I do submit, in this regard, to the inescapable risks of my own arbitrariness, inevitable for any critical argumentation, expository or otherwise, even
for the doubly enchanted who may claim to select illustrative instances "at
random").

One of the first (if not the first) dialectical negations, or critical reflections,
a reader encounters in *Terra Nostra* is an apocalypsis with a deferred eschatology — perpetually deferred, for the eschatology as such never "comes," it is
always (be)coming. The novel, in one if its itinerant plots, in one of its repeatedly
forking paths, is the long-drawn play of that deferring. Opening and "closing"
on a millennial threshold, July 14-December 31, 1999, in Paris, the novel forces
our critical discernment into unfolding as mnemonic exercise, a witnessing in
living recollection (an instance of what Hegel calls *Erinnerung*) the events of
an apocalyptic future whose consummation never dawns. The opening ploy of
this negative reflection consists in *recovering* (in the irreducibly redoubled sense
of that term as "apocalypsis" and "anacalypsis" at once) the force of what has
become debilitated by familiarity. Thus, in a pre-posterous procedure reminiscent
of T. S. Eliot's ("In my beginning is my end"; "In my end is my beginning" —
the proemial verse and coda of "East Coker"), already discussed in our first
chapter, Fuentes tropes the apocalyptic end into inaugural moments of the received
origins, as we read in the proemial lines of *Terra Nostra*: "Incredible the first
animal that dreamed of another animal. Monstrous the first vertebrate that succeeded in standing on two feet and thus spread terror among the beasts still
normally and happily crawling close to the ground through the slime of creation.

Astounding the first telephone call, the first boiling water, the first song, the first loincloth. . . . Pollo Phoibee . . . dreamed these things, and prepared to answer them himself. But then he was visited in his dream by the somber, faceless figure of a monk who spoke for Pollo, continuing in words what had been an imagistic dream: 'But reason — neither slow nor indolent — tells us that merely with repetition the extraordinary becomes ordinary, and only briefly abandoned, what had once passed for a common and ordinary occurrence becomes a portent'.''

The mediate intrusion of the "somber, faceless figure of a monk" who speaks becomes the articulate corrective of Fuentes's text; its proleptic advertance, which steps forward, to the fore of the text, to deliver a premonitory admonition, a forewarning against what Hegel calls "ideal presentation," i.e., what merely *is* as uncomprehended immediacy with passive indifference and the ordinariness of familiarity. In this sense, Fuentes's "faceless monk who speaks" may as well be taken as Hegel himself (I am not claiming that he *is*, only that this is a plausible fiction) who, in his own "Preface" to *The Phenomenology*, militates against the familiar and in favor of what in Fuentes "becomes a portent." Here is Hegel, once again, "What is 'familiarly' known is not properly known, just for the reason that it is 'familiar'. When engaged in the process of knowing, it is the commonest form of self-deception. . . . Knowledge of that sort, with all its talk, never gets from the spot, but has no idea that this is the case. . . . The circle which is self-enclosed and at rest, and *qua* substance, holds its own moments, is an immediate relation, the immediate, continuous relation of elements with their unity, and hence arouses no sense of wonderment. *But that an accident as such, when cut loose from its containing circumference,* — that what is bound and held by something else actual only by being connected with it — *should obtain an existence all its own, gain freedom and independence on its own account — this is the portentous power of the negative*'' (pp. 92-93, added emphases). *Terra Nostra*, with its augural premium on what "becomes a portent," comprises a desultory agglomeration of such Hegelian "accidents" that break all internal encirclements and dislocate all possible centricity within its textual fabric. Fuentes's work figures as critical precipitation of such an "accident," as already noted: a cutting "loose from its containing circumference," that is, from the *terra nostra*, our received Western tradition of culture, historicity, and writing. This is why, I suspect, Fuentes's text opens with an "accident" at its greatest powers of generality: an apocalypsis — but an apocalypsis which is not Absolute, transcendental, or overdetermined Telos. Rather, it displays an apocalypsis which has been wrought by the "accidents" of culture — the *heretical millennialism* of the Medieval sects, those discussed by Norman Cohn's *The Pursuit of the Millennium*,[8] a book which profoundly informs Fuentes's text, as he notes in his "Acknowledgements." Fuentes's proemial apocalypsis, if the oxymoron be allowed, is an "accident" that does not "close the circle," but one that haunts endlessly as yearning, as timelessly desired timelessness, a passionate uchronia, mediated perpetually through the *election* (the Greek etymon of "heresy" means just that) of the force of desire.

In masking his textualizing procedure with a transparency that allows us to see not an "ideal representation" but the process of his text's becoming, Fuentes abysmally reflects, echoes, as negative or dialectical counter-term, the figurations traced by the text itself, the plots, that is, woven by this process of self-display. In the spectral inversions of that dialectic, Hegel's "portentous power of the negative" becomes subjected to hyperbolic exacerbation, beyond Hegel's wildest dreams or self-conscious nightmares: The gargoyles of Notre Dame come to life to sass, with their cleft tongues, twelve million Parisians; the entire façade of the Sacré-Coeur appears painted in black; the Louvre turns into transparent crystal; the Basilica changes color, in its paintings the figures change race, the paintings and sculptures in the Museum take on an opacity in contrast to the crystalline walls, floors, and ceiling, the Victory of Samothrace finally takes wing ("those wings were finally justifying themselves"); the Arc de Triomphe turns into sand, the Eiffel Tower into a zoo, et cetera. Beyond the chastisement of the familiar by the negative image, the inverse reflection of surfaces; beyond this Rabelaisian carnival of *renversement*, all possibility of "ideal presentation" becomes proscribed through the capacitation or enabling of the characters as subjects of active self-consciousness, capable of critical dialectic and of becoming, in their spectral selves, "the portentous power of the negative." That power of independent unfolding, of self-becoming of the characters and their world, subsumes the privileged presence of authorial subjectivity — of Fuentes. But, as spectral supplements of that authorial authority, they reflect the illusionary nature of their own putative power. As a consequence, no individual or constellation of individuals within the novel attains to the privileged status of controlling center, just as the author, Fuentes, recedes into effaced desultoriness, lest he emerge as transcendent idealogue with the text as *his* "ideal presentation." Bent on dwelling this side of the Hegelian absolute telos — the totalization of Being or of knowledge — the subject, whether author, character, or authorial character, in the Fuentes enterprise, haunts, in fragments, behind the limitations of illusionary power. Or, as Hegel himself phrases it, "the artificer is still the inner, hidden reality, which *qua* entire is present only as broken up into active self-consciousness" (p. 705).

If "ideal presentation" thus becomes interdicted, so does an ideal unity or totality, an attainment of absolute insight into the self (whether novel, or character, or author) as Being. Hegel's peregrination toward that goal of plenitude reads: "As the work comes closer to itself in the coming together of its aspects, there comes about thereby at the same time the other fact, that the work comes closer to the self-consciousness performing it, and that the latter attains in the work knowledge of itself as it truly is" (p. 705). Aside from the obvious fact that in a work of fiction or in strong criticism what "truly is" comprises what is *not* "truly" but fictionally (the truth of fiction), as tropical self-apprehension of illusion, Fuentes's enterprise, *qua* modern, self-critical, relentlessly "negative," anxiously *excludes* from its itinerary a "coming closer to itself in the coming together of its aspects." At best, any such plenary cohesion or "coming together" occurs only as adjacency, or as paratactical contiguity, where, we must add, those contiguities figure as dialectical counter-terms, as reciprocal negative supplements. Within the plots of the novel, those contending oppositions prove staunchly unsynthesizable. They do act as supplements, but not to the extreme of mutual eradication. There is a mutual sublimation of contiguous oppositions, but not a fusion into a "beyond" which irrevocably does away with individual terms and their intermediations. All tentative approximations of enclosure or encirclement in the novel which come to the verge of privileged centricity break apart on that very threshold. In this sense, *Terra Nostra* is composed of an agglomeration of such liminal contiguities. The proscription of those would-be totalizations and the sundering of cyclical closure at those liminal points are invariably wrought by the agency of writing, by the abysally compounded mediation of the writing *of* the novel, the writing *in* the novel, the superscriptions and palimpsests we read *through* the novel. I do not intend by this to privilege "writing" as analogue to Hegel's "mind," "spirit," or any "transcendental signified" of the sort. I merely note that in a process of dialectical mediations, of supplemental adjacencies, writing emerges as threshold, as bridging liminality. Writing, that is, emerges as connective linkage and, simultaneously, as dialectical interstice, as bridge which points to the gap, the "breach-between," the empty space (in the sense of Lezama Lima, discussed in our first chapter, of "gnostic space") that affiliates contiguities. The constitutive nature of such writing is mnemonic, that is, encyclopedic in the sense that it arrogates to itself the power of necessity (the impetus of an insufficiency) to recall and recollect, to appropriate by force of the possessive the myriad contiguities of historical consciousness. Self-conscious of its own historicity, of the "historical" nature of its own activity, this *encyclopedia* (this "cyclical" or "revolutionary lesson") of writing can include itself in its compilation, but it can never overcome its own liminality; its own self-consciousness that its activity opens yet another breach, another instance of desultory adjacency, rather than closing an encyclical. If, then, *Terra Nostra* and its writing(s) move toward the figuration of an encyclopedia, that very movement, by dint of its tireless kinaesthesia — its consciousness of being mobile — images the impossibility of such a configuration. In this sense, the plots of the novel are never "ideal representation," but an endless unfolding in themselves. Endless because the perspicacity of that process of unfolding is embedded in the dialectical self-consciousness of those plots. Thus, the novel perpetually breaches its self-identity, that is, it never attains to a similitude to itself (another way of saying that it never becomes immutable myth). Rather, in its mnemic strategies, it "remembers" itself also and, in doing so, always remains other, or different, to itself as "re-membering" (as *articulate*) member. In that reflective vocation, Fuentes's enterprise could be read in the spirit of one of the most commonly invoked Hegelian apothegms: "The pallid shades of memory struggle in vain with the life and freedom of the present."[9] The historical "necessity" or unrequited force of desire for re-collection, recovery, appropriation, and mastery embedded in the *nostra* of *Terra Nostra*, however, renders the "present" within the Hegelian *sententia* irretrievably problematic. The novel's plots become what Hegel himself terms in the same work a "spectacle of passions" ("Schauspiel der Leidenschften"). We obviously must read "spectacle" here, as we did earlier in the cases of Emerson and Borges, both as unfolding dis-play and, in keeping with its root etymons, as *phantasmata*, or *imagines*. It is precisely in the haunting and haunted spirit and in the problematic letter of this procession that I choose, on this occasion, to read the writing(s) of *Terra Nostra* as liminal bridge and breaching "negativity."

Accordingly, from the opening frames of the novel, we can see Pollo Phoibee, "one of the heroes" (he is legion), in a quest for self-remembrance, as de-cipherment or self-reading, written into the plot as palimpsest, seeking after an identity only to find self-difference, bridging and breaching a gap between spectral graphemes — the text of Ezra Pound/the con-texts of *Terra Nostra*: "Pollo from A to Z. Here . . . look . . . where could that book of poems be? Where does it say my name is Pollo? Written by an old madman who confused all symptoms with all causes. The poet Libra, a Venetian phantom, exhibited in a cage, a recluse in an American asylum. Gray eyes, eh? The gray eyes of this girl recognized him, but her lips formed soundlessly, a different name: 'Juan' . . . 'Juan'" (p. 34). *Terra Nostra's* Pollo Phoibee reads "himself" in "Cino," one of Ezra Pound's *Personae* (1926); he is recognized by the gray-eyed Celestina — Fernando de Rojas's *Celestina* (1499) — as Juan, of Tirso de Molina's *El Burlador de Sevilla* (1630) and José Zorilla's *Don Juan Tenorio* (1844), and, (why not?) Byron's *Don Juan* (1819-1824).

The haunted reflection of the hero Pollo Phoibee in this spectacle are accompanied by an attendant reflection, or spectral imaging, in the textualizing process imputed to the weaver of one of the received "precursor" texts — "an old madman who confused all symptoms with all causes." The "confusion" ascribed to Ezra Pound emerges as spectral reflection of *Terra Nostra's* own procedure, here and throughout. We can read in this "con-fusion" the proscription of metonymic causality, the foreclosure of reduction to a dynastic succession of texts. We cannot claim, instead, a synchronous immediacy, a privileged "present" on a continuum in the Hegelian sense referred to above. Rather, in keeping with the process by which *Terra Nostra's* plots unfold, we have to speak of a *uchronic* co-incidence — the timelessness of the novel's textual space where writings become spectral contiguities in the writing, as we see in the passage just cited. Any temporality which insinuates itself into the utopic space of these fictions' intermediations is either a function of our expository language or of the plots' narrativity. Thus, just as Pollo Phoibee in this recognition scene encounters the mutually reflecting self-differences in self-identity, and as the writing of Fuentes's text colludes with these "other" writings in spectacular adjacency, Celestina (Rojas's Celestina, Pound's gray-eyed woman, Fuentes's Celestina — the procuress, the go-between, the enchantress, the hymenal healer) carries out her mediating task, for the first and innumerable time, in a timeless scene of writing. In this sense, rather than as character, as subject, Celestina functions as *discourse*, a written discourse, the writing tattooed on her lips — mnemonic grapheme which bridges, as erotic force, the dialectical oppositions, Hegel's "spectacle of passions." Her (re)encounter with Pollo Phoibee is as necessary (born of the force of desire, of writing's self-seeking), as it is fortuitous ("Chance has determined that it was here you would be born, spend your youth, and live your years. Your life and this time could have coincided in a different space. It does not matter" [p. 14]). Celestina in this and in numerous other instances is the go-between; the writing tattooed on her lips affiliates those desultory "times" with "different spaces" — the topo-graphic spaces, the landscapes of textuality — even as she serves to differentiate, to breach through the (re)structuration of a mediate membrane between those spaces by her intercession as writing and as hymenal re-caster.

Significantly, Pollo Phoibee's and Celestina's re-encounter, one of an indeterminate number, occurs at the midpoint of the Pont des Arts (curiously enough, the site of fortuitous encounters in another textual landscape of Latin America's incunabula — the meeting place of Horacio and of another "Maga," in Julio Cortázar's *Hopscotch*). In the light of this logistical stratagem, Pollo and Celestina's encounter becomes the text's self-encounter: a bridge of art's self-breaching, a pleonastic counterpoint (bridge/writing), a *speculum*, where writing becomes its own "enunciation," its own "pronouncement" in the etymological sense of *nuntius*, meaning *mediation* or message-carrying go-between; an enunciation in which message and messenger are *spectrally* self-same, albeit not identical. Lest this *pontifical* moment of self-mediation become privileged locus, or a *topos* of an immediate "ideal presentation" in which the "Pont" of the writing art becomes usurped by its own reflection as plenitude, as transcendental "Pontifex" or mystified *nuncio*, the symmetry is shattered, the encirclement broken, the liminal centricity sundered on that very threshold of recovery or re-encounter, not to be countenanced again until the "end" of the novel and, there, glimpsed only to be denied, negated, remanded to its status as "mere writing" once again:

> — Aren't you tired Pilgrim? You have travelled far since you fell from
> the bridge that afternoon and were lost in the waters that tossed you onto
> the shore of the Cabo. . . .

— . . . That isn't true, I've been shut up here, I haven't left this place, I haven't opened my windows since summer, you are telling me things I've read in the chronicles and manuscripts and folios I have here in this cabinet, you've read the same things as I, the same novel, I've not moved from here. . . .
— Why not believe the opposite? . . . Why not believe that we two have lived the same things, and that the papers written by Brother Julián and the Chronicler give testimony to our lives?
— When? When? . . .
— During the six and a half months that passed between your fall into the river and our meeting here, tonight. . . .
— . . . There wasn't time. . . . All that happened centuries ago. . . . These are very ancient chronicles (p. 774).

Inside the seven hundred and some page abyss, within the six and a half months' gap, between the encounter on the Pont des Arts and this re-encounter in Pollo Phobee's flat in the Hotel du Pont-Royal on the eve of the second millennium, yawns the abysmal space, the timeless river which receives Pollo Phoibee in his Icarian fall from the Pont des Arts, carrying him to the Cabo de los Desastres. We bridge that abyss from Pont des Arts to Pont-Royal in reading the critical (the Hegelian "Negative") supplement of the "chronicles and manuscripts and folios" Pollo has in his cabinet, the compendium we share — "you've read the same things as I, the same novel" — but which neither of us can master. We cannot do so because that compendium, that putative "encyclopedia," *the novel*, is included in the novel which is its supplement, *Terra Nostra*: a synergesis (as opposed to a Hegelian synthesis or totalization), in other words, a writing which will always be greater than the sum of its parts and greater than the sum of our multiple readings. That surfeit, that supplemental yield, constitutes the critical ("negative") difference between *Terra Nostra*, on the one hand, and, on the other, the itinerary of its plots, its palimpsests, usurpations, textual superscriptions and their baneful histories, the *via dolorosa* of its supernumerary pilgrims. The constitutive *materia*, the map, of that itinerary, as in the itinerary of Pollo Phoibee's bottomless fall, is a relentless history that always repeats as wheel of strife, forever foundering on a tempestuous Cape of Disasters, as we shall see in short order.

Pollo Phoibee's fall into the river from the liminal edge of that self-recognition scene becomes synonymous with our fall into historical consciousness, the history that unfolds simultaneously with Pollo's floating downstream in the spectral reflection of the writing tattooed on Celestina's lips, that mnemonic grapheme unfolded in mirror image: "This is my story. I want you to hear my story. Listen. Listen. Netsil. Netsil. Yrots ym raeh ot uoy tnaw I. Yrots ym si siht" (p. 31). What becomes unfolded in this imagistic echo is historical consciousness *as* history, the history of *Terra Nostra* with our own consciousness of its figuring as critical movement in that history. In the timelessness of this exhausted space, in the uchronia of the text as mirror, we witness ourselves as the on-lookers looking on the "spectacle of passions," in Hegel's phrase. Extending through the ternary divisions of the novel — The Old World, The New World, The Next World — and encompassing the Rome of Tiberius, the Jerusalem of Pontius Pilate, Philip II's Counter-Reformation Spain, pre- and post-Columbian America, Central America in Vietnam-style futuristic warfare, and bi-millennial Paris, the character of that spectacle is always the same: unremitting tragedy. The players may or may not change; the plots never do; the "script" remains "constant," constantly faithful to its own specters. Thus, in Pollo's and Celestina's re-encounter, in the Pont-Royal, lived and remembered history fuse; historical reflection as autoscopy and historical consciousness conflate — "the kiss of the girl with tattooed lips; you are filled with memories, Celestina has transmitted to you the memory that was passed to her by the Devil disguised as God, by God disguised as the devil . . . you remember you did not read it, you lived it." And the dire revelation of that Luciferian gnosis, legacy of an over-reaching Angel, or of a self-effacing God, speaks to the immutable nature of historical mutabilities, to the repetitions that wright the ahistoricity of history as such: "history has had its second chance . . . a few places changed, a few names . . . differences of shading, unimportant distinctions, history repeated itself, history was the same, its axis the necropolis, its root madness, its result crime, its salvation . . . a few beautiful buildings and a few elusive words. History was the same: tragedy then and farce now, farce first and then tragedy, you no longer know, it no longer matters, it was all a lie" (774-75).

In this self-summation of its own itinerary, Fuentes's narrative irreverently conflates Hegel, for whom history constitutes a tragic plot in which men strive, as through a vale of strife, to find a tragic fate, and Karl Marx. First Hegel: "If we go on to cast a look at the fate of world historical personalities . . . we should find it to have been no happy one. They attained no calm enjoyment; their whole life was labor and trouble; their whole nature was nothing but their master passion. When their object is attained they fall off like empty hulls from the kernel. They die early, like Alexander; they are murdered like Caesar; transported to St. Helena, like Napoleon."[10] And now, Karl Marx, "Hegel remarks somewhere that all facts and personages of great importance in world history occur, as it were, twice. He forgot to add: the first time as tragedy, the second as farce."[11] Dramatically dilating Hegel's view of history as tragic plot and, at the same time, exacerbating Marx's programmatic seriality by deliberate obfuscation of what comes first and when, Fuentes manages in this conflation to salvage only one thing: "a lie." Or, in the words of Pollo Phoibee's raving, "a few elusive words," which we take as the critical (self-conscious) surfeit, or remainder; the supplement of our history's tragic plots of whose nature the novel *Terra Nostra* partakes, with which it is of a piece. Against Hegel's "ultimate truth," then, Fuentes deploys the truth of fiction. And, within the play of irony which lies in that "truth," the tragedy of history becomes transumpted into *comédie humaine*. Against Hegel's "ultimate design" which governs history ("In history, we must look for a general design, an ultimate end of the world. . . . We must bring to history the belief and conviction that the realm of the will is not at the mercy of contingency. That world history is governed by an ultimate design, that it is a rational process"),[12] Fuentes unleashes innumerable contingency and incontinent madness. Rather than celebration of Hegel's "divine and absolute reason," *Terra Nostra's* superscriptions and their emplotments of history sing the Erasmian praises of folly via Cervantes and Quevedo — the first encoded in the text as writing consciousness, the ironic court Chronicler, whose polysemic texts provoke dread in his obsessed master and king, Philip II, who sends him off to the galleys; the second, Quevedo, enciphered as citational apothegm of an unhappy, Quixotic consciousness: "Nada me desengaña. El mundo me ha hechizado" ("Nothing [un]deceives me. The world has bewitched me"). Concurrently, those enchanted plots of history celebrate the reticent hedonism and cataleptic self-consciousness of the Stoics, epitomized here by Teodoro — scriptor of Tiberius and witness to Caesar's baleful madness.

Indeed, both Fuentes and Hegel, *mutatis mutandis*, partake of a tragic view of history; and the Stoics and Stoicism serve as their contrapuntal locus of crossing and disjunction. In *The Phenomenology* Hegel dedicates part of a chapter to the Stoics, whom he considers as an early station in the pilgrimage of the Spirit toward "absolute consciousness" ("Freedom of Self-consciousness: Stoicism, Scepticism, and the Unhappy Consciousness," pp. 241-67). And, in the "Introduction" to the *Philosophy of History*, Hegel directly seeks to contravene the Stoics' *eimarmeny* ("fate," or "natural necessity"), insisting that "Contingency is the same as external necessity, that is, a necessity which originates in causes which are themselves no more than external circumstances. In history, we must look for a general design, the ultimate end of the world, and not a particular end of the subjective spirit or mind." There is a consonance between Hegel and Fuentes on the Stoics: where Hegel, in the above mentioned chapter of *The Phenomenology*, sees in Stoic consciousness "a freedom which can come on the scene as a general form of the world's spirit only in a time of universal fear and bondage." Since *Terra Nostra's* plots repeatedly evolve as constellations of "a time of universal fear and bondage" that agreement is not difficult to comprehend. With regard to the Stoics' historical consciousness, however, in *Terra Nostra* Fuentes is far from relegating Stoicism to an early or primitive stage of the pilgrimage, as Hegel is wont to do.

What attracts both Hegel and Fuentes to the self-reflective Stoics, I suspect, is a measure of the enterprise of each as process of unfolding whose itinerary is itself the enterprise. Hegel sees an insufficient liberation from or negation of "determinate notion" in the Stoics. By which he means that their thought or freedom falls short of absolute self-sufficiency, thereby still remaining vulnerable to "necessity." For Fuentes, on the other hand, the absolute freedom which is the telos of the Hegelian program represents no more than a fabulous arithmetic, a programmatic illusion. As Fuentes's Stoic scriptor notes (and I think we can read his equivocal insight as equally valid for Fuentes and his response to Hegel), "my kingdom is not that of necessity but that of whatever fragile liberty I can gain for myself in spite of necessity" (p. 689). Fuentes evinces an ambivalence toward Hegel's philosophy of history. Perhaps because of the equivoque embedded there, Fuentes's "Hegelian" project is not without a modicum of irony and his deployment of the Stoic Theodorus could be read as amphibolous strategy, as dialectical counter-statement against Hegel. I offer a cento from that spectral prosopopeia of self-consciousness as troped in the latter part of *Terra Nostra*:

1. A man like myself, who understands these things, must, nevertheless, choose between two attitudes as he writes history. Either history is merely the testimony of what we have seen and can thus corroborate, or it is the investigation of the immutable principles that determine these events. (p. 688)
2. Before these truths and these disjunctions, I choose to be witness to the fatal chance represented by my master Tiberius. (p. 689)
3. I know that my questions imply a temptation: that of acting, of intervening in the world of chance and placing my grain of sand upon the hazardous beach of events; . . . my kingdom is not that of necessity. (p. 689)
4. My stoic spirit dictates to my hedonistic hand the last words of these folios, and I say that in every good action what is praiseworthy is the effort; success is merely a question of chance, and, reciprocally, when it is a question of culpable acts, the intent, even without the result, deserves punishment by law; the soul is stained with blood though the hand remain pure. (p. 698)
5. The true history perhaps is not the story of events, or investigation of principles, but simply a farce of specters, an illusion procreating illusions, a mirage believing in its own substance. (p. 699)

In this quintessential cento it is difficult to mistake Fuentes's problematic usurpation of Hegel and the exacerbation of the Hegelian program. Unmistakable in this sequence (and the numerical assignations above are intended to be symmetrical to the numbering which follows here) are Hegel's progressive delineations of: 1. historical consciousness in itself; 2. "original history," Hegel's first variety, as he outlines in the opening pages of his "Introduction" to *The Philosophy of History*; 3. reflective history of the critical kind; 4. reflective history of the pragmatic kind; 5. philosophical history, which for Hegel's schema represents historical consciousness at its acme. While the first four fragments above construe with Hegel's first four categories in this programmatic propaedeutics, the fifth fragment from *Terra Nostra* follows Hegel's fifth and final historical category only far enough to swerve from it in order to achieve its exacerbation, to image Hegel, in spite of Hegel, as yet another manifestation of "Comic" Stoicism, still caught, like Fuentes and Theodorus, in the cataleptic entanglement of dialectical consciousness and its insurmountable but *desired necessity*. That desideratum is the acute perspicuity of insufficiency, or the Negative, seeking after substantiation of a "mirage," a transcendence beyond the "farce of specters," or, as Hegel himself puts it, beyond "the spectacle of passions." I suspect, and *The Phenomenology* gives ample and subtle grounds for the suspicion, that Hegel, like Fuentes, was not insensitive to the lurking possibility that the "meaning" of that "transcendence beyond" may dwell this side of the Comedy and ironic consciousness of the truth of fiction — whether this be troped as philosophy or as novel, as philosophical cipher or as poetic figuration. "In Comedy," Hegel tells us in *The Phenomenology*, "it [self-consciousness] is conscious of the irony lurking in this meaning" (p. 746). This may well be why Hegel's Absolute as ultimacy remains just that, a desired telos, his own Stoic *necessity* in historical unfolding. That futurity is troped in history, this side of historical "completion," as ironic presence, as odyssey of discovery (a common epithet for *The Phenomenology*). In the course of this pilgrimage, the critical and creative Negative must always reject and seek to divest itself of the "determinate notion," dissolve the ideal form, undo what Hegel calls the "other," "the mask," the "abstract universal." And that is why, I suspect, toward the end of *The Phenomenology* Hegel manifests a penchant, an unambiguous preference, for Aristophanes and Comedy (pp. 745-49) over the Fateful, epic plots of tragedy (pp. 736-44): "The individual self [in Comedy] is the negative force through which and in which the gods, as also their moments (nature as existent fact and the thoughts of their determinate characters), pass away and disappear. At the same time, the individual self is not the mere vacuity of disappearance, but preserves itself in this very nothingness, holds to itself and is the sole and only reality. The religion of art is fulfilled and consummated in it, and is come full circle. Through the fact that it is the individual consciousness in its certainty of self which manifests itself as the absolute power, this latter has lost the form of something ideally presented [*vorgestellt*], separated from and alien to consciousness in general — as were the statue and also the living embodiment of beauty or the content of the Epic and the powers and persons of Tragedy" (p. 748). If we turn Hegel on Hegel and historicize this climactic manifestation of "absolute power" with Hegel's own *sententia* on history as "The pallid shades of memory struggl[ing] in vain with the life and freedom of the present" (*Philosophy of History*, p. 6), we can see more clearly how Fuentes's unorthodox Stoicism skews the apex of Hegelian historical consciousness, "true history," as simply a farce of specters, "an illusion procreating illusions, a mirage believing in its own substance" (p. 699).

We can appreciate, too, how *Terra Nostra's* "culmination" as Dantesque *commedia*, as passion play of ecdysiastic masks in the enactment of the twenty-fifth Canto of the *Inferno*, reads as exacerbating trope on Hegel's valuation of Comedy. In Comedy, Hegel tells us, "The pretentious claims of the universal abstract nature was shown up and discovered in the actual self; it is seen to be caught and held in a concrete reality, *and lets the mask drop* just when it wants to be something genuine. The self, appearing here in its significance as something actual, *plays with the mask which it once puts on*, in order to be its own person; but it breaks away from this seeming and pretense just as quickly again, and *comes out in its nakedness and commonness, which it shows not to be distinct from the proper self, the actor, nor again from the onlooker*" (*Phenomenology*, p. 745. Emphases added).

This ecdysis, or stripping of masks, at the end of *Terra Nostra* figures as the text's redoubling back on itself — a re-encounter which is a self-encounter, where the self as acting and the onlooking self as *spectating* reflection coincide. In that conflation, in that collusion, the desultory fragments of history and historical necessity become transformed from "spectacle of passions" to passion of "nakedness" — the "nakedness of Comedy," in the sense of Hegel's insight. Significantly enough, the passion dance of Pollo Phoibee and Celestina (and their transformation into androgynous copula) takes its choreographic score, as already noted, from the *Inferno's* twenty-fifth Canto of Dante's *Commedia*, the canto on the transformations of the sinners: "The masks fall . . . ed eran due in uno, ed uno in due . . . without sin and with pleasure" (pp. 777-78). In that transformative conjunction ("Transformed utterly:/A terrible beauty is born"), we must read "yet another" co-incidence — that of the weaving of the fabric, of the texturing and of the text, unfolding as Comic passion's self-fecundating hedonism, disseminating passion's pleasure as critical ("negative") perspicacity, as self-mediating dis-play of unending supplemental necessity. And this perpetual endlessness, too, is wrought into the itinerary, as liminal edge of suspended apocalyptic millennium — "Twelve o'clock did not toll in the church towers of Paris" (p. 778). The mythical Apocalypsis, the transcendental eschatology, becomes displaced and subsumed by self-conscious recognition of self as questing passion, as erotic unmasking, as the genitive force of desire, or the "portentous power of the Nagative." The fecund negativity, the portentous power of the self-inseminating androgyny that transforms the force of the possessive's desire — the *Nostra* — into secreted commodity for its own ends (the self-seeking text, or writing, become object of its own passion), gloats in the genesiac hedonism, "without sin and with pleasure," of its own copula. Or, as Hegel might say, "feasting on its own offering, that *itself* is the Fate to which the secret is betrayed" (*Phenomenology*, p. 746).

If in this Comedy the fate of the text is to be itself the Fate, what "secret is betrayed" by it to itself? When the self-mediation becomes so Hermetic, what does it steal to itself, what does it secretly arrogate as property proper to itself? In other words, if we press etymology thereby uprooting "betrayal" as "excessive delivery," can we chart the excess, the surfeit of desire's appropriation? The force of this variously stated question aims at that remainder, at that "secreted" excess, or capable posture(ing) that enables a text's, or an author's, reaching after self-mastery of self. The question is directed at that self-conscious and self-directed power play which we could descry as negative or critical supplement. The stratagems, the ploys of this enabling surfeit in *Terra Nostra* take on innumerable guises. I refer to only three of those ruses, to me, the most obvious: 1. Contagious, illusionary insight, ironically troped within the text itself as "candid pride" or as "culpable innocence." 2. Reticent contrition and cataleptic, but knowing, perplexity. 3. Insistent self-effacement. We could readily identify instances which exemplify each of these strategies, respectively. 1. "the Chronicler believed only in the poetic reality of what he had created; any relationship that could not be reduced to the resolute struggle to impose his invented words as the only valid reality was as foreign to him as it was incomprehensible: candid pride, culpable innocence. And thus the strength of his conviction convinced the others of the documentary truth of what he was reading to us" (p. 238).

2. "I confess here that the only temptation to which I shall truly succumb is that of presenting myself to myself — when I write about myself in the third person — in a more worthy, more sympathetic light. The truth is not so beautiful.

But that temptation to act . . . that all too human temptation" (p. 689).

3. "That isn't true, I've been shut up here, I haven't left this place . . . you are telling me things I've read in the chronicles and manuscripts and folios I've here in this cabinet, you've read the same things as I, the same novel, I have not moved from here. . . . There wasn't time. . . . All that happened centuries ago. . . . These are very ancient chronicles. . . . It is impossible" (p. 774).

The individual instances of this ternary cento (which, collectively, figure a spectral parable for the authorial predicament and self-serving strategy of Fuentes himself, as we shall see shortly) appertain, in the same order, to Miguel, Chronicler in the Court of Philip II; Theodorus, scriptor of Tiberius Caesar; Pollo Phoibee. In all three cases we can read a crossing point of conjunction and disjunction, a momentary and tactical collusion between individual fate and the strategic situation of the text — between desultory strategies engaged in the production of the novel and the novel as such. In the first, the chronicler in his conviction (his belief in poetic reality as the sole reality) construes the text of *Terra Nostra* and this, his own constituting thread, which he is engaged in writing, as abysmal and congruous spectacles. But there is also an incongruous, artful disjunction, a generative surfeit; for the Chronicler's masterful self-assertion "means" its dialectical opposite, an act of self-betrayal which leads to his being condemned, simultaneously, to the galleys of the Spanish ships by his master, and to the galleys of the printing press by his friend and traitor (yet another amphibology) Julian the Court Confessor. In either fate, the self-supplemental disjunction engenders a text — that of the naval galleys yields the *Don Quixote* of Miguel (de Cervantes) after being maimed in the naval Battle of Lepanto; that of the printer's galleys yields a part of the *Terra Nostra* text we are engaged in reading, which also subsumes and displays within it the production of the *Quixote* in process.

In the second instance, Theodorus' self-presentation to himself in dark lucubrations, we see reflected the text's self-presence to itself, again, *en abîme*, as we also witness the negative supplement, the critical disjunction, or difference, which engenders the text of *Terra Nostra* we are in the process of reading — "I, Theodorus, the narrator of these events, have spent the night reflecting upon them, setting them down upon the papers you hold, or some day will hold, in your hands, reader, and in considering myself as I would consider another person" (p. 687).

Finally, in the third instance, the novel recedes into self-conscious self-effacement. It yields primacy to "chronicles and manuscripts and folios" whose identity is troped as self-same, the difference and diffidence of critical self-effacement notwithstanding, with the novel *qua* the novel we have read and go on reading.

I limit myself to these three instances to exemplify the performative and problematical mediation of critical supplements embedded within the proper covers of the text entitled *Terra Nostra*; "Negative" mediations, or creative "self-negations," which strategically serve to re-iterate the text as attempted exercise in self-mastery, as self-engendered and self-serving enterprise. Incontinent obsession that it is, however, the force of the critical supplement, of the negative reflection, overflows the proper book-ends of the book. And now I should like to turn to that overflow, that surfeit or excess "beyond" the novel, but still within its purview. I am referring to the two versions of *Don Quixote, or the Critique of Reading*,[13] a text which, I should like to suggest, might best be read as dilated, critical *speculum*, in the manner of the pasages just cited, to Fuentes's enterprise in *Terra Nostra*. I propose to move toward such a reading and, in doing so, justify my proposal by holding Fuentes up to Hegel's mirror, once again, in order to illustrate the degree to which these Fuentes texts overlap, as each other's legerdemain in that spectral reflection.

Reduced to its skeletal plot, Fuentes's argument in *Don Quixote, or the Critique of Reading* (*Cervantes, o la crítica de la lectura*) consists in a "naive" and idolatrous identification, or synonymizing, of Cervantes with *Don Quixote* (as the differential substitution in the English and Spanish titles clearly suggest) and, subsequently, in a consideration of that compound trope an equivalent of critical self-consciousness, or of the Hegelian Negative. Fuentes follows Hegel's own plotting of this Cervantine itinerary, as well as Hegel's chronological framework in which the historical unfolding of the Cervantes project *qua* critical and self-mediated enterprise is located. I should hasten to add that Hegel is by no means a cicerone whom Fuentes follows blindly. Nor is he the sole intellectual lens through which Fuentes views Cervantes. Hispanic students of the *Quixote* and of Spanish history, such as Americo Castro, for example, rival Hegel in this regard. Given that the thrust of my discussion is aimed at Fuentes's ambivalent and equivocal dialogue with the Hegelian project, I confine my discussion to this limited task. I shall move, then, first to description of the two versions of this critical text and second to an exploration of the textured mediations which obtain between these versions and *Terra Nostra*. In the process, I shall be remarking and speculating on the paradoxical predicament of Fuentes's self-presentation via the screen of his trope for Cervantes, a predicament which, as I have suggested already, becomes a negative theology (by which I mean a sacralized map of critical self-consciousness) salvageable only by a generous dose of counter-self-directed irony.

The English version of Fuentes's critical study, *Don Quixote, or the Critique of Reading,* construes only partially with the Spanish *Cervantes, o la crítica de la lectura.* The disparity is more suggestive, as we shall see, than the fact that the English is an earlier fragment of the more extensive and subsequent Spanish version. Thus, the two versions, English and Spanish, of the essay make the text problematic in itself, much less in its relationship to *Terra Nostra.* To begin with, the English version is not properly a version in a double sense. It is neither a translation, nor is it a quantitative equivalent of the Spanish. The English was written first by the author in this language. It was subsequently re-worked in Spanish and into Spanish, and interpolated into the more extensive Spanish language, Mexican edition. The author's "Advertencia," his "Preface," to the Spanish language edition may help clarify, preliminarily, some of the confusion, while creating more suggestive problems. I translate the final paragraph:

> The text which I entitled *Cervantes o la crítica de la lectura* gathers, re-elaborates, and unifies texts which I previously used for my inaugural address as a member of the Colegio Nacional; during a colloquium at the Woodrow Wilson International Center for Scholars in Washington, D.C.; for the occasion of the Hackett Memorial Lecture at the University of Texas (Austin); and in a series of articles entitled "Tiempo hispánico," published in *El Sol de México.* Although the central theme is Cervantes and his work, I do not, for that reason, refrain from reviewing here, in the manner of a memento [*recordatorio*] from a definite moment of Spanish history, divers aspects of Spain's life in the epoch that historically *is inscribed* [*se inscribe*] between 1499 and 1598 and literarily *is written* [*se escribe*] between two dates that collect the past, inhabit the present, and announce the future: the publication of *La Celestina* in 1499 and that of the *Quixote* in 1605. (p. 12)

The English text *Don Quixote, or the Critique of Reading* comprises an expanded version of Fuentes's mentioned Hackett Memorial Lecture at the University of Texas, delivered on the night of January 27, 1975 and published by the Institute of Latin American Studies of the University of Texas in 1976 as part of this annual Memorial Lecture Series that dates back to 1954. Fuentes's actual lecture was entitled "Cervantes, the Founding Father." The final Spanish text *Cervantes o la crítica de la lectura*, then, derives its title by a strategic displacement, a suggestive oscillation between the title of the spoken address and that of the published text. We can read in this strategy a breach or a tactical substitution which *betrays* (i.e., "excessively delivers," in the etymological sense of the term we gleaned earlier from Hegel) Fuentes's critical self-consciousness within the scene of a family romance, a writing scene with its attendant politics and antithetical problematics. The two principal stratagems deployed by Fuentes for that tactical breach amount to suppressing, or "secreting," dialectical difference and accommodating antitheticality. This diatactic, in turn, leads to two corresponding consequences. First, it privileges a historical process: the decentering operation of critical reading through the powers of the "negative." Second, it serves to privilege a myth of conciliation with the antithetical antecedents, the prior or anterior presence which he tropically invokes: the conquistador, the ambivalent father, the founding father. This equivocal procedure constitutes an ambivalent problematics very much alive in *Terra Nostra*, as we have already seen, and as we shall see further in what follows. Accordingly, we find Fuentes's opening gambit betraying a distinct consonance between the necessary diatactics of his discourse and its adversative rhetoricity, on the one hand, and the antithetical or dialectical declaratives of the discourse itself on the other. I translate the first paragraph of his "Advertencia"; "Our relationship with Spain is like our relationship with ourselves: conflictive. And of identical character is Spain's relationship with Spain: unresolved, masked, frequently manichaean. Sun and shadow, as in the Iberian arena. The measure of odium is the measure of love. One word tells all: passion" (p. 9).

Fuentes speaks here as a Mexican, a coherent, though, as he obviates, a contradictory and conflictive condition. I opt for reading his shorthand term "passion" which "tells all" as *desire*. In doing so, I am extending to Fuentes Jacques Derrida — "coherence in contradiction expresses the force of desire," a formulaic condensation wrought by Derrida from Freud who understands "symbols" as contradictorily desirous of fulfilling and suppressing a given impulse.[14] My reading in this sense finds particular grounding in the opening of the paragraph which follows. There Fuentes tells us that the relationship between Spain and Mexico has its origin in a "trauma," the Conquest. But this, too, becomes ambivalent, an expression of "the force of desire," for we read: "Spain, cruel father: Cortés. Spain: generous father: Las Casas." In the figure of the military conquistador and that of the benevolent Dominican missionary, the desire, or "coherence in contradiction," which traces Mexico's family history and the history of Fuentes as Mexican is schematized into manichaean dialectic. But, and here is the adversative of the *advertencia*, the "Founding Father," Cervantes, becomes secreted, he goes unmentioned. The real adversative, the true antithetical "father," is sublimated by Fuentes and troped here as the antitheticality which obtains between these two figures (Cortés and Las Casas). The eristic *figura* of this sublimation — Cervantes — is shielded or screened out by the tactic deployed in the cited first two paragraphs, i.e., a substitution of the historical self for the authorial self, Fuentes the Mexican for Fuentes the novelist. The telltale signs of this self-betrayal, betrayed, too, to the discernment of the critical reader through this breaching, in this oscillation of accommodating, are two-fold. First a substitutional displacement of titles mentioned already: "Cervantes the Founding Father" supplanted by *Don Quixote, or the Critique of Reading* (a clear swerving from the personal to the institutional, from the authorial to the *oeuvre*), suggestively re-combined into *Cervantes o la crítica de la lectura*.

The second telling sign is furnished by Fuentes in the final lines of his "Advertencia," which I have translated above, and figures as a function of the difference between the two verbs Fuentes opts for in referring alternately to historical and to literary discourse: *inscribir* for history, *escribir* for literature. My delineation of this distinction would follow along the general lines of *inscription* viewed as founding act, as received myth, presence, mystified and mystifying structure; while *writing (scribing)* could be seen as act or operation that subverts and problematizes inscription with the suppleness of decentering play and the openness of critical performance. The first, we could say, constitutes a hypomnesic function, or memorialization of the historical; the second a mnemic process, or conscious activity with no "memento" or memorial baggage. The difference between the two verbs, strategically enjoined here by Fuentes, comprises the actual adversative in the author's "Advertencia" and this, of course, is what goes undeclared, *proscribed*. This contentious dialectic resides in the problematic space between received *inscription* — the historical memento, the *patrimony* from the "Founding Father" — and its eristic negation, its creative betrayal in critical re-marking, in Fuentes's writing. The antithetical politics of this dialectic become "secreted" and that occultation itself becomes the mediate act which "betrays" the elision, the secret of what is muted. Thus, that act of self-betrayal opens the prefatory text to what is left unsaid — an enunciation, as preface, of the text to come in which the secret, what Hegel called "the fate of the text" is perpetually left unsaid. Perhaps this may serve as a correlative to Gayatri Chakravorty Spivak's way of understanding prefaces when she tells us, in her own putative "Preface" to her translation of Jacques Derrida's *Of Grammatology*, that "the preface harbors a lie" or that "it might well be the insertion of an obvious fiction into an ostensibly 'true' discourse."[15]

In Fuentes's case, as is usually true with highly self-conscious textual strategists, the inserted fiction, of course, is not so obvious. And as for the "ostensibly 'true' discourse" into which this "obvious fiction" might well be finding its way, we had best underline the adverb *ostensibly* and emphasize the quotation marks around "true" as an indispensable precaution. We had better do so, because, as I have noted here, the text which follows the prefatory "Advertencia" may well constitute the deflected "truth," or secreted "lie," that follows the adversative term, the *advertencia* and its implicit fiction. In other words, it may well be that the *ostensibility* of "truth" in critical discourse of the text which follows has already decentered that discourse and pro-scribed any "truth" the text might declare. "Ostensibly," after all, means, literally, to "show before," which makes it self-same as the "Advertencia" and that, as we have seen, points "beyond" itself, to the mirror or negative of itself, literally "it is about" a fiction, it circum-scribes, or "harbors a lie." In this sense, then, we must read the text of *Cervantes o la crítica de la lectura* as yet "another" fiction of the novelist-critic Fuentes, just as we would read the "self-presenta-tions" of Theodorus the Scriptor, or of Miguel the Chronicler — as one more thread in the macula of *Terra Nostra*. In its negative perspicacity, in its critical reflection, the text of the "essay" on Cervantes may well be read as spectral extension of *Terra Nostra*, its differential surfeit, its supplement, yet another superscription of the palimpsest. Thus, we could say that, in his critical circum-spection, Fuentes *no inscribe, sino escribe;* he does not inscribe, *rather* (adver-sative) he writes; his discourse ensues from, flows from an adversative stance, an ambivalent dialogue, whose ambivalence he seeks to elide, a dialogue with patrimony before which he stands as before a mirror, a stance which turns his "dialogue" into soliloquy, a self-writing not unlike the autoscopy of the Stoic Theodorus whom we have already read.

In this regard, the texts, *Cervantes o la crítica de la lectura* and *Terra Nostra* are interfaced, "parallel" fictions which we must read as texts written "simul-taneously." The composition of the two is, in fact, contemporaneous. The author's datelines for the first read as Mexico, D. F., July 1972; Paris, August 1975 and, for the second, Hampstead Hill Gardens, London, Winter, 1968; Chesterbrook Farm, Virginia, Winter, 1974. In addition, Fuentes appends a "Joint Bibliography" to *Cervantes o la crítica de la lectura* in the heading of which he explains, "To the extent that the present essay and my novel *Terra Nostra* are born of parallel impulses and obey common concerns, I indicate below the identical bibliography for both works" (p. 111). Clearly, the generic distinction which Fuentes would like to retain between the two texts is problem-atic, not to say moot, particularly in view of his admission that "the present essay is an offshoot of the novel I have been working on for the past six years" (I cite from the English *Don Quixote, or the Critique of Reading*, p. 23; p. 36 in the Spanish). Some of the items in his bibliographical listing would indicate that Fuentes is not altogether naive regarding the problematics and theoretical concerns which occupy the present discussion. I am referring, for example, to items such as articles by Jacques Derrida, Hélène Cixous, Sylvére Lotinger which appeared in the Paris-based *Poétique*, as well as such disparate works as Umberto Eco's *L'Opera Aperta*, Michel Foucault's *Les Mots et les Choses*, Harry Levin's *Contexts of Criticism*, and, of course, authors more immediate to the Hispanic tradition in which Fuentes is, unmistakably, writing: Cervantes, Quevedo, Ortega y Gasset, and Octavio Paz. Hegel, I might point out, is not mentioned. Fuentes does know Hegel's work, however, and he indicates elsewhere the period in which be became familiar with the German philosopher's writings.[16]

Having taken Fuentes's lead here and momentarily assigned to these two works the status of parallel texts, I must make known my serious reservations about the very notion of parallelism of texts in general, not to mention of contemporaneously conceived and executed texts by the same author. As we have already seen, the relationship between such texts is inevitably more problematic than that of two lines or streams that run without convergence. For this reason, rather than as parallels, it might be more appropriate to consider the two texts as intertwined, serpentlike, about each other, without the Hermetic caduceus, that is, without a fixed center, heralding each other in a compensatory and mutually vicarious relationship of supplementarity, spectral negativity and self-conscious mediation.

I opt for the terms compensatory, vicarious, supplementary with which to suggest the interrelationship between these works, because these terms amplify the adversative procedure I have already outlined, and they speak further to Fuentes's strategy in these texts: what we could summarize as a dialectical ploy of the optative mode. Like all strategies, however, the one deployed by Fuentes involves a ruse, a devious artifice. By this stratagem, Fuentes converts the options he dialectically posits from alterity to mirrored synonymy, or to mutually substitutable terms, even while the trace or suggestions of the alternatives perdure. The most blatant demonstration of this strategy is in the titles *Cervantes o la crític de la lectura* and *Don Quixote, or the Critique of Reading* in which the alternative conjunction *o*/or must be read as what it is even while it enjoins us to read it as its opposite, and/*y*, thereby transforming the options or alternatives into correlative terms; that is, terms which are reciprocal and, therefore, individual while, at the same time, they become spectrally substitutable supplements to each other.

With dialectical insistence, Fuentes's opening gambit in his discussion of Cervantes offers an invitation to the reader to consider the alternate possibilities of an ingenuous or a deceitful Cervantes, a naive iconographer or an impious hypocrite. The verdict (Fuentes-induced); both and neither — an ironic iconoclast in the Humanist tradition of Erasmus's *The Praise of Folly*. Be that as it may, our subject is not Cervantes and his critique of reading, *ostensibly* at any rate, but, and foremost, Fuentes and his critique of Cervantes's critique of reading, though "Cervantes" here be a trope and his critique Fuentes's fiction. And here, again, we cannot afford to relent in our critical virgil of the ostensibility which an author deploys as self-serving or as self-corrective screen. To succumb, credulously, to the authorial ploy, to accept an author's gambit at face value would mean a capitulation to the awesome authority a practitioner critic, in this case a novelist-critical reader, wields. It would mean a surrender to the blindness which such authorial authority seeks relentlessly and unavoidably to force upon us as readers, compelling us to overlook the internal tensions and problematic equivocations embedded in the author's texts. The peril of such entrapment is particularly acute in Fuentes's case since his discourse directs itself at the very activity in which we are engaged: critical reading. Lest we forget the admonitions of one of the most consummate professional prevaricators, D. H. Lawrence, who warns us that "an artist is usually a damned liar," and enjoins us to "never trust the artist. Trust the tale. The proper function of a critic is to save the tale from the artist who created it" (*Studies in Classical American Literature*); lest we forget the sound counsel of this highly suspect counselor, we must follow in our task a more embattled, a more properly antithetical procedure. A response in keeping with such a procedure consists in our seeing through Fuentes's stratagem and in that perspicacity perceiving the author's own self-enshrinement in the canonization of his subject, Cervantes. Moreover, we must detect the ironic naiveté (whether calculated or actually naive) in a strategy which privileges and sacralizes "negativity," that is, a strategy which idolatrously mystifies demystification and consecrates critical agnosticism. In this chiasmus, Fuentes emerges as a "naive" insofar as he sanctifies Cervantes and his iconoclastic work as *epic* of "negativity," of self-decentering, critical reflection. The irony of the paradox here becomes exacerbated when we remember that *epic*, as Fuentes himself notes, means normativity, univocality, mystified presence, a myth, and what is mythologized in Cervantes is the very activity of de-mythification, equivocality, dialectical self-mediation, and pluralistic, critical reading. In his catachresis, Fuentes engages in totemism, in ancestor worship, where the forefather, or "Founding Father," as Fuentes calls him, is consecrated into an originary model, into a paradigm of critical modernity. Fuentes's discursive itinerary consists in tracing the passing from epic and classical tragedy to medieval heresy and pluralism which eventuate in the ironic, self-critical spirit of the *Quixote* that, in turn, becomes the paradigm for Joyce's voices, with which Fuentes's plot in *Cervantes o la crítica de la lectura* resoundingly ends.

The measure of Fuentes's naiveté is problematic in itself, however, insofar as it is a measure of the naiveté of his specular subject, the subject of his consecration, whom he subsumes and in whom he looks as in a mirror. And we know from reading the *Quixote* that the "naive idealism" of Cervantes and of his knight-errant hero is *vicarious*, that is, a substitution, a turn or a figure of speech, an adversative, a trope on the Medieval romance of chivalry (*vicarious* is derived from the Latin *vicis*, a turn, to turn), and a trope, Harold Bloom has taught us, is a "willing error."[17] So is counter-self-consciousness, or ironic naiveté, for it is self-consciously wrought. In that sense Fuentes's "blindness" constitutes a turn on a turn, a trope of a trope, what the Alexandrian Hellenistic rhetors called a *metalepsis* and what Harold Bloom recoups as "transumption." In this abysmal endlessness of substitutions, Fuentes reads Cervantes's work as a parable on reading, with Fuentes's own peripaedeudics of reading — the deflections of his discursive commentary — becoming a tropical allegory of the *Quixote* and Cervantes's critique of reading. In turn, *Cervantes o la crítica de la lectura* and *Terra Nostra* become each other's compensatory substitutions, vicariously taking each other's place, breaching each other's "otherness," breaking the optativity that their alleged genre differentiation would afford them.

If Miguel de Cervantes protagonizes Fuentes's tropical paean on critical reading, he also figures prominently, as we have seen, as "Miguel" the court Chronicler and scriptor in *Terra Nostra*, confronting in this text, too, the enigmas of *lectura* and *escritura*, expressing, at times in identical utterance, the problematics of reading and writing uttered by the critical persona of Fuentes in *Cervantes o la crítica de la lectura*. In this compensatory relationship of textual economy we re-view the problematics of a vicarious relationship between reading and writing as performative and as constatory (as immediate and as mediate) acts. Viewed in this manner, *Cervantes o la crítica de la lectura* and *Terra Nostra* do not "explain" each other, as some critics, overcome by the author's awesome power, wishfully believe.[18] On the contrary, they take us further from "explanation." Each may construe the "other," at best, and *only* if their discrete existence could be maintained, but such construing compounds the complexity of our task. Construing is itself a constructive, or structuring activity and, as such, it furnishes yet one more term, yet another structure with which we have to contend. It is precisely this interstitial term that we have been tracking after here, a term of rhetoricity which calls up the tropes or figurative turns that I alluded to above as compensatory, vicarious, supplementary; the figures that underlie and overlay the spectral and mutually substitutable constructions of these texts. "The method of construction," Lévi-Strauss reminds us, "adds a supplementary dimension."[19] And this is the dimension I should like to continue to pursue.

The nature of this supplementary dimension in Fuentes should be familiar to us by now. I have referred to it variously as critical perspicacity, self-mediating dis-play, quest for self-mastery, and as the surfeit of desire's urge for self-appropriation. If, as I have tried to show, *Terra Nostra* is a novel born of the dramatization of the strategies deployed in its own production as novel, an enterprise, that is, which evinces the creative negativity or critical self-consciousness of a Hegelian project, *Cervantes o la crítica de la lectura* is yet one more thread, one more clew in the fabric, one more prismatic facet of the self-mirroring textuality. The editorial contingencies which happen to find this thread between separate covers from those of *Terra Nostra* may be attributable to authorial (and graphic) obsession with spectral imaging, with self-re-iteration as the spectacle of self become its own self-differential viewer; a desire of writing to become its own monumental object; an author's scripture wishing to become its own inscription in the very act of self-de-scription. Screened through Cervantes, Fuentes's enterprise figures one more instance, another station of a self-conscious itinerary on the pilgrim's endless highway. The traces of Hegelian dialectic in this spectacular odyssey masquerade cryptographically within and between the interstices of *Cervantes o la crítica de la lectura* and *Terra Nostra*. The *de-scription* of the "Founding Father" in the first is isomorphic and spectrally tantamount to the subsuming and appropriation of Cervantes, to his inscription as novelistic character in the second. Both ploys constitute one strategy, the strategy of Fuentes's own self-contemplation, his project's self-consciously working itself out. The specular attempt at self-mastery, whether the text's or the textor's, then, amounts to an attempt at mastery over the subsumed "Founding Father." Or, at the very least, it becomes a search for an accommodation whereby the "Founding Father," subjected to the mediations of Fuentes's and his enterprise's self-willing into becoming, is rendered an inscription, a memento, a hypomnesic reminiscence of the Fuentes enterprise. Thus, Cervantes becomes another liminal and lapidary element, one which breaches *Terra Nostra* and *Cervantes o la crítica de la lectura*. Fuentes, however, screens out the arrogations of his power play be tactically privileging Cervantes, the object of his mediation, as paradigm and ancestral source for the stratagems he himself deploys in his project. And here, Hegel's observations on mediation become extremely serviceable in understanding Fuentes's strategy. "Mediating," Hegel writes in the "Preface" to *The Phenomenology*, "is nothing but self-identity working itself out through an active self-directed process; or, in other words, it is reflection into self" (p. 82).

Hegel's applicability to Fuentes, I repeat, must be vigorously qualified. As we have seen, and shall see again, Fuentes deliberately problematizes, antithetically confronts Hegelian dialectic and its program as it might have proved ideologically totalizing and normatively absolute for his own project. The most significant qualification to be stressed is that in invoking Hegel I do so only in the name of a demonstrative methodological procedure, without any intent to impute a Hegelian view of history or the Spirit of history to Fuentes. The undeniable relevance of Hegel to the Fuentes enterprise, as we have seen, is entailed in the procedures of dialectical, creative negation common to both. Fuentes's itinerary follows closely the Hegelian "odyssey of discovery," the concept as the "biography" of its process of conceiving and being conceived, philosophy as the record of the project of philosophizing, as the "excess," the surfeit or remainder of a process. In other words, what links Fuentes to Hegel is the latter's view of his own enterprise as tactically and procedurally consonant with the creative itinerary of literature followed by Fuentes. I am specifically prompted to invoke Hegel and his dialectics by the observations he makes (and the observations he precipitates in others) on philosophical discourse and literary discourse in *The Phenomenology of Mind,* predications appropriated, inverted, and displaced by Fuentes. I am also moved by Hegel's observations on Cervantes and the *Quixote* in his later work, *The Philosophy of Fine Art,*[20] to which I will refer by the conventional shorthand title of *Aesthetics,* observations assimilated, directly or indirectly, by Fuentes. To vindicate my claims for Hegel in this enterprise, I would like to note briefly a sampling of very divers readers who have confronted the problem of textualization, in Hegel himself and in others, in Hegelian terms: the late Jean Hyppolite, French translator of *The Phenomenology* and one of the most lucid expositors of Hegel;[21] Jacques Derrida, particularly in *Of Grammatology* and in *Dissemination,* already referred to above; and M. H. Abrams, who, in his *Natural Supernaturalism* refers to Hegel's dialectic as "self-moving and self-sustaining system" with particular relevance to literary discourse.[22]

In *Of Grammatology* Jacques Derrida duplicitously elides Hegel into a trace which becomes its own "sublation" (Hegel's term), its own sublimation. With the opening peal of his later *Glas,*[23] he renders Hegel into the hollow tolling of a bell which tolls for a Hegel become Godot. In *Dissemination* Derrida keenly exploits Hegel's studied hesitations on the inalienability of the process of philosophizing from philosophy, of conception from concept, to illustrate the impossible "exteriority" of textual elements which we would conventionally identify as "extra-textual," e.g., prefaces, epilogues, commentaries "surrounding," or "about" the text. Less drastically, M. H. Abrams reads Hegel as the "sublimated identity" [dies aufgehoben Desein] of the protagonist whose odyssey configures the spiritual history of *The Phenomenology,* which Abrams, following Josiah Royce, characterizes as a *Bildungsroman,* more accurately as a *Bildungsbiographie.* In an equally suggestive observation, Jean Hyppolite notes, "this Hegelian voyage of discovery, *The Phenomenology of Mind,* is a great novel of culture."[24] These three commentators, so different from each other, uniformly present us with a specular Hegel. The consonance among these readings may be instructive, although not surprising. Hegel himself tells us in his "Introduction" to the *Aesthetics* that "in the works of art, mind has to do with its own."[25] In his earlier *Phenomenology* Hegel had assigned such self-reflective attributes to philosophical discourse when he compared this to literary discourse, prompting Hyppolite's following misreading: "just as the *Divine Comedy* of Dante, the *Don Quixote* of Cervantes, or the *Human Comedy* of Balzac are works whose structure and organization of discourse we can study, thus in these philosophic works of Hegel [*The Phenomenology of Mind* and the *Science of Logic*] we may also consider philosophic discourse as such. The comparison with literary works is all the more indispensable since Hegel drew it himself; however, the difference between a literary discourse and philosophical discourse is very important. While literary discourse is an imaginative speculation, philosophical discourse contains its own criticism within itself. . . . In philosophic discourse someone speaks . . . but he also speaks *about* his own speech. . . . And the speech about the speech is an integral part of philosophic language."[26] Hyppolite's adversative addendum, the distinction between the two discourses which he extrapolates, is problematic at best, particularly in view of the literary works he cites as examples. This distinction is clearly deauthorized and eradicated by Hegel himself in his "Introduction" to the *Aesthetics* when he tells us that "in the works of art, mind has to do with its own." Given the overall concerns of the *Aesthetics* with the languages of the fine arts, it would be dehegelianizing Hegel only minimally, or not at all, if we trope "mind" here as "language" within this passage. Thus, the "imaginative speculation" which Hyppolite equates to literary discourse becomes truly "speculative," or specular — a process projecting its own critical reflection in its unfolding. In this sense, the desultory refractions of that Hegelian *speculum* find their way into *Cervantes o la crítica de la lectura* (we have already seen them in *Terra Nostra*), in Fuentes's discursive characterization of a "new" way of reading which, he says, is offered us by *Don Quixote*: "A critique of reading that projects itself from the pages of the book toward the outer world; but also, and above all, and for the first time in the novel, a critique of narrative creation contained within the work itself: a critique of creation within the creation."[27]

The logical extension of Hegel to Fuentes (an extension prompted by Fuentes himself whose observations on the *Quixote* follows so closely, and so problematically, those of Hegel) cannot fail but point up a *compounded* "unhappy consciousness," which Hegel describes as "the consciousness of self as a divided nature, a doubled and merely contradictory being" (*Phenomenology*, p. 251). This antithetical self is Fuentes's *aporia*, his self-conscious elaboration of a repetitive and repeating equivoque: the critique of a critique of reading which is *Cervantes o la crítica de la lectura*, on the one hand, and, on the other, the dramatization of the irreducible doubleness of language, particularly written language since its signature indelibly leaves a mark, which is the odyssey of Cervantes in the perpetually untotalizable project of *Terra Nostra*. That project is untotalizable by virtue of compounding, by dint of the supernumerary, palimpsest-like mediations it incorporates into itself, mediations its own language must perpetually endure: Cervantes's *Don Quixote* for one, in addition to the textual traditions of Spain's Judeo-Arabic patrimony, as well as the novels of chivalry and of the picaresque tradition, compounded by the texts of Erasmist Humanism and Utopian reveries which mediate in the *Quixote* itself. If, as Hegel tells us, the *Quixote* is a modern epic which suffers the mediations of textual accretions springing from Medieval and Renaissance Europe, Fuentes's *Terra*

Nostra, in subsuming Cervantes and the *Quixote*, is a hyperbolically compounded *bricolage*, or gleaning, that gathers all that mediates in the *Quixote*, plus the textual tradition that is precipitated and has accrued since, including Hegel. The insight into its own untotalizability, into the impossibility for closure or completion of its textual odyssey, then, also becomes self-consciously woven into the fabric, into the map of *Terra Nostra's* itinerary.

In the *Aesthetics*, at that juncture where Hegel deals with the epic and the novel, we read with reference to the latter, "What fails us here is the *primitive* world-condition as poetically conceived, which is the source of genuine epos. The romance or novel in the modern sense pre-supposes a basis of reality organized in its *prosaic form*, upon which it then attempts, in its own sphere, so far as that is possible from such a general point of view . . . to make good once more the banished claims of poetical vision" (IV, p. 171). On a number of other occasions (II, p. 373; IV, pp. 188-89), Hegel suggestively observes that Cerventes, like Ariosto, is already possessed of the insight into the blindness of the Medieval and chivalric attempt *consciously* "to make good once more the banished claims of poetical vision." That ambivalently antithetical insight is what Fuentes critically reads in Cervantes as the "critique of reading." "The profounder romance of Cervantes," Hegel perceptively tells us, "already assumes knight-errantry to be a Past behind it; which, consequently, can only enter into real prose and presence of life as vanity in its isolation and fantastic folly" (IV, p. 189). Hegel, and Fuentes who follows him in this regard, reads the *Quixote* as a scene of (re)cognition which adumbrates its own antithetical self-consciousness and prosaic dialecticality. As *prose*, and as the pre-posterous opening to the "prose of the world" (in the limited Hegelian sense of the phrase now become a shibboleth), *Don Quixote* stands as the violent undoing of "primitive presence" or "unmediated notion" (again, Hegel's terms, like the previous one, in the sense of the Hegel citation above). *Don Quixote*, in other words, as Fuentes's reading obviates, becomes the disruptive, dislocating, and decentering instrument which shows up the blindness of Medieval and chivalric romances to all that mediates within their language and concept, interdicting, thereby, the *illusion* of "unmediated notion" and "primitive presence." *Prose*, or the prosaic formulation as such, carries within itself precisely this antithetical dialectic for Hegel who equates prose with "science," that is, with conscious knowledge and re-cognition — an equation reminiscent of Vico's symmetry between "scienza" and "conscienza" discussed previously. (Hegel's discussion on "The Composition of Poetry and Prose" is suggestive in this regard. IV, p. 20 and the next two chapters.) This quality of prose, this self-conscious doubleness which condemns, once and for all, the "primitive presence" and "unmediated notion" of the Epos to mediation and an "unhappy consciousness" is what Hegel's own prose shares with the novel and, to this extent, we can understand Hyppolite's characterization of *The Phenomenology* as "a great novel of culture," as well as Abram's consideration of this Hegelian work as a *Bildungsbiographie*. Beyond this point of consonance, however, the relationship of Hegelian prose to what Hegel termed the "prose of the world," our modern novel that is, becomes problematic. In Hegel the sundered state which ensues from reflection and its antithetical dialectic is successively transcended [*aufgehoben*] in a dénouement, however provisional, or pro-visional, of homecoming, in which the pilgrim spirit of knowing attains the absolute goal of "being at home with itself" [*Beisichsein*] within the conciliatory third term of a triad in which the dialectical antitheticality becomes transcended. However, the prose of the novel initiated by Cervantes arrives in the "end" at a baneful and melancholy compounding of self-consciousness, a scene of recognition in which the consciousness of itself is not an absolute and comprehended whole but, as Fuentes observes with respect to the hero Don Quixote, a knowledge of itself as "doubly enchanted."[28]

The hero, as Fuentes reminds us, reads himself in the novel and knows himself to be read by others. But, finally, when the world dons the garb of his enchantment (when Dorotea disguises herself as the Princess Micomicona, when the Bachelor Carrasco confronts Don Quixote disguised as the Knight of Mirrors, when the Dukes stage the enchanted realm of Don Quixote's reverie and make it consubstantial), in this "playing with the masks" of Comedy, as Hegel would say, the double enchantment does not attain to a homecoming but to an enchanted disenchantment, an illusionary dis-illusionment, what the polyvalent shorthand equivoque *desengaño* suggests in Spanish. The alternatives at this juncture are two, and Fuentes incorporates both, equivocally, into *Terra Nostra*, thus compounding an already compounded "unhappy consciousness" thereby compounding the impossibility of ever attaining to homecoming. The first alternative belongs to Cervantes and to Don Quixote: death by virtue of reason and falling into history, a *desengaño* or renewed enchantment in which, as Dostoyevski observed about Don Quixote (and Fuentes cites the Russian novelist in his *Cervantes o la crítica de la lectura*), Cervantes's hero *betrays* a "nostalgia for realism," that is, in Hegelian terms, for an unmediated earliness, for a primitive world of the Epos.

The second alternative belongs to Francisco de Quevedo, Cervantes's younger contemporary and that other face of Spain's Golden Age. In this sense Quevedo may be closer to the troping and ironic punning of a Hegel which Derrida, and even Abrams, descry in oscillating Hegelian terms, such as *aufhebung* — at once annulment, preservation, transcendence— and *Er-Innerung* — remembering and internalizing. Except that in Quevedo (and, by extension, in Fuentes by whom he is subsumed) the trope of irony becomes exacerbated into "conceit," a hyperbole of mediation and acerbic wit, as we read in one of Quevedo's "Sentencias" appropriated by *Terra Nostra*: "Nada me *desengaña*, el mundo me ha hechizado" ("Nothing 'disenchants' or 'disillusions' or 'reveals the truth of the deception' to me, the world has 'enchanted' or 'bewitched' me''). This is truly an "unhappy consciousness" compounded by the self-recognition and re-collection, or *Er-Innerung*, of its own lucid and discerning "unhappiness." In this sense Miguel the scriptor-Chronicler in *Terra Nostra* (as well as the authoring Fuentes who has subsumed Miguel's fate in subsuming his vocation and obsession) emerges as a vicarious persona — an authorial mask, or hypomnesic inscription, a spectral memento mirroring Fuentes. He emerges, in short, as a sublimation of Quevedo (as much as an avatar of Cervantes), whom Borges has penetratingly characterized as a being purely of language, "less a man than a vast and complex literature," one who "continually aspired to attain a kind of stoic asceticism."[29]

Like Hegel, Fuentes portrays Cervantes in "both" his texts as iconoclastic self-consciousness cognizant of its belated arrival on a scene of writing and reading to which the "primitive world-condition" and epic naiveté have been lost. And so, as Miguel the Chronicler sets out to complete his chronicle, which turns out to be the self-problematizing *Quixote* in Fuentes's novel *Terra Nostra*, he begins with a transumptive bow, a recognition of the texts which mediate in his text from the outset: "Everything is possible" and "Everything is in doubt" (p. 668), from Marsilio Ficino and John Donne, respectively. In *Cervantes o la crítica de la lectura* Fuentes elucidates this metalepsis, or compound trope, of *Terra Nostra's* Chronicler. I cite from Fuente's own English rendition in *Don Quixote, or the Critique of Reading*:

> Between these two sentences, pronounced more than a century apart [the Spanish reads: "In the midst of these oscillations of Humanism" — the rest conforms], the new literature appears as an opaque circle where Hamlet can represent his methodic madness, Robinson Crusoe his optimistic rationalism, Don Juan of Seville his secular sexuality and Saint John of the Cross his celestial eroticism: in literature all things become possible. In the Medieval cosmos, each reality manifested another reality, in accordance with symbols that were homologated in an unequivocal manner. But in the highly unstable and equivocal world that Copernicus leaves in his wake, these central criteria are forever lost. (p. 36; p. 71 in the Spanish).

Within the Hispanic tradition in which Cervantes wrote and Fuentes writes, "the Medieval cosmos . . . homologated in an unequivocal manner" harkens to what Hegel terms in the *Aesthetics* "the Epos of a unified totality" (IV, p. 152), in which the German philosopher considers Spain's national epic, *The Cid*, as the "blossom of national heroism in the Middle Ages" (IV, p. 102). Fuentes tropes this Hegelian "unified totality" as the illusionary, mystified, epic of a *restorative* goal within Spain's Siglo de Oro (the Golden Age — another restorative illusion of language), the Spain of Cervantes and of Philip II, whose calamitous history parades as "spectacle of passions" through the pages of *Terra Nostra*. In the *Critique of Reading* Fuentes echoes his own novel once more:

Like the necrophiliac monarch [Philip II, in whose court Miguel serves as Chronicler] secluded at El Escorial, Don Quixote both pawns and pledges his life to the restoration of the world of unified certainty. He pawns and pledges himself, both physically and symbolically, to the univocal reading of the texts and attempts to translate this reading into a reality that has become multiple, equivocal, ambiguous. But because he possesses his readings, Don Quixote possesses his identity: that of the knight errant, that of the ancient epic hero. (p. 37)

Unlike the "necrophiliac monarch secluded at El Escorial," however, Don Quixote, in his double enchantment, suffers a demystification which allows him to see through the illusionary character of this restorative enterprise. And if not Don Quixote, for certain, Cervantes is unquestionably possessed of this perspicacity and affords his protagonist the opportunity to discern his own ironic figuration. "Because he possesses his readings," Don Quixote possesses not only "his identity" of knight errant, of "ancient epic hero," but he also knows that identity to be in and of reading — a graphic, paper identity as such. Not only does he read himself and know himself to be read by others, but in the Second Part of the novel Cervantes's hero visits a printer's shop in Barcelona. There Don Quixote witnesses his own paper reality, the printing of the *Quixote*, and its infinite dissemination — "my character will be multiplied to infinity," Don Quixote avers. Thus, unlike Philip, Don Quixote crosses from one "horizon" to another, managing, in the process, the impossibility of totalization or closure, attaining the guarantee of a perpetual quest and a perpetually deferred homecoming in the endlessly disseminated landscape of textuality. In this way, Cervantes's enterprise and its protagonist manage to elude what would have been a completed history of a completed past, Hegel's totalized "finished history," and become projected into the infinite disseminations of indeterminate futurity. In one of those desultory futures, a disseminated fragment of that projection will have been *Terra Nostra* and the itinerary of its own impossible "homing." The "necrophiliac monarch," on the other hand, erects for himself and for his past the stone monument to and of a clausura. El Escorial becomes symbol and reality of completion and of absolute history. Like Tiberius Caesar, portrayed in *Terra Nostra* as baleful madman obsessed with the infinite dispersion of Rome's unity so that he might be the culmination of his genealogy, Philip II desires nothing less than radical peroration (despite, or because, of the fact that his father, Charles V the Holy Roman Emperor, sought to restore Imperial Roman Unity). Philip becomes the epitome of Nietzsche's *epigone*, the late arrival to a concluding world, a Hegelian final scene of history.[30] Accordingly, Philip's motto reads: "Brief Life, Eternal Glory, Unchanging World." His impatience for that finality is expressed in his byword: "Nondum."

Committed to the mystified cipher of an unchanging, univocal, and normative myth of totalization, Philip II finds his quietus in an excremental death — the closing of a circle, since Fuentes telescopes Charles, the Holy Roman Emperor, and his son Philip into one, thus having the "necrophiliac monarch" of El Escorial undergo his father's birth in Flanders to Juana the Mad, shat by her in a Flemish latrine. We could read this stratagem as a play on Fuentes's part on "the malady of history" (Nietzsche's phrase), a catachrestic pleonasm aimed at Hegelian historicism and its totalizing movement.

Don Quixote, Fuentes notes, is the "Spanish extension of the Praise of Folly identical to the praise of Utopia" (*Critique of Reading*, p. 46; p. 87 in the Spanish). In this obvious metalepsis, Fuentes betrays his insight into Erasmus's irony: the dedication of *The Praise of Folly* to Erasmus's Utopian, English friend Thomas More, whose name is inscribed in the original Latin title Erasmus gave his work — *Moriae encomium*. In extending Erasmus's tropo-graphy to Cervantes through his own compound trope, Fuentes connects Old World utopiography with the New World topography. In that linkage, he inevitably suggests the problematics we examined in our opening chapter. In other words, he points to Utopia's exacerbated historical itinerary in the New World. It would appear, then, that for Fuentes the identity of "Folly" and "Utopia" which he descries in Don Quixote's u-topic enchantment finds its topos, its "place," in the land-scape of the New World and its baneful history. Thus Utopia of ironic and oscillatory enchantment, in other words, seeks and finds its consubstantial and problematic correlative in a *geo-graphy* — the embattled and tropical space of New Spain and the New World. In this sense (a sense whose significations I have discussed more fully in chapter one), the trope-object of Fuentes's troping game becomes a demonstration of tragic repetition. That repetition, in Hegel's words cited earlier, is fated as "*primitive* world-condition as poetically con-ceived," fated to know that its attempts "to make good once more the banished claims of poetical vision . . . can only enter into real prose and presence of life as vanity in its isolation and fantastic folly." This, then, is the fate of the epic of America, a "new," and therefore hopelessly self-conscious, heroic age in the jungles of the New World, whose heroes carry with them the Utopias, the utopic incunabula, of Tommaso Campanella and Thomas More in their saddlepacks. In his ironic allusion, as already noted, to Giambattista Vico, Hegel, and Marx, Fuentes observes with reference to repetition that "history repeats itself, but in Spain the second time it is not repeated as farce; it is tragedy once again."[31] History's repetitions fare no differently in New Spain. And that "tragedy" in the New World, we could say, is the failure, the necessary failure whose necessity inheres in repetition, of Utopia: the failure of the sixteenth century Humanists to find/found the Golden Age Don Quixote one night tells a group of goatherds about — an age of justice, equity, and communalism which was the Renaissance dream; the failure to find Campanella's City of the Sun, the legendary Adocentyn which dates from another Renaissance fiction — Hermes Trismegistus. It is the failure of the good Bishop Vasco de Quiroga's experiment in Utopia Moriana within the Arcadia of the New World. Utopia succumbs to strife and fratricidal conflict — the indispensable ingredients for primal tragedy since Aristotle's prescription in the fourteenth book of *The Poetics*. I read in this Fuentes trope the implied and, I believe, admissible suggestion that *Don Quixotes*, as the threshold to the "new novel," to "the prose of the world," in Hegel's phraseology, which spelled a *coup de grâce* to the epic of chivalry and its blindness to the mediations within it, ironically enough, also becomes the textual correlative of a "new" epic, a "nascent poetry of heroism" — albeit, like that textual correlative, an epic already fated to the self-consciousness which obtains in its founding as repetition, as "new." This is the topo-graphic epic of the "New" World, the topothesia of a new fiction, as noted previously in chapter one. The *text* of this Epos, the *incunabula*, in Lazama Lima's sense discussed earlier, is the Space of the New World as such, the antipodal, "other" World which invaded European historical consciousness and received its utopiographia only to exacerbate it *à outrance*. Some two centuries after Cervantes, Hegel will look Westward, still, for what he calls the Epopee of the future. "If we lift our eyes beyond Europe," he remarks, "there can be only one direction, America" (*Aesthetics*, IV, p. 133).

The "Joint Bibliography" appended to *Cervantes o la crítica de la lectura* includes one item in particular which is treated at some length by Fuentes in his earlier collection of essays entitled *Tiempo mexicano*, already referred to in the notes. The entry in question is an essay by Eugenio Imaz, *Topía y utopía*.[32] Fuentes's exegesis, which I shall follow closely here, of this treatise attests to the intensity of Hegel's infusion into the thought of this Mexican who has been so important to the intellectual development of Fuentes. Modern reason, according to Imaz, is conceived in order to attain a mastery over the physical world, the world of space. The French Revolution makes present the world of history, that is, the world of time. Thought passes from space over to time and with this passing, logic is converted into dialectic. Dialectic is logic applied to becoming. The concepts of time and space are no longer juxtaposed, rather they germinate in each other contradictorily. In time there is *no place* and thus, by definition, there can be Utopia, which is "no place." Fuentes then observes, "Imaz' reasoning explains perfectly why Renaissance Utopia failed in America. The system of ideas of the epoch . . . is a thought system of space; the discovery, conquest, and colonization of America was not an act in time but an extension of space. Utopia is time and it could not fit within that spatial epic."[33]

The debatable historical (chronological) accuracy of Imaz's scheme is not my main concern here. What is important for our purposes is the scheme itself and, particularly, as it is rendered and accommodated by Fuentes. In this regard, a number of things become readily apparent: First, a clarity of correspondence — an interlinking of time-history-Utopia-novel, on the one hand, and space-epic, on the other. Second, the passing from a reason of space to a reason of time constitutes a falling into history, a fall from being into becoming and into a dialectic of historical consciousness. Third, Utopia dwells in history and history, in turn, is loosed by Utopia's necessary placelessness from a fixed locus, or a firm center, to float in contingency, to move freely in the *Numsquama*, the Nowhereland of Utopia — a Utopia whose praise issues, according to Fuentes's earlier accession to Erasmian Humanism, from the "folly" of our "new novel" that dates from Cervantes, as Hegel and Fuentes, who follows him in this regard, would have it. Now, the programmatic, teleological Hegel may have just turned over in his grave in the face of this unfettered floating in a sea of contingency and decenteredness. But here is how Fuentes sums up these Hegel-inspired cogitations: "The foundation of our modern prose [Hegel's 'prose of the world'], which is the transgression of the epic norm by the utopic heresy: epic/space violated by novel/utopia which creates its own time."[34]

The creation of "its own time" is the creation of its own history. And this brings us back to the compounded, or "abysmal," equivoques and antitheticalities which I indicated earlier as the spectacle of self-consciousness and its self-supplementing pilgrimage, the unending quest of self-perpetuating fictions. For in creating its own time, the "novel/utopia" creates not only its own history, but it also creates its own *prose*, which is none "other" than the itinerary of that history, its own self-conscious language, the generative language of, as Hegel wouldl say, an "unhappy consciousness." We can designate this process by the antithetical, the irreducibly mirrored, or reflective term, *revolution*. The term is a proper equivoque for an equivocal process that simultaneously entails rupture ("transgression") and repetition (*revolvere*). The creative performance, the "negative," or critical quest of the trope novel/utopia constitutes an originary act that self-consciously knows itself not to be wholly original but a repetition of a founding act which it violates, which it transgresses. The process I outline here is indicative of the family romance, the filial line linking Latin America's fictions. As such, it accurately described, too, the Fuentes project under discussion, which is part of that family history. And Fuentes, in a passage which betrays the preponderant ghost of Giambattista Vico in his work, reveals as much when, in his observations on *Topía y utopía*, he notes that given the cultural pluralism of a country like Mexico, it becomes quite possible to think in terms of "a generous and revolutionary Utopia . . . creation of *a poetic spiral* in which time and language, mutually withstanding each other, do not repeat the past, rather, they *found anew the origin*."[35] In the catachrestic peripeteia of founding *anew* without repeating the past, through a poetic spiral, one unavoidably senses the resonance of that most characteristic of Vichian terms at the heart of *The New Science: ritrovare* — a scene of recognition, re-finding, and, most significantly, of re-inventing; a task of invention rehearsed by Fuentes, with Cervantes and the tradition of critical or creative negation as his object; a task, too, in which the subject of the Fuentes enterprise (whether text or textor) becomes its own pursued object.

In the refracted mirrors and multiplied reflections of that autoscopy, of that self-seeking quest, I propose that we read the space, such as it is, "between" Fuentes's *Terra Nostra* and *Cervantes o la crítica de la lectura* as the supplemental difference which obtains within the repetitive act of (self) founding anew without repetition. In the pursuit of such an undertaking, we will have deciphered and, necessarily, re-enciphered, the spectral figures that haunt in the force of desire, or "passion," as Fuentes calls it, for found origins, the conflictive origins which are conflictive because of our vigilant insight (our self-consciousness) into the mediations which haunt there. I suggest, that is, and hopefully have demonstrated my own suggestion, that we take these "two" books as each other's extended spectacle or spectral continuity, each perpetuating the force of questing desire, a desire inscribed as unrequited passion in the pertinacious possessive of *Terra Nostra* and pre-scribed, or already anticipated, in the title of *Cervantes o la crítica de la lectura* as endless self-mediation, or reflection into self.

Taken thus, these textual figures, like the texts we have been examining throughout this study, serve to extend their own incompletion, or untotalizability. Rather than texts which mutually explain or determine their identity, they become one amphibolous strategy deployed for the sake of its own ever-extended indeterminacy. In other words, the self-corrective or auto-exegetic attempts of the practitioner-critic, Fuentes, make the critical mediation "present to itself" *but*, like the self-problematizing texts we examined previously, only to be denied, deflected, or subverted outright by virtue of the fact that the very mediate intrusion constitutes yet another term, another turn or figure of invention, thereby guaranteeing the perpetual quest of the (self)critical supplement for its desiring object of desire. Thus, in revolution as regressive, cyclical movement, or as dialectical process of self-mirroring, self-reflective mediation becomes exacerbated by and into "poetic spiral," which is neither linear, progressive, ultimately totalizable in the resolution of the dialectic (as in Hegel or Marx), nor is that movement hopelessly doomed to repeat in cyclically determinate invariability (as in Spengler). This is what, I suspect, Fuentes means by the hope to "found anew the origin" through time and language. Clearly, I believe, this is what he achieves (consciously or by the delusions of self-consciousness) in the itinerary of his enterprise. His accomplishment extends the quest of the family romance toward an impossible homecoming. And Fuentes writes himself as yet one more pilgrim on the path of endless peregrination, the perpetual odyssey of Latin American fictions toward a home of *incunabula's* homelessness.

Notes

Notes

Foreword

1. The great currency of the story in English is revealed by the fact that it appears in the most general of Latin American histories; see, for example, Hubert Herring's *A History of Latin America* (New York: Alfred A. Knopf, 1972), p. 278.

2. An example ready to hand would be Juan Goytisolo's essay, "Captive of Our 'Classics'" (*New York Times Book Review*, May 26, 1985). He ends the essay with the sentence "The battle against what is 'typically' Spanish will be a hard-fought one, but I am convinced that sooner or later new literary realities will carry the day" (p. 24). Admittedly, he is striving for acceptance of a plurality of representations as opposed to a single authoritative one, but he still clearly conceives of the issue as one of conflicting representations — thus the formulation interms of 'agnostics' about which description will most accurately represent the current "literary realities."

3. Julio Cortázar, "Amérique Latine: exil et littérature," in *Littérature Latino-Américaine d'Aujourd'hui*, ed. J. Leenhardt (Paris: U. G. E. 10/18, 1980). This was Cortázar's contribution to a Cerisy Colloquium on Latin American literature. Page references will appear in the text.

4. It should be noted that the inversion mentioned here bears a significant resemblance to Kierkegaard's concept of "repetition," and that in Kierkegaard's terminology "reality," sometimes *Realitet*, is frequently rendered with *Virkelighed*, which would more closely approximate the movement of Cortázar's text: the English text, for example, generally translates *Virkelighed* as "actuality" (and of course the German cognate of the Danish is the well-known *Wirklichkeit*), intimately bound with the *act*. See for example the recent translation of *Fear and Trembling* and *Repetition*, trans. H. V. Hong, and E. H. Hong (Princeton: Princeton University Press, 1983).

5. Until Kadir's introduction of certain aspects of the problem in Fuentes's work, neither *Terra Nostra* nor *The Recognitions* has ever been read with an eye toward the mechanism of representation that is the central concern of both books. Although *The Recognitions* is beginning to draw academic readers, critics devote themselves almost exclusively to tracking down sources and speculating about Gaddis's intended meaning; see, for example, *In Recognition of William Gaddis* (Syracuse: Syracuse University Press, 1984).

The following references from *Terra Nostra* are taken from the English versions, trans. Margaret Sayers Peden (New York: Farrar, Straus, Giroux, 1976); the second page reference in each citation refers to the Spanish *Terra Nostra* (Barcelona: Editorial Seix Barral, S. A., 1975).

6. The hegemonic powers of such historical schemas — schemas equating belatedness and a lack of self-consciousness and using them to describe non-European societies — have recently received some critical attention: in Edward Said's *Orientalism*, Johannes Fabian's critique of anthropology in *Time and the Other*, and Bryan Turner's *Marx and the End of Orientalism*.

Chapter 1. Overture: Errant Landscape/Untimely Pilgrimage

1. Harold Bloom, *The Ringers in the Tower: Studies in Romantic Tradition* (Chicago: University of Chicago Press, 1971), p. 3.

2. Edward Said, *Beginnings: Intention and Method* (New York: Basic Books, 1975).

3. Octavio Paz, cited from a 1970 interview by Rita Guibert, *Seven Voices* (New York: Knopf, 1972), p. 244. For a lucid discussion of this problem in Anglo-American letters, see Malcolm Cowley's *Exile's Return* (New York: W. W. Norton and Co., 1934).

4. Octavio Paz, "A Literature of Foundations," in *The TriQuarterly Anthology of Contemporary Latin American Literature*, eds. José Donoso and William Henkin (New York: E. P. Dutton, 1969), p. 4.

5. Octavio Paz, *Children of the Mire: Modern Poetry from Romanticism to the Avant-Garde*, trans. Rachel Phillips (Cambridge: Harvard University Press, 1974), p. 2, *et passim*.

6. Carlos Fuentes, *Tiempo mexicano* (Mexico: Joaquín Mortiz, 1971), p. 9. My English rendering; emphases added.

7. Harry Levin, *The Myth of the Golden Age in the Renaissance* (New York: Oxford University Press, 1969), p. 93.

8. In Harry Levin, p. 93.

9. Richard Burgin, *Conversations with Jorge Luis Borges* (New York: Holt, Rinehart, Winston, 1968), p. 64.

10. Carlos Fuentes, pp. 10-11.

11. Jorge Luis Borges, "The Life of Tadeo Isidoro Cruz (1829-1879)," in his *The Aleph and Other Stories, 1933-1969*, trans. Norman Thomas di Giovanni (New York: E. P. Dutton, 1970). All citations from this edition shown parenthetically in the text.

12. For a concise and lucid discussion of the relationship between Borges and the *Martín Fierro*, see the incisive article by Enrico Mario Santí, "Escritura y tradición: el *Martín Fierro* en dos cuentos de Borges," *Revista Iberoamericana*, 14 (1974), pp. 303-19.

13. See the "Autobiographical Essay" and "Commentaries" appended to the English translation of *The Aleph and Other Stories, 1933-1969*.

14. T. S. Eliot, "Tradition and Individual Talent," in *Selected Essays 1917-1932* (London: Faber and Faber, Ltd., 1932).

15. For Derrida's version of the *supplement* see his *Of Grammatology* trans. Gayatri Chakravorty Spivak (Baltimore: The Johns Hopkins Press, 1974), especially Part II, chapter 4, pp. 269 ff.

16. José Lezama, *La expresión americana* (Havana: Instituto Nacional de Cultura, 1957; re-edition Madrid: Alianza Editorial, 1969). This volume is the collection of five lectures originally delivered by the author in January 1957 in Havana's Centro de Altos Estudios. One of these, "Image of Latin America," appears in the English translation by Mary G. Berg of *Latin America in Its Literature* César Fernández Moreno, et. al., eds. (New York: Holmes and Meier Publishers, Inc., 1980), pp. 321-27. All references to Lezama's Spanish text are indicated parenthetically by page number in the text and the English translations are my own. Where Mary G. Berg's translation is cited, the essay's English title is indicated before the page number. Some of Berg's translations have been altered for greater accuracy and consistency with the Lezama text.

17. My reading of Lezama is at great variance from those who would sacralize Lezama's *terminus technicus*, canonizing it with theological catholicity, pagan or otherwise. See for example Emilio Bejel, "Cultura y filosofía de la historia (Spengler, Carpentier, Lezama Lima)," *Cuadernos Americanos*, 239, No. 6 (Nov.-Dec., 1981), pp. 75-89. For a reading of Lezama more consonant with my own, see Severo Sarduy, *Barroco* (Buenos Aires: Sudamericana, 1974).

18. Harold Bloom, *A Map of Misreading* (New York: Oxford University Press, 1975).

19. *The Use and Abuse of History*, trans. Adrian Collins (New York: The Liberal Arts Press, 1949).

20. Ralph Waldo Emerson, "The American Scholar," in *Essays and English Traits*, Harvard Classics (New York: Collier and Son, 1909), p. 11.

21. Roland Barthes, *S/Z*, trans. Richard Miller (New York: Hill and Wang, 1974).

22. Ernst Robert Curtius, *European Literature and the Latin Middle Ages*, trans. Willard R. Trask (Princeton: Princeton University Press/Bollingen Foundation, 1973; original German edition Bern: Verlag, 1948).

23. *The New Science of Giambattista Vico*, trans. from the third ed., 1744, Thomas Goddard Bergin and Max Harold Fisch (Ithaca: Cornell University Press, 1961).

24. Roberto González Echevarría, *Alejo Carpentier: The Pilgrim at Home* (Ithaca: Cornell University Press, 1977), p. 21. Subsequent references cited in the text.

25. Emir Rodríguez Monegal, ed. *The Borzoi Anthology of Latin American Literature*, 2 vols. (New York: Knopf, 1977), vol. 1, p. 2.

26. Emir Rodríguez Monegal, *El otro Andrés Bello* (Caracas: Monte Avila Editores, 1969).

Chapter 2. Borges's Ghost Writer

1. Michel Foucault, "What is an Author?" in *Textual Strategies: Perspectives in Post-Structuralist Criticism*, ed. Josué V. Harari (Ithaca: Cornell University Press, 1979), pp. 141-60.

2. Paul Valéry, *Oeuvre* (Paris: Gallimard, 1960), vol. II, p. 413.

3. Jorge Luis Borges, "El inmortal," *El Aleph* (Buenos Aires: Editorial Losada, 1949; numerous subsequent editions by Emecé Editores). Since this lead story of the original Spanish edition does not figure in the English translation of the collection, I am citing from *Labyrinths: Selected Stories and Other Writings*, eds. Donald Yates and James E. Irby (New York: New Directions, 1962). All references noted parenthetically in the text by page number.

4. "Perhaps universal history is the history of a few metaphors"; "perhaps it is a mistake to suppose that metaphors can be invented. The real ones . . . have always existed; those we can still invent are the false ones, which are not worth inventing." *Other Inquisitions: 1937-1952*, trans. Ruth L. C. Simms (Austin: University of Texas Press, 1964), pp. 6, 47.

5. *The Aleph and Other Stories 1933-1969*, trans. Norman Thomas di Giovanni in collaboration with the author (New York: E. P. Dutton, 1970).

6. "The certainty that everything has been already written nullifies or makes phantoms of us all." *Ficciones*, ed. Anthony Kerrigan (New York: Grove Press, 1962), p. 87.

7. Roland Barthes, "From Work to Text," in *Textual Strategies*, p. 78.

8. *Other Inquisitions*, p. 90.

9. "Everness," in *Selected Poems: 1923-1967*, ed. Norman Thomas di Giovanni (New York: Dell Publishing Co., 1968), p. 187.

10. Ronald Christ, *The Narrow Act: Borges' Art of Allusion* (New York: New York University Press, 1969).

11. In *Plato: The Collected Dialogues*, eds. Edith Hamilton and Huntington Cairns, Bollingen Series, 71 (New York: Pantheon Books, 1961).

12. See George K. Anderson, *The Legend of the Wandering Jew* (Providence, R.I.: Brown University Press, 1965), p. 19. In Wendover's *Flores Historiarum*, Anderson tells us, the Wandering

Jew bears the name "Joseph, honored in the scriptures. Before baptism he was called Cartaphilus, an appellation generally broken down into *kartos* and *philos*, roughly translated as 'strongly' or 'dearly' and 'loved'." Anderson indicates, *ad hominem*, that "there has been general agreement on this etymology" (note 14), and there may well have been. Borges, however, as I suspected from the evidence in the story and as he has indicated to me in conversation, favors a varying etymology which skews the one sanctioned by Anderson. Borges would syncretize the Greek *philos* — loved, dear, a friend — with the Latinate *charta*, which has its root etymon in the Greek *khartēs* — a leaf of paper or a layer of papyrus, or, metaphorically, a piece of writing — a clever collusion that educes Cartaphilus' graphic or papyrus identity; a book peddler and bibliophile, himself a figure of the palimpsests he disseminates and perpetuates.

13. See Mary G. Berg, "The Non-Realistic Short Stories of Lugones, Quiroga, and Borges." Unpublished Ph.D. dissertation, Harvard, 1969, p. 435.

14. Ralph Waldo Emerson, "Self-Reliance," in *Essays and English Traits*, The Harvard Classics (New York: Collier and Son, 1909), p. 73.

15. Emerson, "Nature," in *The American Mind*, eds. Harry R. Warfel, et al. (New York: American Book Co., 1937), p. 532.

16. Christ, p. 192.

17. Harold Bloom, "Borges: A Compass for the Labyrinth," in his *The Ringers in the Tower: Studies in Romantic Tradition* (Chicago: University of Chicago Press, 1971), pp. 211-13.

18. In *Borges: A Reader*, eds. Emir Rodríguez Monegal and Alastair Reid (New York: E. P. Dutton, 1981), p. 312. Emphases added.

19. In *Borges: A Reader*, p. 284. Emphases added.

20. Giambattista Vico, *The New Science*, paragraph 386, p. 80. Further references cited parenthetically by paragraph number.

21. I am not unaware of Jacques Derrida's discussion on "Hors Livre" in his *La Dissemination* (Paris: Editions du Seuil, 1972). To try and expatiate Borges strictly in terms of Derrida, however, would amount to hyperbolic and illusionary back-formation since the Derridaean canon, and I am cognizant of the eristic character of the term here, is already writ in the Borges tropography.

22. Emerson, "Nature," p. 533.

23. The Qabalist resonance in the name does not escape Ronald Christ's allusive referentiality. *The Narrow Act*, p. 212. Saul Sosnowski, *Borges y la Cábala: la búsqueda del verbo* (Buenos Aires: Ediciones Hispamérica, 1976), p. 41, note 56, decries Ronald Christ's linking of this Nahum Cordovero to Moises Cordovero as misguided and as an emanation of Christ's "own qabalistic reading on the name given by Borges." Sosnowski's own talmudic corrective of Christ has its purported basis in Borge's *verba*. It would appear from what he says that Sosnowski has credulously accepted Borges's implausible denials in an interview about having knowledge of the Spanish Moises Cordovero, the greatest systematizer of the Qabala and, as teacher of Luria, the immediate precursor of Lurianic qabalism. The truth must lie everywhere (and endlessly). Be that as it may, Borges knows full well that Nahum is a prophet and already *a book* in the Old Testament.

Chapter 3. Erotomania: Mexico's Gothic Family Romance

1. Carlos Fuentes, *La muerte de Artemio Cruz* (Mexico: Fondo de Cultura Económica, 1962). References are to Sam Hillman's translation, *The Death of Artemio Cruz* (New York: Farrar, Straus, and Giroux, 1964), and will be cited parenthetically in the text by page number.

2. Juan Rulfo, *Pedro Páramo* (Mexico: Fondo de Cultura Económica, 1955). Trans. Lysander Kemp, *Pedro Páramo* (New York: Grove Press, 1959). Subsequent references cited in the text.

3. Otto von Simson, *The Gothic Cathedral: Origins of Gothic Architecture and the Medieval Concept of Order*, Bollingen Series 47 (New York: Pantheon, 1956). And Paul Frankl, *The Gothic:*

Literary Sources and Interpretations through Eight Centuries (Princeton: Princeton University Press, 1960).

4. John W. Aldridge, *After the Lost Generation* (New York: McGraw Hill, 1951).

5. Irving Malin, *New American Gothic* (Carbondale, Ill.: Southern Illinois University Press, 1962).

6. J. Douglas Perry, "Gothic as Vortex: The Form of Horror in Capote, Faulkner, and Styron," *Modern Fiction Studies*, 19, No. 2 (1973), 153-67.

7. "Same Voices, Other Tombs: Structures of Mexican Gothic," *Studies in Twentieth Century Literature*, 1, No. 1 (1976), 47-64.

8. See, for example, Paul Westheim, *La calavera*, trans. from German by Mariana Frenk (Mexico: Ediciones Era, 1971); and Jesús Angel Ochoa Zazueta, *Muerte y muertos* (Mexico: Set/Setentas, 1974).

9. Octavio Paz, *El laberinto de la soledad* (Mexico: Fondo de Cultura Económica, 1959). References are to Lysander Kemp's translation, *The Labyrinth of Solitude* (New York: Grove Press, 1961), p. 196.

10. Paz, p. 25.

11. Cited by Perry, p. 155.

12. Carlos Blanco Aguinaga, "Realidad y estilo de Juan Rulfo," *Revista Mexicana de Literatura*, 1, No. 1 (1957); Mariana Frenk, *"Pedro Páramo,"* *Revista de la Universidad de Mexico*, 15, No. 11 (1961); Hugo Rodríguez Alcalá, *El arte de Juan Rulfo* (Mexico: Instituto Nacional de Belles Artes, 1965), pp. 113-25.

13. Malin, Chapter III.

14. Northrop Frye, *Fables of Identity* (New York: Harcourt, Brace, and World, 1963), p. 15.

15. Paz, Chapter II.

16. Martha Banta, "The House of the Seven Ushers and How They Grew: A Look at Jamesian Gothicism," *Yale Review*, 57 (October, 1967), p. 65.

17. Banta, p. 65.

18. Cited in Banta, p. 62.

19. Paz, p. 54.

20. The utterance is so ideologically overloaded in Mexico's historico-cultural linguistics as to be untranslatable into English. The best one could do, and the term is so translated by Anglo-American translators of Mexican works, is the comparatively innocuous and univocal "motherfucker."

Chapter 4. Baroque, or the Untenable Ground: Quest as Self-Reminiscence

1. Lezama Lima, "Image of Latin America," p. 326.

2. Roberto González Echevarría, *Alejo Carpentier*, p. 22. Emphases added; subsequent references cited in the text.

3. Michel Foucault, *The Order of Things: An Archeology of the Human Sciences* (New York: Random House, 1970; Vintage Books edition, 1973).

4. T. S. Eliot, "The Metaphysical Poets," in his *Selected Essays, 1917-1932* (London: Faber and Faber, Ltd., 1932). Eliot's essay first appeared in the *Times Literary Supplement*, October 20, 1921.

5. Morris W. Croll, "The Baroque Style in Prose," in *Style, Rhetoric, and Rhythm: Essays by Morris W. Croll*, ed. J. Max Patrick (Princeton: Princeton University Press, 1961), p. 208.

6. Heinrich Wölfflin, *Renaissance and Baroque*, trans. Kathrine Simon (Ithaca: Cornell University Press, 1966), p. 14.

7. Carlos Fuentes, "El barroquismo de William Faulkner," *Revista de la Universidad de México*, 24, No. 1 (1969), p. 3. My translation; emphases in original.

8. Alejo Carpentier, *The Kingdom of this World*, trans. Harriet de Onís (New York: Alfred A. Knopf, 1957; Collier Books, 1970). I shall be citing from the first Collier Books edition. References cited in the text.

9. For a treatment of the Metaphysical poets other than T. S. Eliot's, see Odette de Mourges, *Metaphysical, Baroque, and Précieux Poetry* (Oxford: The Clarendon Press, 1953); Frank J. Warnke, *European Metaphysical Poetry* (New Haven: Yale University Press, 1961). For specific commentary on T. S. Eliot's essay, see Frank Kermode, "'Dissociation of Sensibility': Modern Symbolist Readings of Literary History," in his *The Romantic Image* (London: Routledge Paul, 1957).

10. "Lo real maravilloso americano," in *El reino de este mundo* (Mexico: EDIAPSA, 1949). An expanded version of the essay, from which I translate here, appears with the same title in Carpentier's collection of essays *Tientos y diferencias* (Montevideo: Arca, 1967).

Emir Rodríguez Monegal dates the phrase "lo real maravilloso" to the Avant-garde, specifically to the Italian Futurist Massimo Bontempelli. Carpentier makes of the concept an autochthonous American ontology. As Rodríguez Monegal documents, however, Carpentier cannot free himself or the phrase from his Surrealist associations which he tries to put behind him in his essay. See Emir Rodríguez Monegal, "Lo real maravilloso y *El reino de este mundo*," in *Asedios a Carpentier*, ed. Klaus Müller-Bergh (Santiago, Chile: Editorial Universitaria, 1972).

11. I am thinking of Jean Hyppolite, "The Structure of Philosophical Language According to the 'Preface' to Hegel's *Phenomenology of Mind*," in *The Language of Criticism and the Sciences of Man: The Structuralist Controversy*, eds. Richard Macksey and Eugenio Donato (Baltimore: The Johns Hopkins Press, 1970); of Jacques Derrida, *La Dissemination* (Paris: Editions du Seuil, 1972); and of Gayatri Chakravorty Spivak's self-problematizing prefatory essay to her translation of Derrida's *Of Grammatology* (Baltimore: The Johns Hopkins Press, 1974).

12. Paul de Man, *Blindness and Insight: Essays in the Rhetoric of Contemporary Criticism*, 2nd ed., revised (Minneapolis: University of Minnesota Press, 1983), p. 165.

13. For a discussion of the concepts of *bricolage* and *bricoleur* see Claude Lévi-Strauss, *The Savage Mind* (Chicago: University of Chicago Press, 1966). For a corrective commentary on Lévi-Strauss's notion, see Derrida, *Of Grammatology*, pp. 101-40.

14. See Emir Rodríguez Monegal, note 10 above.

15. Frank J. Warnke, *Versions of Baroque* (New Haven: Yale University Press, 1972) p. 54. Emphases added.

16. Warnke, *Versions*, p. 53.

17. See González Echevarría, Chapter 3, for a detailed correlation of events in Carpentier's narrative and the events of the historical period covered by the novel. González Echevarría sees a symbiosis of historical incident with historical narrative, bound by the metaphor of nature and natural cycles. But he acutely notes that as in all cosmic (i.e., theological) metaphors, the order which evolves from this schema is an "imposture."

18. Alejo Carpentier, *El recurso del método* (Mexico: Siglo XXI Editores, 1974), p. 99.

19. Wylie Sypher, *Four Stages of Renaissance Style* (Garden City, N.Y.: Doubleday and Co., 1955), p. 187.

20. *El recurso del método*, p. 22. My translation. An English translation of the novel does exist, Frances Partridge, *Reasons of State* (New York: Writers and Readers, 1981).

21. Wylie Sypher, *Rococo to Cubism in Art and Literature* (New York: Random House, 1960). p. 13.

Chapter 5. The Quest's Impossible Self-Seeking

1. See, for example, Paz's Charles Eliot Norton Lectures, delivered at Harvard in 1971-72 and published as *Children of the Mire: Modern Poetry from Romanticism to the Avant-Garde*, trans.

Rachel Phillips (Cambridge: Harvard University Press, 1974); or his earlier (1976) essays, in which our epigraph originates, *Alternating Current*, trans. Helen R. Lane (New York: Viking Press, 1973).

2. Paul de Man, *Blindness and Insight: Essays in the Rhetoric of Contemporary Criticism*, 2nd ed., revised (Minneapolis: University of Minnesota Press, 1983).

3. Enrico Mario Santí, "The Politics of Poetics," *Diacritics* (December, 1978), pp. 28-40.

4. Paz, *Alternating Current*, p. 131.

5. Paz, *Alternating Current*, p. 132.

6. Carlos Fuentes, *Terra Nostra* (Mexico: Joaquín Mortiz, 1975). Trans. Margaret Sayers Peden (New York: Farrar, Straus and Giroux, 1976). All references cited in the text parenthetically by page number.

7. G. W. F. Hegel, *The Phenomenology of Mind*, trans. J. B. Baillie (New York: Harper and Row Publishers, Harper Torchbooks, 1967), pp. 82-83. Subsequent references cited in the text parenthetically.

8. Norman Cohn, *The Pursuit of the Millennium* (New York: Oxford University Press, 1957).

9. G. W. F. Hegel, *The Philosophy of History*, trans. J. Sibree (New York: Dover Publications, 1956), p. 6.

10. Hegel, *Philosophy of History*, p. 31.

11. Karl Marx, *The Eighteenth Brumaire of Louis Bonaparte* (New York: International Publishers Co., Inc., 1963), p. 15.

12. Hegel, *Philosophy of History*, "Introduction," p. 18. *Pace* Hegel's prescription here, in the same "Introduction" we read: "What experience and history teaches is this — that people and governments never have learned anything from history, or acted on principles deduced from it."

13. Carlos Fuentes, *Don Quixote, or the Critique of Reading* (Austin: Institute of Latin American Studies, University of Texas, 1976). *Cervantes o la crítica de la lectura* (Mexico: Joaquín Mortiz, 1976).

14. Jacques Derrida, *Writing and Difference*, trans. Alan Bass (Chicago: University of Chicago Press, 1978), p. 278.

15. Jacques Derrida, *Of Grammatology*, trans. Gayatri Chakravorty Spivak (Baltimore: The Johns Hopkins Press, 1974), p. x. Spivak's allusive dialogue here is as much a conversation with the text she has translated as it is with Derrida's discussion of Hegel and the problematic notion of prefaces in "hors livre," *Dissemination,* trans. Barbara Johnson (Chicago: University of Chicago Press, 1981).

16. See Carlos Fuentes, *Tiempo mexicano* (Mexico: Joaquín Mortiz, 1971), particularly the chapter entitled "Radiografía de una década: 1953-1963," pp. 56-92.

17. Harold Bloom, *A Map of Misreading* (New York: Oxford University Press, 1975), p. 93.

18. See, for example, the otherwise sensitive essay by Lucille Kerr, "The Paradox of Power and Mystery: Carlos Fuentes's *Terra Nostra*," *PMLA*, 95 (1980), 91-102, specifically note 8.

19. Claude Lévi-Strauss, *The Savage Mind* (Chicago: University of Chicago Press, 1966), p. 24.

20. G. W. F. Hegel, *The Philosophy of Fine Art*, trans. F. P. B. Osmaston (London: G. Bell and Sons, 1920).

21. See note 11, chapter 4.

22. M. H. Abrams, *Natural Supernaturalism* (New York: Norton, 1971), pp. 147-77; 225-37.

23. Jacques Derrida, *Glas* (Paris: Galilée, 1974). No English version exists to date. For a discussion of this text and Hegel's significance to it, see Geoffrey H. Hartman, *Saving the Text* (Baltimore: The Johns Hopkins Press, 1981).

24. Jean Hyppolite, "The Structure of Philosophical Language," p. 164.

25. *The Introduction to Hegel's Philosophy of Fine Art*, trans. Bernard Bosanquet (London: Kegan Paul, Trench and Co., 1886), p. 22.

26. Jean Hyppolite, "The Structure of Philosophical Language," pp. 158-59.

27. I translate from the Spanish, p. 15, since the passage in the English *Don Quixote, or the Critique of Reading* is truncated and somewhat less explicit.

28. Like the Hegelian triad in which the dialectic passes on, through a conciliatory third term, Fuentes deploys a ternary strategy in *Terra Nostra* . The third term of a successive series of triads (including the novels three principal divisions — "The Old World," "The New World," and "The Next World"), however, invariably signifies sundering, dispersion, and dissemination, rather than re-integration. The third term in Fuentes's triadic world is, ironically enough, the fulfillment of a curse — the curse of Tiberius Caesar cast upon the successors of Rome, that is, upon the future, individuated hordes of an "unhappy consciousness": "Let Agrippa Postumus, multiplied by three, one day be revived from the bellies of she-wolves, so he may contemplate the dispersion of the Empire of Rome; and from the three sons of Agrippa may another nine be born, and from the nine, twenty-seven, and from the twenty-seven, eighty-one, until unity be dispersed into millions of individuals, and as each will be Caesar, none will be he. . . . And let these things all come to pass in the ragged reaches of the Empire, beneath the secret sands of Egypt where are buried the trinitarian mysteries of Isis, Set, and Osiris, beneath the arid sun of rebellious Spain" p. 697.

29. Jorge Luis Borges, *Other Inquisitions,* pp. 39 and 42.

30. Friedrich Nietzsche, *The Use and Abuse of History*.

31. I translate from the *Cervantes o la crítica de la lectura*, p. 39. The passage does not figure in the English.

32. Eugenio Imaz, *Topía y utopía* (Mexico: Fondo de Cultura Económica, 1946).

33. *Tiempo mexicano*, p. 40.

34. *Tiempo mexicano*, p. 41.

35. *Tiempo mexicano*, p. 40. Emphases added.

Index

Index

Abrams, Meyer H., 131, 134

Acevedo, Francisco Xavier, 20

Aesthetics (G. W. F. Hegel). *See Philosophy of Fine Art*

Aldridge, John W., 72

"American Scholar, The," (Ralph Waldo Emerson), 24-25

"A New Refutation of Time," (Jorge Luis Borges), as radical irony, 11

Apion, Homer in, 48, 64

Apocalypsis: and *ancalypsis*, 109; as deferred eschatology, 109; as inaugural movement, 109; non-teleological, 110; suspended, 120

Aquinas, St. Thomas, 6

Arabian Nights, The, 60

Ariosto, Lodovico, 133

Aristeia, 47

Aristotle, 8, 138

Arnold, Matthew, 24

Articulation: as re-membering, 113

Augustine, St. of Hippo, 8, 25

Author: aphanisis of, 40, 41, 46, 67; apocryphal, 69; as apostrophe, 42; as *auctoritas*, 61; and authorial function, 40, 41, 44; and authority, xxii, 55, 106, 111, 128; in Borges, 39-61; as breach, 130; as character, 45; and demystification, 54; disappearance of, 40; in discourse, 55; economy of, 67; as extra-vagant, 66; feint of, 66; as grapheme, 45; Homer as symbol of, 45; as Homeric avatar, 46; and indeterminacy, 55; as interdiction, 67; as liar, 128; and mastery, 54, 121, 130; as mirror, 154; and narrative voice, 44; and necessary falsity, 65; and novelty, 42; and oblivion, 42; "paper author," 41; as persona, 135; as phantom, xxii; phantomness of, 41; as practitioner-critic, 128; predicament of, 121; privilege of, 40; and property, 62; and proprietorship, 61; as questing subject, 69; and the reader, 44, 66; as scriptor, 58; and self-delusion, 107; self dramatization, of, 62; as self-inscription, 30; and signature, 43; as spectacle, 66; as specular remainder, 61; and subsumption, 45, 69; and succession, 130; as superfluity, 65; as synergism, 68; as text, 63; and thanatopraxis, 41; as trace, 36; as wanderer, xxii; as writing subject, 46

Bacon, Sir Francis, 42, 43, 44, 47

Balzac, Honoré de, 25, 131

Banta, Martha, 81

Baroque, 86-104; as absence, 6; and Afro-American élan, 102; as *bricolage*, 93; as compensation, 86; and Copernican revolution, 90;

Djelal Kadir was born on the island of Cyprus. He earned his B.A. in philosophy and Latin American studies at Yale University in 1969, and his Ph.D. in Ibero-American studies with a specialization in inter-American literary relations at the University of New Mexico in 1972. Kadir is Professor of Spanish and Comparative Literature and Chairman of the Program in Comparative Literature at Purdue University. His previous publications include *Triple Espera: Novelas Cortas de Hispanoamerica* and *Juan Carlos Onetti*.

Terry Cochran is humanities editor at the University of Minnesota Press, and translator of José Antonio Maravall's *Culture of the Baroque* (Minnesota, 1986).